Nobody's Children

SISTER GREEN

Nobody's Children

The Recollections of a Nurse in India in the Last Years of the British Rule

Irene Green

LEONAUR

Nobody's Children
The Recollections of a Nurse in India in the Last Years of the British Rule
by Irene Green

FIRST EDITION

Leonaur is an imprint of Oakpast Ltd

ISBN: 978-0-85706-878-1 (hardcover)
ISBN: 978-0-85706-879-8 (softcover)

http://www.leonaur.com

Publisher's Notes

Contents

Introduction   9

How It Happened   11

Early Days   14

Nasirabad   27

The Ever-Welcome Cuppa   32

Bacchanal   37

Neemuch   47

Return to Mhow   61

Hard Times   71

Trainee—Green Belt   79

"The Mouse" and Pamela   93

The Second Year   101

Breaking Out   106

Ward Life and Death   113

Frontier Nurse   122

Burra Club, Kala Jugga and Band Nights   130

Mummies, Feuds and Infidelity   136

Fairies in the Khyber   141

Pasteboard Memories and Preparation   150

Politics and Piety	158
Frontier War	163
Afridis—and Guest Nights	170
Murder by the Stairs	175
Frontier Finery	181
Summer Madness	184
Off With the Old	199
Indolent Interlude	207
Nostalgic Moments	215
Things That Go Bump in the Night	219
Indore	225
Mendicants and Wedding Bells	234
Charlotte's—Here I Come!	242
The Purser's Table	263
More Adventures Afloat	280
The Ghoom Road Shelter	288
Epilogue	314

DEDICATED

TO THE MEMORY

OF

MY BELOVED PARENTS

I have written the Tale of our life
For a sheltered People's mirth,
In jesting guise—but ye are wise,
And ye know what the jest is worth.

Kipling.

The governor-general's sympathy for the Anglo-Indian[1] community took the practical form of encouraging its members to enter the Government Service, where their promotion for good work was assured. From the day when Lord Hastings promoted Skinner, descendent of the Scotsman Hercules Skinner and the Rajput girl he married, from Captain of Irregulars to Lieutenant-Colonel, Anglo-Indians have served the Government of India loyally and well.

---

1. The definition of the term Anglo-Indian was:—
"A resident British subject (not being pure European) who is of European descent in the male line, or who is of mixed Asiatic and non-Asiatic descent, and whose father, grandfather, or more remote ancestor was born in the Continent of Europe, Canada, Newfoundland, Australia, New Zealand, the Union of South Africa or the U.S.A." (*Ind. Stat. Commission Report*, Vol. I. p. 45). The term Anglo-Indian was used by Sir John Malcolm in 1826 *(Political History*, Vol. II. pp. 260-265).
Ref: Sir George Dunbar's *History of India*, Vol. II. p. 441.

Introduction

Irene 1906–2002

My mother told her story "like it is"; no beating about the bush nor trying to hide the uncomfortable bits. Her life back "Home" from 1950 until her death was not easy. She had grown up accustomed to staff cooking and cleaning for her—at home and at work; and suddenly found herself doing absolutely everything for herself and for her family in what was a very "foreign" environment.

One of her greatest joys was her garden. Wherever we were her gardens were admired by passers-by, many of whom stopped, discussing gardening lore and forming good friendships; but her Indian up-bringing was deeply ingrained and it was a source of embarrassment to her adolescent children that whenever horses passed our homes our mother would scuttle out with bucket and shovel to collect the precious manure for her beloved roses.

It is sad that her story was not published during her lifetime but her family is proud and grateful that it is now in print. That achievement is largely due to Irene's daughter-in-law, Suzi Edwards, who first read the manuscript in the early 1970s, never forgot the impression it made on her and when Irene died was nothing short of terrier-like in her determination to save the story and have it reproduced for the family. The result is this book.

Suzi, in turn, is grateful for the help, encouragement and advice she received from Tony Rundell and Charles Radford in pointing her in the right direction.

John Edwards

April 2012

CHAPTER 1

How It Happened

"Keep out of the sun, girls, you don't want to get any browner than you are," called my mother. This was the first beauty hint drummed into our young ears. My sister and I would dutifully hurry into the shade of the *neem* tree to continue our games. We were Anglo-Indians or Eurasians, whose most highly prised possession was a skin that was slightly lighter than the Indian's.

This community came into being as a result of the inter-marrying or condoned misalliances of the early European adventurers to India. The Portuguese came on the scene first in 1498, followed by the East Indian Company, which obtained its charter in 1603. The French, Dutch and Danes all had settlements at one time or another in various parts of this sub-continent. In all these instances there were never enough European women to balance the exiled male population, and what followed was a natural sequence of prevailing circumstances.

Through the centuries this 'mixed' population gradually increased as the militant adventurers, having fought and decided, who was the victor, were replaced by an established army, civil service and trading community, or '*box wallahs*' as the army and civil service called them. But, there was always the scarcity of European women. Due to the circumstances of his birth the Anglo-Indian generally had an opportunity to acquire a better education then the average Indian and he could, of course, speak English. As communications started to develop in the country he became the automatic choice for positions of driver, guard and clerical worker on the railways. The post and telegraph sections also began to absorb him. As these sections expanded so he took over more responsibility.

In time the girls started nursing and practically monopolised this profession in the civilian hospitals. If it had not been for them, the medical profession in India would not have advanced very rapidly. In effect the railway, the posts and telegraph services became the preserve of the male Eurasian, whilst the girls did the nursing, and on occasions, acted as nannies to the army and civil service families.

As India became industrialised and British and foreign capital was invested in the country by large European firms, the Anglo-Indians found fresh opportunities as chargehands or foremen who could control Indian labour and act as the interpreters between the temporary European bosses and the local workers, There was nobody more loyal to the British Crown and Empire than this community. They played their part during the First and Second World Wars and it was during the latter that they came into their own. They had the privilege and amenities offered to the European military or civil defence personnel and were not hampered by any colour discriminations. Perhaps they should have realised it was too good to last.

There had been talk of "Home Rule," "*Swaraj*" or an Independent India for years, when the British would be kicked out and it would be India for the Indians, But nobody took this seriously, least of all the Eurasians. After V.E. day and the general election of 1945, the grapevine began to get rumours around that the labour government was quite prepared to hand over India lock, stock and barrel. This was at first treated with contempt by Anglo-Indians. Further developments, however, soon convinced them that there was to be a "sell out." Those of the Anglo-Indians who could see ahead, and had the means to do so got out of the country as soon as they were able. Many on the railways and in the telegraph services collected their provident funds to pay their passages and those of their families and migrated, mainly to England to start afresh. Those who had done war service were granted a free passage to England for themselves and one dependant.

The new Indian and Pakistani Governments were rather perturbed at the mass exodus that was occurring amongst the personnel of services vital to the efficient running of two newly created states. They persuaded many that thought of leaving to stay on telling them that there was nothing to worry about, and that their jobs were secure. The pattern changed when they had trained sufficient of their own kind. Constant moving about from one station to another on transfers that were without justification, and other annoyances to make life feel insecure were inflicted upon them to try and persuade them to collect what was due to them and get out.

This is a brief outline of how the Anglo-Indian community origi-nated, played its part in British India, and has practically disintegrated, to be scattered in European countries that were willing to absorb them, and where a colour bar was not in operation. The majority have migrated to England. The following story is an attempt to portray my own life as a child, a young girl and an adult in the Anglo-Indian community, and those with whom we had to work and live outside our own circle.

CHAPTER 2

Early Days

It is a far call from a child born in India in 1906, to a middle-aged housewife today running her Yorkshire home.

My father was born in India of English parents. He was what the dictionary defines as an Anglo-Indian. Then again, people who have lived in India for many years, preferring the climate to that of this damp and misty isle, called themselves Anglo-Indians, and so the issue is somewhat confused. My father married a widow with several children, She was half Portuguese, half Indian. His mother strongly disapproved of this marriage, and her biting comments: "The basket of ready-made children," "A woman of the country," and "Trace of the tar-brush!" were, unfortunately, repeated to my mother, who was hurt. Colour prejudice, the cause of the unhappiness, burnt bitterly into my soul, and that bug-bear of most Anglo-Indians, an inferiority complex, was born. This complex made us (when noticed by Europeans) feel highly flattered, and being oversensitive, when ignored we felt snubbed, imagining gibes when perhaps none was intended.

My mother, who always referred to herself as an ignorant woman, was gentle and kind with natural good manners, and a wealth of commonsense topped with plenty of good humour. When asked how she came to possess such a fine nature her reply was, "By reading the Bible and other good books." The lessons learnt from my dear mother were to be kind to all regardless of colour or creed; to take a pride in our work no matter how lowly; and above all else, to pray daily. I owe much to her and am proud of the spiritual heritage she passed on to me. My mother told me she was very pleased when I was born, a near-white with green-grey-blue eyes end very fair hair. She thought I would escape the trials of the colour bar, but I have often thought how wrong Mama was. She went on to tell me that after my birth in the Lady Lyle Hospital at Agra, of Taj Mahal fame, she and I were travelling to Bandikui, a railway settlement, to join my father who was stationed there. On the train my mother met an old acquaintance. He knew my mother had remarried but had never met my father. When he noticed me in my mother's arms he casually enquired whose baby I was.

"She's mine," proudly exclaimed my mother.

"Go on!" said he, "You're pulling my leg! She is some European's child and you are the nanny!"

"No, she is not, she is my baby."

And my mother found it very difficult to convince him. A year later my sister Doreen was born, a pale beige. I well remember a description once given of an Anglo-Indian family. They were likened to a bunch of flowers, all colours! And this fact was the cause of much unhappiness in families, especially amongst girls, but my mother in her wisdom managed to prevent this type of bitterness amongst us. When Doreen was two or three days old, the English matron of the same hospital at Agra, on a routine round of the wards, saw my mother looking in a puzzled way at her baby. "Now, Mrs. Green, I know what you are thinking. Why is this second baby so much darker than the first? Just wait and see, this child is going to be beautiful one day."

And she was right. My sister Doreen, with her lovely well-shaped nose and other clear-cut features, turned out a classic beauty, enhanced by large brown eyes and black hair; whilst I, with a small pug nose which kind people called '*retroussé*,' teeth which protruded very slightly, a round baby face, hair that commenced as gold but soon changed to brown, was 'Mouse' or 'Mousey-Face' to my pals, when I became a nurse.

My earliest memories of Anglo-Indian or Eurasian life as lived on the railways goes back to when we lived in Bandikui, a railway colony. My father was in the traffic department, and although his parents were English, the fact that he was born in India made the road to promotion long, and difficult, He worked for many years as a ticket examiner, then as a guard, and did not get his first appreciable step-up until 1914. With the First World War in sight the authorities decided to make better use of the white Anglo-Indians and these were moved to the garrison stations. Before this the official and senior subordinate posts were ear-marked for men from the United Kingdom, mostly under covenant or on contract, and this was a very sore point with those Anglo-Indians and Eurasians whose parents had spent hard, earned money on their education.

It was a well known fact that many of the covenanted men were barely able to sign their names, and when it came to writing a report in English the subordinate was given the work. However by having the covenanted *wallahs* amongst us we had the advantage of the Railway Institute or Social Club which had originally been provided by the Railway Company in most colonies for the benefit of the exiles. These centres were open to all except the purely Indian. The amenities provided generally consisted of tennis, bowls, a billiard table, bar and library. This was not all provided free and those using the Institute paid a subscription for the 'privilege.' The only Europeans in the junior grades were 'Tommies,' who having married Anglo-Indian, Eurasian and even Indian, women preferred to settle in India rather than face the chance hostility of the colour bar at home.

In centres consisting entirely of railway personnel, schools were provided by the railway, and taking into consideration the lack of funds generally the standard of education was restricted. Commencing with infant classes it stopped at what was known as standard IV (form IV). Children whose parents were better off financially usually sent their children to hill schools, which were first class. Education was very costly in India, and many an Anglo-Indian family was beggared on retirement, having spent their hard-earned money on their children's education. Scholarships were a rarity, in fact there were no facilities for advanced education. For school dress we wore ordinary clothes but clean pinafores were a kind of uniform. We wore these with a long sleeved dress to protect our arms from burning in the very hot sun and then, most important of all, the solar *topee*—with a final pat on its crown—was set upon our heads.

Everyone in India seemed to wear these, except the Indians—they had more sense. The Indian Christian gradually took to these thereby raising, as he imagined, his social status to that of a Eurasian. At first this very ludicrous European headgear gave him a somewhat top-heavy appearance, but this, plus the discomfort, was off-set completely by the added prestige gained when he was mistaken for a *topee wallah* or Eurasian, and a further thrill was experienced when a '*pugree*' clad Indian *salaamed* and called him '*Sahib!*' My mother insisted upon veils being worn with our *topees*. Green silk knotted round the brim cascaded over face and neck to protect the skin from darkening. Our plea that we could hardly see and that these made us hot, had no effect. As we said our goodbyes, my mother always had the last word, "Now keep out of the sun, girls."

Years later, on joining my husband, in Malaya, I was reminded of those *topees* and veils. Chinese girls working in the fields under the hot sun wore large straw hats. They also wore long sleeves to their jackets, and something I had never seen before, flaps sewn to the cuff ends to fall over the back of the hands. I pointed these out to my husband who said, "Oh! They don't want to get sunburnt!" Back switched my thoughts to the colour problem. Even the Asian girls wanted to be as fair as possible. In India one is often able to see advertisements on the following lines in the local press:—

Refined Indian gentleman in government service England re-turned, failed B.A., requires a young English-speaking bride with authentic Indian look, moon face and doe eyes. Good dowry expected, must be very fair.

The last few words indicate that the degree of the skin pigmenta-tion is even a problem in the marriage stakes in Asian countries. It is impossible for them to understand the mentality of the sun-starved Britisher or other European who anoints himself or herself with oil and fries in the hot sun to acquire a tan.

The men having gone to work and the children to school, the housewife had plenty of leisure and she used this in different ways. A gossip with the next door neighbour, or a visit to a friend, after the servants, each in turn, had been given their day's work. Often the housewife sat on the verandah supervising the *dirzee*. This character squatted on the floor on which a thin old carpet had been spread, and repaired old clothes and odd bits of linen on a very old sewing machine, usually a vintage 'Singer' which had been handed down for generations. Fashion books sent out monthly from England and sold on the railway station bookstalls were bought by the women. Now there was an added interest, patterns would be studied and as the *dirzee* could not read English 'Memsahib' would have to explain. The result was a very good copy by an illiterate Indian tailor of a fashion model.

Anglo-Indian or Eurasian women rarely went out to work in those days as it was considered unseemly. The exception was being a nurse or a nanny to the army officers' children. Between the first and second world wars they gradually entered more into the business life of the community and took on clerical and secretarial appointments and even started serving in the large European stores in the cities as sales assistants. The Second World War, of course, emancipated them completely and they did jobs that they would never have thought of accepting a few years earlier. Girls in India matured early and as a result married quite young. The prospect of a home of their own was something to look forward to besides easing the strain on the one wage earner in the family.

Midday would see us children racing down the hot dusty roads, homeward bound from school. Our minds fixed on the chopped melon sitting on crushed ice, with lashings of sugar and lemon juice. Or the green coconut that bearer would crack open over a bowl to catch every drop of the delicious clear, cool fluid which we would drink before sharing the soft semi-transparent flavoured coconut meat scraped off the inside of the shell with a teaspoon. After *tiffin* everyone, except the '*mad dogs and Englishmen*,' went for their *siesta*.

Towards the cool of the evening most young people would make for the institute to play games, or just sit around and chat. The swings and slides were always popular with the children. At most of the larger railway centres there was a railway stores, a sort of co-operative venture run by the Railway Company mainly for the benefit of its own employees, although anybody could acquire a nominal share and make use of its services. This 'shop' was generally by the institute and proved popular with the children for sweets and bottles of 'pop'.

The Indian railway staff were not allowed to join these institutes which were called 'European,' though ninety-five *per cent* of its members were coloured. In some stations the Indians had their own institutes. They did not suffer this indignity alone because the colour bar seemed to be in operation everywhere to a greater or lesser degree. In cantonments some clubs were barred to us, so there we were, a community which considered itself in terms of national status superior to the Indians yet unacceptable in an all white community. We were positioned, as my mother remarked, "*between the devil and the deep sea.*"

Returning home after an evening's recreation it was a pretty sight to see dotted here and there tables with white cloths, flowers, vases and silk shaded oil lamps, which the servants had to get ready in each compound. When the heat was intense dining out-of-doors was a pleasure but, attracted by the lamps, the flying insects were a pest. It was bliss sleeping out-of-doors under a sky of black velvet, with millions and millions of stars keeping watch over us. My mother always insisted on us saying our prayers indoors after we had changed into our night clothes and before we got too sleepy. Then we would run out and dive between cool sheets, first making sure there were no snakes under our beds. We would lie chatting happily to each other for a while, then Mama would suggest we close the day by singing a hymn. I remember with nostalgia a little girl staring back at the stars singing 'Now the day is over' or 'Abide with me,' feeling very happy, safe and close to God. All the cruel things of life were far away, though as each day passed, they crept nearer. Sometimes the jackals would wake us; we were a little frightened of these, especially as a pack once attacked my father as he was coming home from work in the middle of the night.

These starving creatures would leave the jungles on the lookout for a stray pi-dog, or a chicken not properly penned. It is impossible to describe their blood-curdling howls and shrieks, but one can only imagine it would be something like tearing babies limb from limb. A pack of these suddenly starting their cacophony by the house whilst on their scavenging trail was enough to frighten any child.

As the monsoon approached sleeping out became more risky and in case of a sudden shower we had to be prepared to grab our bedclothes and dash inside to finish the night on the floor, hoping the scorpions, centipedes and other creepy-crawlies would not notice they had company.

That was life in those far off days, not much entertainment for the young compared with their demands today, but more peaceful for the elders. About once a month, a dance to a gramophone, a whist drive, a touring cinema show or a concert party, would cause much excitement. On such occasions, the railway stores would do a brisk trade in a French make of face powder, and the most popular shade was *Blanche*. So that their skins would appear lighter the women would plaster themselves thickly with this, although why they thought it necessary when their men folk were content, to leave theirs the way God made them, is now a mystery to me, but as a teenager I was just as foolish.

Just occasionally a *fête* or bazaar would be arranged, and, most Eurasians being Roman Catholic, this meant the chapel would benefit considerably. Papa, Doreen and I were members of the Church of England, at my mother's request Doreen and I were baptised as such.

Mama and the children by her first husband were Roman Catholics, so even in this we were a mixed lot. But again Mama, in her wisdom, saw to it there was no discord. After one of the church meetings, Mama came home in great excitement to tell me that I had been chosen to present the bouquet, also to sell buttonholes as assistant to an officer's daughter, who had graciously consented to manage the flower stall. At the time Mama was speaking, I was only interested in the new frock I had been promised. But this was the start of the 'preferential' treatment I got to know so well as I grew older. The important roles such as 'Queen,' 'Fairy,' or 'Bouquet Giver' were reserved for the fair-skinned ones; perhaps it was a good thing for my morale that I was not always chosen, often being beaten by one just a shade or two lighter.

In school concerts, in drills or in a chorus, the poor little brown ones were discreetly pushed to the back, whilst the fair ones would be in the front row.

It was shortly after my debut into this social life that my father came home looking very pleased and proudly announced that he had been transferred, with promotion, from guard to night stationmaster, and posted to Mhow.

Transferred to Mhow! The elder girls, Maisie and Vi, my half sisters, could hardly believe it. They had always wanted to go there after hearing from friends about life in that gay army cantonment. Mama's mind was fixed on the larger pay packet Papa would receive, whilst Doreen and I could only think of the long train journey. "Really miles and miles and miles of it, Papa?" we asked over and over again. We remembered nothing of the previous journeys between Bandikui, Sirsa and Agra, as we had been too young. Janki and Munoo, our cook and *ayah's* children were as excited as we were—they were going with us—the bearer and sweeper declined to move. The journey from Bandikui to Mhow is four hundred and sixty-one miles. The railway allowed us a coach for ourselves, with four berths for sleeping.

The servants travelling in the adjacent *coupé*, with a door opening between, came at night and made a bed on the floor for Doreen and me. Our dogs insisted on sharing this with us, fleas and all! A wagon was provided for our furniture. Mama had ordered cook to make a good supply of duck *vindaloo*—a sort of pickled curry which keeps indefinitely—for part of the journey, also a large roast which, owing to the heat, was eaten first.

There was too much for us to see and do on the big stations, so

WITH YOUNGER SISTER DOREEN, ON THE RIGHT

little time was taken up with eating. The dogs needed exercise and Doreen and I would take them out on leads. The yelps of delight at the prospect of a walk can well be imagined, but this was short lived. Also, at these stops, we had to go along with Papa to our wagon which was at the rear of the train. Papa, who kept the keys, would unlock the wagon and hoist Doreen and me up to feed and water the poultry. These poor things were certainly not at home in wire-covered crates that had been packed in with the furniture, but even so, one or two were obliging enough to lay. All this was exciting and tremendous fun for us, too much perhaps? So, even the imagined lullaby of the wheels,—

Ek ek anna
Do do paiss
Do do paiss
Teen teen rupaye

—as the train rolled on failed to induce sleep, much as we needed it.

Usually, sleep is not possible on Indian railways, the noise at all hours of the night has to be heard to be believed. At all stops vendors with their wares would jostle one another, and rush blindly in their eagerness to make direct contact with the passengers in the short time available. Their shouts of "*Pan-biri,*" "*Char Gurram, Gurram Char,*" "*Ludoo, Para, Jellabi,*" and the base voice of the *Paniwallah* went up like a mighty roar.

Then came the surge forward by illiterate Indian villagers. These would bang, loud and long, on any carriage door, and cases were known during hot summer nights when windows were left open, of villagers pushing their ragged bundles and themselves through these windows on to some sleeping second class passenger! Such incidents were quickly spotted by harassed railway servants, who would then guide these third class passengers in the right direction. These poor souls would have to travel on hard forms, packed closer together than any sardine in a tin. A two feet square cabin with a hole cut in the compartment floor was totally inadequate for their personal needs. So, when the train stopped at any station the third class passengers would get out on the 'off-side' to attend to nature's demands. Here men and women squatted side by side, the women taking care to cover their faces only!

One year Doreen and I were taken to Delhi to meet a party of schoolchildren coming down from Simla. Their parents were unable to meet them, and being; friends of ours, my mother volunteered to go, as our passes for the year had not been used. The children coming home for Christmas were very excited and happy. They glowed with health, all having lovely pink cheeks, whilst we, who had spent the summer on the plains, looked pale and sickly in comparison, but we were shocked at the naughty things they did. The train was a 'Special', chartered for the school party, and would only stop at the big stations. Just before it was due to leave, mysterious long wire hooks attached to canes were pulled out of the bedrolls, and if the sweetmeat vendors had not moved to a safe distance as the train moved off, these were pushed out and '*jellabies*' skilfully yanked off the trays on the vendors' heads.

Naughtier still were the boys with the catapults. Throughout the journey these were in action. Station lamps were an easy target, but if on looking out they saw villagers using the railway embankment as a lavatory, or another train pulled up at a small station and the third class passengers using the space between parallel trains for the same purpose, they would call out: "Frogs coming up!" and rush to the windows and 'ping' away at the exposed unoffending bottoms. All this was known to the school authorities as yearly complaints were sent from the different stations. Before leaving school the boys would be searched and 'cattys' being unlawful they would be confiscated, and the culprits 'tanned' in public. A second check was made sometimes at the station but all this was foreseen and plans made. '*Chokras*'—Indian boys—were given *buksheesh* to take the 'cattys' to the station, and as the train drew out, these little devils would run alongside and pass them in.

My brother-in-law, a scholar from St. Joseph's College in Naini Tal, told us some of these and other school stories when we were still very young.

We arrived at Mhow too soon, at least Doreen and I thought so, but the four grownups and two dogs had other views. Then came the work of unloading the wagon. My father went off to report for duty leaving my mother to supervise this. The *coolies* from the station were commandeered. The cook using his influence as the night stationmaster's servant, bullied these poor little men. The big girls, with Doreen and I leading the dogs, ran down the road excitedly to inspect our new home. This stood very near the station and the military police, on his way to duty there, got word around that there were young ladies in the new family. Invitations to dances, whist drives, tin and bottle tournaments soon poured in, and so we were introduced to the British 'Tommy.' Doreen and I were a little shy and frightened of them at first, but soon grew to love these good-natured men.

Mama was fond of entertaining the soldiers. Meals "*just like mother used to serve up back home*," roasts, pies and stews took the place of the more familiar curries. This gesture was appreciated and reciprocated by bottles of beer and other army rations. The army, from officers down to other ranks were always welcomed to the railway institutes, but this wholehearted hospitality was only returned by the lower ranks. The higher the rank, the stronger was the colour-bar. In these cantonments, the Anglo-Indian and Eurasian men were at a disadvantage. Apart from not being such good dancers as the 'Tommies,' their women folk preferred to dance with the white men. This being 1914-15 my father was kept busy with the army specials.

If during the day we heard the band coming down the road, Doreen and I would run to stand by our wire fence. We soon learned to wave and fly kisses, as sweets and chocolates were thrown to us by the men marching along gaily singing 'It's a long way to Tipperary' or 'Carry me back to dear old Blighty.' We often caught my mother in tears when we returned to the house. Her only son was also serving his king and country in 'Mespot.'

As we lived so near the station, we could not fail to see the arrival of the Red Cross trains with the wounded who were sent to the large army hospital in Mhow. Then another sad sight was a military funeral. The cemetery being directly behind our house we had an uninterrupted view. The gun carriage bearing its flag-draped coffin, and the troops marching behind with guns reversed, to the sad strains of 'Flowers of the Forest' affected us considerably, and Doreen and I would stand quite still and wait until the procession was out of sight before resuming our game. I wonder how many of the parents at 'Home' knew that, when their sons were being buried under a far distant Eastern sky, there were two little Eurasian girls mourning with them. Would they have been comforted do you think?

The Anglo-Indian and Eurasian community proffered to the Crown a loyalty that was firm and true and from this was born a strong desire to serve England. Many an A.I. boy joined the forces, but this was not encouraged to the same extent as it was in the Second

World War. The same thing applied to the girls; nursing and typing were the only ways in which they could serve then, but during the Second World War they were all in khaki serving in all branches where women were accepted.

About this time Maisie showed a keenness for singing, and asked Mama if she could have some singing lessons. "Yes," replied Mama, "but you must pay for them yourself."

To do this Maisie took a job as nursemaid in an officer's household.

"Why this sudden interest?" asked Papa.

"We'll soon find out," replied Mama, smiling, "I suppose there's a fellow in it somewhere."

She was right, too! Maisie had met a young man with a good voice who belonged to the local Choral Society. She joined this after a few singing lessons and started bringing the young man home. My mother was a despot in matters concerning the opposite sex. 'The Gypsy's Warning' was mild compared to her rules. Courting couples were allowed to sit alone but in a well-lit room, and there were no silent interludes, they had to keep talking! My mother would sit in an adjoining room and cough at intervals. The young couple were not allowed out after dark, and could go only to those functions where the crowd was chaperone.

At dances 'kala-juggas' specially built for courting couples were taboo. In a nutshell, she was extremely strict, and how any of her daughters ever collected husbands is a mystery, except that the men concerned were determined and persevering. Years later, Doreen was put through this form of torture, and tells of the evening one of her boyfriends said, "Why doesn't your mother do something for her cough, it seems very troublesome?"

My mother, on being told this next morning, said dryly, "You tell, him to buy me some cough mixture, I'll take it!"

Another asked her, "Why doesn't your mother go to sleep?"

This she was wise enough not to repeat.

I had no boyfriends because they found me dull. It was not until I was a second year student at St. George's Hospital that I collected my first. Perhaps my mother failed in not discussing the facts of life with us without embarrassment. Everyone pretended that sex did not exist, and we only gleaned a little doubtful knowledge through the usual childish prattle of the Indian children with whom we played. They had no inhibitions on the subject and took it all for granted, because the facts were not hidden from them.

"Here comes the bride, fair, fat and wide," Doreen and I would sing to Maisie, teasing her as she went about getting her trousseau ready. Then, my father came home one day looking very pleased with himself. "Maisie," he said, "you had better hurry along your wedding arrangements as we are on transfer again." At the sight of the glum faces gathered around Papa hastened to say, "It is a promotion," but this only pleased my mother who, doubtless, was thinking about the extra money. The wedding was rushed through, Maisie marrying her soldier in Christ Church very quietly, just the family attending.

My mother was very pleased Maisie had married a British soldier, and not a coloured man. "Not that I am snobbish," she hastened to explain, "It's just that I do not want my children being hurt more than is necessary."

CHAPTER 3

Nasirabad

This move was to Nasirabad, three hundred and five miles north of Mhow. On arriving we found our house was situated a short distance away from the station, and a road leading from the station went past our bungalow to the military cantonment. "Not many troops here," my father informed us. We were surrounded by waste land, nothing but thorn, cacti and sisal seemed to flourish in this stony, sandy countryside. However, there were a few fields of sugarcane and corn of a poor quality. When these crops were harvested, we had cows and goats as neighbours, as they were allowed to graze on the stubble. The Indian staff were housed behind the station so were out of sight and sound of us. We were isolated, and being the only Anglo-Indians in Nasirabad had to make our own amusements and interests. One of the highlights was the *purdah* party arranged by my father's head clerk who was anxious for my mother to meet his wife. We had to travel by bullock-cart to his village, which was some miles out of Nasirabad.

On arriving, to our dismay, we found not only our hostess but the entire female population waiting for us. Not a male over six was in sight. *Ram Rams* being exchanged we were escorted to the shade of some large *pipal* trees in the courtyard of the only brick-built home in the village. Smaller mud huts were clustered about, with cows, dogs and chickens in abundance. A few vegetables and flowering plants struggled for existence, A carpet and three *moorahs*, those comfortable split cane chairs, and a small table had been arranged for us, The yard had been freshly *leeped* or faced with a mixture of mud and cow dung. The women squatted on cheap string beds called *charpoys* facing us, the giggling young girls brought out refreshments. We had *paratas*, *achars*, *sags*, curries and sweetmeats.

These items with the unleavened bread, cooked with clarified butter called *ghee*, hot pickles and vegetables were a typical meal for the richer family. My mother being polite used the fingers of her right hand to eat, as the others around us were doing. Doreen and I were too hungry and used the cutlery provided. They laughed at us, but we knew they did not mean to be unkind.

After tea we sat and talked; at least they questioned whilst my mother replied. They wanted to know about our way of life. These women asked the most intimate questions without a blush: not from rudeness, I hasten to add, but from a thirst for knowledge. Their desire to learn about the outside world was pathetic. I remember, some years after this party, I was travelling between Mhow and Bombay and had to share a Second Class Ladies with a number of Marwari women going to a wedding. The Marwaris are wealthy merchant class, originally from Marwar in Central India. The questions I was asked would have made me hopping mad had I not known that rudeness was unintended. "How many children have you?" "Not married!" "Why not?" "What do you think you have been given that body for?" "Are you going to marry?" "When?" "Whom?"

So under the palm trees we endured in patience; after the questions came the inspection. They inspected our clothes, even lifting our frocks to see what we wore underneath. Our long old-fashioned white cotton drawers down to the knees, ending in a frill with lace, made them laugh! Doreen was pink with anger! I looked at her and laughed, and was kicked on the ankle. My mother understood and was patient. I came in for special treatment being the only one there with eyes and hair of a different shade. They asked Mama if I could see properly. "Poor thing, perhaps she is a little blind," they added kindly. As this was a special occasion, my long hair hung free to my waist, "*Sona! Sona!*" exclaimed the women, stroking the unusual golden coloured hair.

Nasirabad was rich in game birds; we were never fed so well nor so cheaply as when we were there. Villagers came around with huge baskets on their heads crammed with live grouse, partridge, quail, pigeon and even peacock. This bird, being held sacred by some, should not have been trapped. I suppose the villager got round this by the well-known method of palm-greasing. We had large cages standing in the compound where these birds would be released, fed and watered, to be killed by cook as required. The peacock or peahen was brought in weekly to be killed right away and roasted, the feathers being discreetly burned. It is a royal and succulent dish, rather like turkey but not as dry. We enjoyed this for months until some silly women visiting us from Ajmere told my mother that peacocks ate snakes. That settled it. No more peacock, much to the disgust of the family.

Carry me back to dear old Blighty,
Put me on the train to London Town.

This song would be wistfully sung by the 'Tommies' who, out of sheer boredom with nothing to do in that dreary place apart from the routine of drills and other army duties and games, would wander down to the station to see the trains go by, and talk to my father. Occasionally, a travelling concert party from Bombay or Calcutta would visit these cantonments and break the monotony. Papa was usually given complimentary tickets in exchange for helping in some way; arranging accommodation in the *dak* bungalow or, if full, the waiting rooms. If no refreshment room service was available, our cook was put at their disposal.

"Jane, I am bringing a couple of boys home to dinner tomorrow night," we would often hear Papa say. My parents thought it was their duty to give what hospitality they could to these lonely men, especially in war time. This seemed to be appreciated, even if there were no young ladies about. Doreen and I were concert crazy at this time. I suppose those touring shows were to blame. Being shy, and not much good at acting or dancing, I was stage manager and general factotum. Doreen was versatile, a splendid mimic, and very soon after our show began she would have the men laughing. We taught Janki and Munoo some English songs, and it was funny to hear Janki sing "*You called me Baby Doll a year ago,*" especially when you realised she did not understand the words. At the 'you' we taught her to point at a soldier, and the 'Tommy,' with his great sense of humour, loved it. Our public consisted of our parents, the one or two 'Tommies,' some of my father's staff and our servants. They were all charged a small entrance fee which we collected for our War Fund.

We learned the lesson one day of that adage which says something about Satan finding mischief for idle hands. Mama had gone into Ajmere to shop, *ayah* was left to turn out cupboards after a dust storm. After finishing the lessons we had been set, we wandered off to the servants' quarters to find Janki. She was grinding fresh henna leaves. Indian women use this to paint their hands and feet; apart from being a beauty aid, it is said to be cooling. Mohammedan pilgrims, who have visited Mecca, also use this on their beards, getting a red tint.

They are then addressed as "*Hajji*" or better still "*Hajji Sahib*," and are treated with great respect. We sat watching Janki, till she had ground the leaves to a fine pulp. She then proceeded to dab this on her toes, keeping her feet still until they dried. She then did her left hand, and I volunteered to do her right hand. Then Doreen had an idea.

"I think I'll have some on my toes."

"Don't be silly, you know the red does not come off easily."

"Still, it will be fun, and we'll be asleep when Papa and Mama come home tonight. In the morning *ayah* can scrub it off. Come on! Irene, you get some on also."

"No, I'm too frightened."

"Cowardy, cowardy, custard," she called.

That challenge had to be met, so I stuck my toes out as well, and Janki smeared us both.

We were barefooted, and as it was very hot, only wore long drawers and bodices, our hair being drawn back into one long plait. We had our hands painted as well, and then decided to do the thing properly, and asked for the *tika* to be placed on our foreheads. This is the red beauty spot worn by girls and married women but not by widows. To our confusion Mama, who was not expected back until late that night, had been able to finish her shopping earlier, and now accompanied by Papa was walking up the road from the station. It was too late for us to do anything about it. I wanted, to run away and hide.

"No," said Doreen, "Come on, we'll go down, and meet them."

Holding her hands up before her face and bowing low, she said? "*Ram Ram.*"

I, following meekly behind, did the same. We must have looked very peculiar to say the least, A military policeman, riding by on his bicycle on the way to the station, wheeled round and laughed. He called to Papa, "What have you got there?"

"Two little rascals who should be locked up."

But as he and Mama were smiling, we knew all was well.

As we were going to miss the usual generous railway Christmas programme, our parents were wondering what they could do for us. Obviously we could not go into Ajmere for all the functions, though they made the effort and we were taken in for the 'tree' on the 24th. Then Papa had an idea: "Jane, I'll ask the officer next time he visits the station to see the M.P.s on duty and find out if the girls could be asked to the sports and 'At Home' being held during Christmas week."An invitation duly arrived, and we were thrilled! Mama saw to it that we were well scrubbed, and in our best party dresses of white voile we left home happily, with *ayah* as escort, After taking us up to the *shamiana*, *ayah* deserted us to join the others seated behind the tent. Then we felt the blast: what a chilly reception we were given, if reception you could call it. There we stood silently staring at the army officers and their families seated in rows of chairs facing the field.

We were anxious to sit down so that we could watch the event taking place just then, but we knew we should not do so until invited. We also knew we should say "Hello" or "Good Afternoon" and shake hands perhaps with someone, but with whom? No one approached us so we waited, awkward and shy. It was some time before a young officer detached himself from a group and came up to welcome us, but it was too late. I was old enough to feel the slight. Once seated, however, we soon forgot the unfriendly crowds and thoroughly enjoyed the events taking place.

At the tea interval, one or two of the army '*memsahibs*' came up enquiring if we had been served; this was done in the usual condescending manner we had grown to expect and accept. Though they need not have bothered, the bearers had seen to it that we had more than enough. *They* were not taking part in any social distinctions that afternoon. Always on occasions such as this we would try and smuggle a cake or two home for Janki and Munoo, who would eagerly look out for our return. We would wrap them in our handkerchiefs, hoping no one would notice. I expect if one of those '*memsahibs*' that afternoon did see us walking away with this loot, she would have turned her friend and said, "Those poor little half-starved half-castes, so sad, don't you think?" On returning home and giving our report instinct made us refrain from talking about the cool treatment we had received. We did not want Papa to be hurt.

Early in the New Year to our delight, and this time even the servants were glad, my father came home to tell us we were on transfer to Sojat-Road. "A bigger place than this, where there will be neighbours and children for you to play with." Then noticing *ayah* he added, "And she'll have company for her pan-eating sessions."

"Hah Umma?"

"Yes Mother?"

CHAPTER 4

The Ever-Welcome Cuppa

Sojat-Road, about ninety miles away, was a welcome change from Nasirabad. It was not so dry and barren, and was a bigger railway colony. There were six to eight families on the senior staff. We were a mixed crowd, mostly Eurasian with just one European couple, a "near white" family, and the Samuels, an Indian Christian family with three children who were to be our playmates. This place boasted a tennis court where most evenings everyone collected. This *Kutcha* tennis court consisting of a bed of gravel smoothed over with a layer of earth plastered with a mixture of mud and cow-dung got Doreen and me into trouble.

One morning soon after our arrival we saw some women working on it, and went over to investigate. They had bowls of fresh cow-dung, which had been mixed with mud. Starting at one end of the court and working together in a line, they took a handful of this 'cowpat' mixture and with the palm of the hand smeared it over the surface to give a renewed smooth playing area. Doreen and I stood watching intently but only for a moment; soon we succumbed to the temptation and were trying to do the same but, of course, unsuccessfully. We were in a mess, blobs and smears of the 'plaster' all over our legs, arms and faces, and when it was time for us to go home, we realised the state we were in and did not feel too happy. Fortunately, my father on his way home to lunch met us, and took us round to the servants' quarters, asking *ayah* to clean us up before my mother saw us.

Education in Sojat-Road presented quite a problem as there was no school. Mama asked Mrs. King if she would give us lessons attending to our spiritual needs as well; this she kindly consented to do. So every morning after breakfast, wearing clean white pinafores and our horrible *topees* complete with hideous veils, we would be marched off for lessons until lunch time. Mr. King was the loco foreman there. Their youngest child, a boy, was in boarding school. We met him during the holidays, and, Doreen being the little flirt she was, soon had him heading her list—her first sweetheart.

My father got to know the local chief 'Thakur Sahib,' or 'T.S.' as he was called by his friends. He was very wealthy and owned a village and a sawmill. He also traded in goats, sending these to the butchers in Ajmere. This was a good trading line, sold as 'mutton,' goat meat was eaten practically all over India. Also, in the course of his work, Papa was able to assist T.S. by arranging accommodation on trains, allocating goods wagons to move his timber which, in the normal course, would have had to wait its turn. By way of appreciation for all my father did for him, T.S. often sent us lovely fruit: mangoes, guavas, pomelos and bread-fruit from his gardens. Occasionally Doreen and I would be presented with a goat each, which we were allowed to keep. They would then mysteriously disappear. In later years I realised the goats were either sold or given to the servants to provide meat for their *Burra Din*, (festivals).

One morning my father was given warning of an approaching Army Special which was due in the following afternoon. Actually there were two trains passing through with a short interval between them. He always had a fondness for the 'Tommies,' and as these men were going on active service, he decided Sojat Road must do something to show its loyalty. He rushed home to tell my mother to approach Mrs. King and the other women for help, provisions and money, whilst my father and some others would visit T.S. and the rich *Setes* in the bazaars for contributions. In this they were very successful, all contributing well; even the Indian staff added their mite. Co-operating well the families and servants got together and cooks were kept busy all that day and the next making meat rolls, sandwiches, cakes, pies and pastries. We children, the three Samuels were with us, were very excited hindering and helping for all we were worth.

Next day we waited patiently for the last passenger train to pull out before the army specials were due. "Please Mr. Guard, wave your green flag and take this train away quickly," said Doreen, dancing up and down. The train had hardly disappeared before the *coolies* carried all the dining tables we could muster on to the platform. These were not nearly enough so office tables were used. These tables covered the length of the platform, and did not look too bad when draped with white cloths. Then gallons and gallons of tea were brewed. Mrs. Maxwell (European), was given the honour of serving tea to the officers, and my father's office was cleared for this purpose. Mrs. Maxwell had arranged vases of flowers on her tables and Doreen and I wanted some for the troops, but my father said, "I think you'll find the 'Tommies' will prefer an extra bun to a vase of flowers." Perhaps he was right. The look on the faces of the men gazing out of the coach windows as the train drew into the station soon changed from boredom to amazement. Very quickly every window was crammed with faces.

My father as stationmaster saw the C.O. and explained. He told the officer we would be honoured if he would allow the men to take tea as our guests, the offer was cordially accepted.

When the order to 'fall out' was given, no train emptied more quickly. And now for us the fun began: we and the Samuel children raced round and round the tables serving. Everyone had to work quickly as time was short. We were pleased at the results. The men did full justice to all that was set before them. It must have been whilst we were busy clearing the tables that a whispered word was passed along. Before they entrained the C.O. said a few words of thanks on behalf of all, which was expected, but the rousing 'three cheers for Sojat-Road' that followed, surprised and delighted us. As the train drew out we heard the strains of 'Auld Lang Syne,' and in spite of the difficulty in swallowing experienced just then by most of us, we sang with them. My father meanwhile stood at attention, hand at the salute, with the rest of the senior staff grouped about him. Then, we had to start all over again, fixing the tables for the second contingent.

Now, to our confusion, we found we had been too generous with the first batch, but there was no time to do anything about it. The second sitting had to have our goodwill with whatever was left over. Though as there was plenty of '*char*,' which, the British 'Tommy' always enjoys, face was saved! A day or two later my father received a telegram from the C.O. expressing his appreciation. He was very proud of this. I would like to think that there are still some of these men, somewhere, who remember that little group of loyal Anglo-Indians and Eurasians, and their war effort on that far distant isolated railway platform.

We seemed to feel the heat more as we grew older, and my mother being sensible, allowed us to run around uncluttered by many clothes.

Indoors we wore just bodices and drawers, our feet bare. A very light muslin dress was added for out-of-doors. For playmates we had Janki and Munoo, and the children of the neighbours' servants. Sometimes the three Samuels joined us. In order to keep our heads clean the use of a dust or fine tooth comb became a daily routine. Occasionally the *ayah* spotted one, she would then start a 'Madras hunt.' With a satisfied exclamation she would pick it out, pinching the scalp in the process which made us squeal. Then placing it neatly between her two thumb nails she would crack a big black louse. It was obvious it had fallen off the Indians as those which hatched out from nits on Anglo-Indians or Eurasians were smaller and of a lighter colour.

About this time, Maisie and her family paid us a surprise visit. They had been moved to Agra, and had left Vi with friends to continue her job in the military office. About two days before the visit was over, Maisie decided to take me back with her. They were living in the fort, and she assured Mama I would be happy and safe playing in those grounds. How they came to terms with Doreen I cannot imagine, but there were certainly no tears or sulks, my mother, no doubt, dealt with the situation in her own wise manner. So it came about that as a little girl I lived in that historic fort and played in the shade of the famous Taj Mahal. Sitting on the ramparts one could see the *Taj* across the river.

After a time I met a girl called Ivy Chipdale who had recently come out to India; her father was a sergeant, I think. She must have been a little older than I was, she was certainly a lot more precocious! During my visit a very big *fête* was organised somewhere outside the fort. It was called the 'Our Day *Fête*'—held on December 12th, 1917 all over India, in aid of the war sick and wounded. A dance was also arranged the same night, the two being connected. Maisie asked me which I would prefer, the *fête* or the dance.

"You can't go to both as you'd be too tired." She was being diplomatic. I do not think the final choice would have been mine as I was only eleven, but she knew—though I did not,—that Ivy was being taken to both. "There will be swings and shies, merry-go-rounds, and dips and lots for you to see at the *fête*," she tempted.

"Oh, the *fête*, please," I cried.

"Good! Now what about a dress for you, you haven't a decent thing to wear."

As there was no ready cash, she had to be enterprising. Standing still in the centre of the bedroom she meditated, whilst I fixed my eyes on her. Suddenly, the bedclothes were stripped off the nearest bed, and asking me to help, she pulled the mattress case away. This was cut up, and in a few hours I had a new white dress. From her rag bag she managed to find enough blue material to make a sailor collar and a pair of cuffs. I wonder how the loss of 'one case army mattress for' was later explained! Though the material was thick and coarse, I felt very proud of my new dress, proud, that is, until I saw Ivy Chipdale. She wore white silk and a string of pearls, and looked like a princess, I thought, with her white skin, blonde hair and blue eyes.

Every evening, the *ayah* with baby and I would go down to play on the lawns below and Ivy would join us there. After a while a couple of 'Tommies' followed; *ayah* now moved away with the pram. Even at her early age Miss Ivy appeared to have her boyfriends, but all this was beyond me and made me feel rather uncomfortable, especially as I was warned by Ivy not to speak about these meetings 'Up-top.' *Ayah* was probably bribed into silence. Thank goodness this situation ended quite suddenly as, with the advent of summer, the families moved to the hills, and I was returned to the safety of my family.

It was a relief to run around again with very little on, especially to have my feet bare, I had missed the homely touches, not having the sound of the trains for a lullaby, or the howling of the pi-dogs and the screaming of the jackals; above all I had missed my naughty little sister. For a celebration, the first day home Mama brought us a huge basketful of those lovely sucking mangoes. I remember sitting round a bunch of those on the verandah floor with Doreen, Janki and Munoo sucking the juice out, and throwing the skins to our pets, the goats watching in anticipation!

CHAPTER 5

Bacchanal

Soon after my return, my father was transferred to Ajmere, as assistant stationmaster. This was not a demotion as it may seem. Ajmere was a very large railway centre, and the experience gained there later helped him to further promotion. Much to our dismay, cook and *ayah* decided now to go back to their village in Bandikui. "Janki is now twelve, and it's time we got her married," explained *ayah*, wiping her eyes with the corner of her *sari*. We were very sad saying goodbye to these faithful servants. As the train drew out, Janki and Munoo, who were running along the platform, called out to us. We guessed what they wanted so we quickly bundled up fruits, sweets and nuts, and threw these packages out to them. We had been unable to pass any over after the "Farewell" as the staff were all around us. We waved to them as long as we could see them, then putting our heads down, Doreen and I had a good cry.

"Now girls, you will have to live like civilised people again, no more running round half naked as you have been doing in Sojat-Road," said my mother on the journey to Ajmere. "And what is more, you will go to school daily."

"You need that badly," added Papa grimly.

"No Janki and Munoo, no pet goats," I sighed.

"No nice pigeon grills, no lovely *jellabies*," added Doreen.

"No sucking mangoes, I don't think we are going to like Ajmere, Mama," I added sadly.

"Well, the *jellabies* and mangoes might be managed on pay day," promised Papa. "But I am afraid the other things cannot be arranged."

After we got to Ajmere, our wagon was shunted to the siding for unloading. There a crowd of servants was waiting to be interviewed by my mother. Papa had informed someone in advance that these would be required. Mama soon chose a cook, bearer and sweeper. We were glad she had decided we were old enough to do without an *ayah*. Hindus were chosen in preference to Moslems or Christians. The Moslem dislikes touching pig meat of any description, while the Christian, apart from expecting privileges, takes umbrage easily. Presently we settled down in our new house, finding ourselves for the first time living in a thickly populated locality.

Ajmere, besides being a big railway centre, had a large engineering locomotive workshop, and the mixed population of Europeans, Anglo-Indians, Parsees and Indians, was enormous. There was a modern hospital, a large school and institute for Europeans and Anglo-Indians. A convent run by the Roman Catholic nuns and a Mission Hospital, looked after the wants of the non-railway population.

We found school here a much bigger place than either of the schools in Bandikui or Mhow, with many more pupils and teachers. It was cheerful and busy and we enjoyed it, finding it pleasant to have companions of our own community again. I need hardly say that we were found backward, and placed in classes with children much younger than ourselves. This did not worry me then but later when it was repeated after we moved to Neemuch, I felt unhappy, as being older, I was sensitive.

In Ajmere, on returning from school, we had to be very prim and proper. We had to bathe and change out of school clothes before tea, then sit to homework, not as much as we should have done. Like most women in those days. Mama was rather inclined to underestimate the value of education for girls. The idea was we would marry, therefore the education would be wasted. "As long as you can check the cook's accounts, and read the bazaar bills, you should do," she said.

Our school, situated on a hill in a better locality, was surrounded by big houses with lovely gardens. These houses were for officers. Some of their children came to our school for a time but were later sent 'Home' to finish their education. I remember being taken by Peggy Tubbs to her house on one occasion. Her home was like a palace compared to ours. They had carpets, lace curtains draped and tied with coloured ribbons; I thought these were grand! Lovely furniture, masses of vases, pictures and ornaments.

When I went home that afternoon, I told Mama all about these, and asked her why we could not have the same. She promised we would one day. "When Papa is a big stationmaster." Our home being on the way, families of these officials had to pass it when going to the institute of an evening.

The girls and young ladies in their lovely clothes getting our admiration tinged with the slightest bit of envy is peculiar to all women, no matter what their age. There were two girls—Myra and Ivy Thomas—who, in winter, wore velvet. They had dresses of red, green and blue. With their red and gold hair and blue eyes, we thought they looked wonderful. To add insult to injury that winter my mother had olive green and navy serge dresses made for us, "Cheap and serviceable," she explained.

One afternoon Doreen and I were having our hair dried after the weekly shampoo. Jai Bai, our cook's wife, was helping Mama with this. Then, hearing a commotion coming down the road, we rushed on to the verandah to investigate.

A party of men were approaching. They had obviously visited the toddy shop to celebrate *Holi*—the Hindu festival of spring and fertility, and were as merry as larks. Accompanied by a drum and cymbals, they were singing and dancing. Their clothes were stained with splashes of red and blue dye which people throw on each other on this feast day. The gay note being added to by the garlands they wore. An old man, completely tight, led the procession. He beat time to the music, smacking his thighs, clapping his hands and lifting his legs in an ungainly step, to thump the hard street with bare feet, he had nearly lost his *pugree*, most of it looking like a broad flat ribbon, stretched away behind him. One or two folds stubbornly clung to his oiled head. A couple of young men beating time to the music were doing an improvised dance, jumping over the billowing *pugree* and crossing from side to side in an exaggerated goosestep. Their *dhoties* flying high in this drunken ballet accentuated their splayed feet and bandy legs.

The old man, blissfully unaware of the sad fate of his once beautifully white *pugree*, danced gaily along. After a while, the *pugree* gave up the struggle and slipped gently down to lie unnoticed in the dust—a mute offering to Bacchus. The procession was now far down the road.

"They are not going to leave the *pugree*, are they, Jai Bai?" asked Mama, shocked.

"Yes, *Memsahib*, but do you see those women following with the *thalis?*" and she pointed down the road. "His wife is probably amongst them, she will pick it up."

Jai Bai was right. The group of women, singing softly, came up to the *pugree* and one, detaching herself from the group, stepped forward and with her toe picked up a corner of it. Then, stooping slightly, she scooped up the *pugree*, which she hastily rolled and placed on her head under the *thali*. The women were on their way to the temple with gifts of sweets, fruit and flowers. They would celebrate the festival by doing *puja*.

"Jane, we are going to have new neighbours! The Blakes are on transfer," said Papa.

"Who is coming here, do you know, Harold?"

"Yes, fellow called Bowman, ex-'Tommy' used to be on the Madras and Southern Maharatta Railway," explained Papa, pushing back his chair, we were having *tiffin* whilst the above conversation took place. A few days later a note from my father, delivered by his *chaprassi*, informed Mama that the newcomers had arrived. He knew Mama liked to send a tea tray with a friendly note of welcome. A few weeks later Mrs. Bowman called on us; she was a very small, thin black woman.

At dinner that night Papa asked, "Well, Jane, what do you think of your new neighbour, the girls tell me she called on you this afternoon? They have no children, I hear."

"No, and not likely to have any."

"Why dear?"

Mama waited until the bearer had left the room before replying, "She told me she wanted a family, but her husband did not want half-black-half-white children."

"Humph! Hardly tactful," mumbled my father.

"Oh, she's all right, Harold; ignorant, poor dear. Probably someone's *ayah* he picked up in the South, she is dark enough for that."

"It is a pity, as she seems a nice little thing," said Papa, removing a moth from his plate—the oil lamp placed in the centre of the table attracted many.

A few days after the Bowmans arrived in Neemuch, Mama arranged a small party for the women to meet Mrs. Bowman. She was particularly anxious for Mrs. Kelly to meet the newcomer, as they were our neighbours, she hoped they would be friends. I well remember her indignant remarks to my father after the party, because at this age I was being made aware of the importance the adults placed on the colour of a person's skin. As a little girl I had realised in school that being just a shade fairer than some of the others had been an advantage. Now I was puzzled by the fact that for some people colour came before most things. Mama said, "I tried to get them together, but they would go into little groups, the covenanted *wallahs* keeping more or less to themselves, just deigning to greet me, their hostess. The fair Anglo-Indian women broke in on this clique, and despite the studied curtness shown to them, they would not budge. The fair ones in turn took no notice of their darker skinned sisters. . . . ."

"And your poor little Mrs. Bowman felt snubbed, eh, Jane?" broke in Papa, rising to leave. "You women are cats," he added, chuckling.

They were 'cats' all right after a meeting such as this or a dance. The following morning the clique would meet at someone's house after rushing the children off to school and giving the servants the day's orders, to sit on the verandah drinking coffee whilst tearing the opposition to pieces.

"Did you see the Kelly girls had new frocks again?"

"I know they are in debt, because my *ayah* tells me their bearer has to chase the *kapra wallah* out of the compound every time he comes presenting his bill."

"And I know their credit has been stopped at the stores, as I was asked to get them some groceries in my name."

"Did you? I'd have sent Mrs. Kelly to Abdulla—the Pathan moneylender."

"Would you now! and what *dasturi*, commission, would you have got? Oh! don't get angry, men, I was only joking."

"I don't like your jokes, Mrs. D'Costa."

"Did any of you notice Jessie Manuel chasing that good-looking Billy Adams—she seems to be getting desperate," said someone to clear the air.

"Oh! But she's wasting her time, she'll never catch him, he wants a white one; he has ambition that young man."

"And, my dear, come nearer, don't breathe a word, but my sweeper woman was told by their sweeper woman that Ma Manuel is expecting again, that makes seven, or is it eight?"

"Really! Well, do you blame Jessie for making her get away from that circus?"

"What can Jane Green be thinking about bringing those two brats of hers to the dance? I hope they are not going to start dancing at their age, it's schooling they need."

"My Maisie can beat Irene at any subject in class, and Maisie is much younger."

"And that little rascal Doreen is forever pulling faces and mimicking the teachers. Instead of dancing, she wants her bottom smacked."

So it went on, and on, and on, Doreen and I heard a little of all this the night before when my mother had been persuaded to take us for the first time to the Hallway Institute to watch the dancing. It was like the droning of bees, making us sleepier and sleepier.

It was through poor frightened frustrated Mrs. Bowman getting sick that I had my first glimpse of hospital life. Her bearer rushed over one morning very agitated, "My *Memsahib* is much sick, master on line. Will Green *Memsahib* come quickly!"

We gave Mama this message and were told by her, "Finish your breakfast quickly, and get off to school, but don't forget your *topees* and veils."

"Bother!" said Doreen, stamping her foot. "She would remember, or we could have forgotten."

That evening at dinner my father was told Mrs. Bowman was in the Mission Hospital.

"Why there, Jane, why not in the railway?"

"Oh, well, you know how it is, Harold, Mrs. B. told me she'd feel more comfortable looked after by the Indian nurses than those stiff starchy swanks in the railway. The thought of the European matron seemed to frighten her." Mama paused to knock the *kebabs* off her skewer before continuing. "I told her she was being silly, but on his return from line, Bowman ordered a *tonga* and drove off with her."

"Well, you and the girls had better visit her occasionally," suggested Papa, whilst helping himself to more *kebabs* and *pilau*. These had been brought with sweets and fruit to us in a *dhali* by one of his Muslim staff whom he had successfully recommended for a pay increase.

"Yes, I have thought of that and we'll go tomorrow after school."

Those visits to Mrs. Bowman were to be an inspiration. A high mud wall surrounded the huge compound of the hospital. Outside the big gates, which always stood open, squatted the inevitable beggar and various pedlars. A *punkah-wallah* selling the palm leaf hand-fans. These she made simply by trimming the fringed edges of the leaves, the more expensive ones had their rough edges bound with coloured material for longer life. For company the fanseller had the *phul-wallah,* whose flower garlands had been strung on a short stick into the rough bark of the date-palm under which he sat. A tray of *pan* and *biris* rested at his feet. Another woman was selling crudely made, garishly painted toys, made from a mixture of mud and cow-dung. These were bought by visitors for the sick children.

Passing through the gates, we saw rows of wards at ground level. The wards were long and narrow, only wide enough to take a single row of *charpoys,* with standing room at the foot for one person only. These *charpoys* faced the front verandah. The back verandah was left free for relations. Here, they were expected to stay all day to cook for the patients, as only liquid diet was supplied by the hospital, as in most Indian hospitals of similar kind. These relations had an uncanny knack of getting in the way of the nurses, but at the sight of a doctor or matron, they scuttled on to the verandah and crept back when the way was clear. Many doors opened from these wards on to the front verandah so that on very hot nights, the *charpoys* could be lifted out easily. A relative had to sleep by the side of a patient to attend to his wants, as only a skeleton staff was on night duty. And the nurses naturally gave most of their time to the serious cases.

Usually only one attendant was allowed to each patient, but I have been in a hospital where the whole family plus chickens, goats and even camels accompanied the patient. The smell from the camels. . . .! but that was later.

My mother asked a nurse whom she saw in the grounds to tell us where we could find Mrs. Bowman, and this girl very kindly took us to the private block. Here we found the patient in a suite, a small bedroom, with a walled-up back yard in which the kitchen and bathroom stood. Furnishing was crude, but it was private. Mrs. Bowman had brought her cook's wife in to prepare the meals, and attend to her when the nurses were busy. There were no overhead *punkahs*, so now we knew why the *punkah-wallah* had positioned herself outside the hospital gates. She did a brisk trade in hand-fans, the unfortunate patients had to fan themselves, if too ill for this, the relative took over. Mama relieved the cook's wife who, happy to hand over the fan to her, squatted outside chewing her *pan*. Doreen and I wandered around, and in subsequent visits got to know the Indian nurses quite well. These girls in their white muslin *sarees* and blouses, with their clean, brown, cheerful faces, were all Christians. I cannot remember now if this was an English, Canadian or Scottish Missions Hospital. We found it very interesting, particularly when we were allowed to help 'fetch and carry' for the nurses.

Then one day we found our way into their tiny chapel, and joined the nurses, patients, and a few inspired white doctors and sisters in prayer. I was now filled with great happiness, and slowly the idea was born; "I shall be a nurse when I grow up."

Mama was unhappy again—this followed after a letter from Grandma in Secunderabad Deccan to my father. These letters always caused trouble, and if we had dared, Doreen and I would have taken them from the postman and destroyed them. Grandma had written to say that Aunt Florrie having married, there was her room going spare, and would Papa like to bring his wife and children on a visit?

"What! After all these years?" said Mama, angry now. "Room could have been found before this," and she gave my hair, which she was combing, a good pull, making me jump.

"Stand still, can't you, Irene?"

"But you pulled my hair," I protested.

"No, thank you, Harold, you can go and take Irene with you," Mama finished plaiting my hair, and pushed me away. So it was arranged, that I should accompany my father to Secunderabad. Doreen was understanding, she made no fuss even though she was being left at home for the second time. Mama made it up to her somehow, I am sure.

The journey of almost a thousand miles *via* Bombay was exciting. For the first time I was to see a large Indian city, and what it had to offer. Papa took me to dinner in the refreshment car the two nights we were travelling. I thought the small tables with damask cloths, flowers, shining cutlery, glassware and silk-shades lamps looked pretty, though I was quite bewildered by the array of cutlery spread before me and fascinated by the way the attendants handled plates of hot soup with the train running at speed. Papa noticed my concern about the cutlery and whispered, "I'll choose first, you copy me."

In turn I whispered, "I wish Doreen could see me now."

"You rascal," but he smiled.

At long last we arrived in Secunderabad.

I was quite prepared to love this old English Grandmama, she was very small and plump, with white hair and blue eyes, "just like Queen Victoria," I told Doreen later, and was always referred to after our first meeting as "Grandma Queen Victoria." Unhappily, she was old, and by

Mrs Green —"Grandma Queen Victoria"

nature cold, and though we were to meet fairly often, she never really thawed. She did make a fuss of Papa; they were seeing each other after twelve years or so. We took a *tonga* round to Aunt Florrie's house. She and her sister Anne were Papa's half-sisters. Aunt Florrie was nicer than Grandma, more friendly. I was greatly surprised when Aunt Annie arrived, she was a typist in a military office. She was nearly brown, well perhaps coffee coloured.

Anyhow, neither of the girls was white, so why the fuss about Mama? I was puzzled, but did not dare question Papa there, they were so happy together, and seeing this I thought of my Mama, and instantly became homesick. Ten days later we returned home and Mama washed my hair, which she was trying desperately hard to keep fair, but failed to do in spite of all her efforts. Alone with her in our bedroom, I questioned her about the aunts.

"Yes, I know one was dark. Your father told me that your Grandma's first husband was an Englishman, and after he died she did not return to England as was expected, but stayed out and married an Eurasian; your two aunts, Annie and Florrie, were children of that marriage."

"Then, why did she make a fuss about you, Mama?" I persisted. "You both did the same thing."

"Oh, well, what's sauce for the goose isn't always sauce for the gander," and Mama smiled.

"What does all that mean?" I wanted to know, taking the comb out of her hand in an effort to get the tangles out of my hair myself.

"Oh, never mind, you run out and finish drying your hair in the sun. Children should be seen. . . ."

"Yes, I know," I broke in impatiently, finishing that old fashioned maxim for her.

We were not back from Secunderabad very long before Papa, was transferred to Neemuch.

He was definitely now on the way 'up,' this move to Neemuch, one hundred and fifty miles from Ajmere, was as stationmaster, and so it pleased us very much.

CHAPTER 6

Neemuch

The Kiss of the Sun for Pardon,
The Song of the Birds for Mirth,
One is nearer to God in a garden,
Than anywhere else on Earth.

(Anon.)

We found the railway colony at Neemuch pretty, most of the houses had some sort of garden, but a few were really lovely, and this is how Papa made ours after we had been there for a short while. The garden had two gates, and the drives from these ended at a low concrete platform built in front of the house. Here, in the cool of the evening, the family collected for a chat, and in the summer our four light cots fitted well to this platform. The drives, both about forty-five feet long and eight to ten feet wide, had narrow borders. In these Papa grew hollyhocks and St. Joseph's lilies, these were my mother's favourite flowers. They looked more beautiful on a moonlit night, and scented the air exquisitely.

At one time, between the drives, a garden bed flourished. We now had the remains, but Papa took this in hand and soon made it lovely. He felt we might be here some time, and so put his heart into it. As we had never been in any place for more than a couple of years, our garden comprised, only of a few potted plants. On a piece of once bare land between our drive and the fence that divided our compound from that of our neighbour's, a Parsee railway doctor, Papa cultivated at fine rose garden. In this plot at one end stood a *neem* tree, as big as any elm in England, on this a swing was fixed up for us: double thick rope for safety, and a strong bit of timber for a seat. I can remember vividly swinging on one occasion after a shower, when the air was

47

delightfully cool, and there was the smell of the clean damp earth. Higher and higher I went rushing through the air until I was able to feel the feathery leaves against my face. The filigree of *neem* leaves, with the golden sunshine trickling through, and the feeling that everything was well with my world, acted like a heady wine making me deliriously happy. I would sing out to Mama if I saw her in the garden or at the bedroom window, but her reply in an alarmed voice, "Come down at once, you are swinging much too high!" was shattering.

On the other side of the house stood a well. This had a ramp leading to it, and the *bhisty's* bullock paced up and down this all day, drawing water which was then stored in a tank by the well. Other *bhisties* would also come and help themselves from the tank, and if any arrangement existed between them and our men, we were never told! Having this water supply at our disposal made life more pleasant. The tank was cleaned occasionally, but before this was done, we would get in and paddle, taking our dogs in with us. In that intense heat, this was a treat. However, once it had been cleaned by the *bhisties* and refilled, we never touched it again so as not to offend the susceptible Hindus.

On this side, under the fruit trees, we grew some vegetables. Narrow channels leading from the tank had been dug between the beds, and the outside *bhisties* using our water were to some extent under an obligation to us, so helped to irrigate our vegetable patch. We had guava, pomegranate, limes, papaya and custard apples. My mother was particularly fond of custard apples, a delectable fruit but for the seeds. The size of shelled almonds, these black seeds could not easily be separated from the custard-like pulp in which they were firmly embedded. One had to work patiently on a mouthful of custard-apple to separate the flesh from the seed, then the 'black beetles,' as we called them, were spat out!

The *papaya* was my favourite fruit, rather like a large green melon, with a sweet well-flavoured orange-coloured flesh. We used to cut these in long slices, and eat them much the way the Africans eat their melons. We opened the papaya by the simple process of banging it on a large stone. Then, sitting in the cool shade of the blossom-laden lime tree—with *bhistie's* bullock padding by and the '*mynahs*'—Indian starlings—chattering in the guava trees for company—we gulped great mouthfuls of the cool sweet fresh fruit.

Behind our house, in a large field, Indian corn and sugar-cane were grown alternately, and when the maize had grown fairly tall, this was a good place to play 'hide and seek.' The landowner had built a *machan* or lookout platform high up above the corn. His wife would sit here all day, banging tins and calling out to frighten away the birds. Doreen and I often relieved her while she went down to feed her baby or to have a frugal meal, a dry *chaupatti* with, perhaps, a red chilli and an onion. She was always glad to see us, and before the corn was ripe, a basketful was picked and given to us. This corn-on-the-cob boiled and eaten piping hot with lashings of butter, pepper and salt, was delicious.

We now started attending school. Neemuch being a small colony did not have a proper school building, the only teacher, a large, red-faced, forbidding-looking Scotswoman with cold blue eyes, shared half a house with the school. It was whilst on my way to school one day that I had my first lesson in gynaecology: in a gutter by the side of a road a cow was in the act of calving. This unusual sight caused a crowd to stop and stare. Then the owner came hurrying along, an old Moslem, who said to us, "*Gaya, butchar dhaytar*"—"The cow is calving"—Fortunately the school bell was heard just then!

After prayers, a small boy dared to tell teacher about this, and asked if what the old men had said was right. "Probably," she replied, fixing him with a cold stare. "But if you want more information about this, you had better go home and ask your mother, I am not here to teach that subject." The little boy was silenced. Here again we were put in class with children much younger than ourselves. I felt this very much but endured it for a year. Then one day we had a visit from a inspector who expressed surprise at seeing a girl of my age in that class. I overheard his remarks and was not flattered. Going home, I told Mama. I said in all sincerity that I did not think we would learn much by staying on as I, for one, was unhappy. She talked this over with my father who agreed to our leaving.

To our great pleasure we found friends—the Pearces, from Mhow, had retired here. They had bought a large rambling house in cantonments. All these houses were built in the Dutch Colonial style. Large rooms with pillars to the roof, all on ground floor level with very large compounds. Outhouses, stables and quarters for the servants were built well away from the house. Mama took the problem of our education to Mrs. Pearce, who agreed that if we were unhappy at school we would gain nothing by staying. She suggested we keep a '*munshi*,' as they were doing, to teach some of their younger children.

The older ones were in the convent at Mhow. Papa did not fancy the 'munshi' idea.

Then Mrs. Pearce very kindly lent us a lot of books for which her girls had no further use. My father now heard of an old lady, the mother of one of his guards, who had been a teacher before she married. Mrs. Morgan took our education in hand. We were happy with her because she made lessons interesting; history became love-ly stories, and geography an adventure. Mrs. Morgan supervised our reading, encouraging us, and gradually this took hold of me until it became an obsession. My mother had been a great reader, perhaps I had inherited this from her.

About this time, Mama had a letter from her sister to say that they were moving to Mhow from Agra. Uncle was going there as Tele-graph Master. Mama was asked to take over Granny. Granny had lived with them for years, but now that the family had grown up, Aunty said that the extra room was needed. "The truth is, Harold," said Mama, putting down the letter she had been reading, "She wants to get her girls married, and means to throw expensive parties. She wants white sons-in-law, and that is why she made Jeff put in for an army station. I know what's in her mind."

"Really, Jane you are a cat!" Here Papa winked at us. "Anyway, I'll apply for passes. Tell her when you reply that we'll be very pleased to have the old lady."

My mother went to Agra to bring Granny, who was very feeble and could only take a step or two at a time. My father arranged for a sedan-chair to meet the train, and supervised Granny's removal from the train to the chair, and walked beside her as she was carried home. Mama was very touched by this, and spoke with pride of it many times after he had died. "He was not ashamed of his Indian mother-in-law," she would say. Aunt Alice sent Granny a small sum of money every month, just to let her feel she was not forgotten. She did not really need any of this as all her requirements, including the services of an *ayah*, were met by Papa. When her 'pay' arrived, as Granny called it, Doreen and I were given one *rupee* each. Mama tried to stop this, but Granny turned so fiercely on her, "Can't I do what I like with my own money?" that Mama had to give in, much to our secret delight.

The rest of the 'pay' was saved in a flat tin that Granny kept under her pillow. We were curious about this and asked her what she was saving for, and though we teased her, she would smile but not reply.

Then, after some months, Granny sent for a jeweller, and the row that followed sent us all flying on to the platform. Papa had had this extension built on the same level as her room, which was at the back of the house so that she could hobble out and sit there in the cool of the evening. There was Granny, banging her cane on the floor and calling the poor cringing jeweller a thug amongst other choice names. When she stopped for want of breath we learnt that she wanted earrings made for us. "Look, Jane, I have plenty of money." She then proceeded to empty the tin on to her lap, and out tumbled dirty old paper currency together with coins. "But he wants to rob me, he is *a thug, chor, daku*" screamed Granny, having worked herself into a rage again.

At last it was agreed that a pair should be made, first for me being the elder, then when enough money had been saved, a second pair would be ordered for Doreen. We later had to submit to our ears being pierced and small pieces of *babul* thorn were pushed through the holes to keep them open, Just as 'sleepers' are used in this country.

The jeweller was thankful to take himself off—all in one piece. He backed from Granny, *salaaming* very low to the ground, but she was still very cross and grumbled for hours. When Papa came home he was summoned to her room and given the whole story. Coming out chuckling he said to Mama, "You had better slip a drop of something into the old lady's glass of milk tonight or neither she, nor we, shall get any sleep."

When my pair of earrings was delivered, Granny carefully wrapped them in cotton wool and slipped them into her tin saying, "You must wait till Doreen gets hers, then you will both wear them new together." I was most disappointed, but knew better than to argue with her.

In the cool of the evening, Granny would hobble on to her platform to sit in a comfortable chair with a foot-stool, and there held 'court.' A small group collected most evenings to squat and listen to her stories; a villager or two, the servants with their families, or a *babu's* wife and friend. Our sweeper's wife was allowed to join in the conversation and jokes, but she knew her place as an untouchable and never ventured on to the platform but sat below in the dust.

Our bearer's grandma was a very old woman, a contemporary of Granny. Moti Bai would be carried here by him balanced on his hip. He would deposit her on the platform, none too gently at times. She would swear at him loudly, calling him a '*sur-ke-bachar*'—son-of-a-pig. "*Wah Umma!*"

"Oh! Mother," he would reply with a laugh, and run off to buy the *pan biris, channa* or sherbets that Granny ordered every evening for her guests.

Sometimes we would stop our games and join Granny's party for a few minutes, my parents, too, did this occasionally instead of sitting out in the front. Returning after so many years to Neemuch—which was a fairly large cantonment—Granny would often talk of the Mutiny; she had been besieged in the fort here with the British wives and children. Grandpa, a Portuguese, had been a veterinary surgeon in the army. Granny's tales of murder, loot and rape were bloodcurdling. These tales were passed on to us by Mama when we were older, with a warning before going to sleep to look under beds, in cupboards, and especially in the tall linen baskets.

Papa used to get quite annoyed at Mama's precautionary antics; a kind of ritual at the end of the day. All doors were examined, and her 'alarms' as she called them, kitchen pots and pans, empty tins and whatnots, were placed lightly against the doors. Often one or other of these 'alarms' was blown down or knocked over accidentally by the dogs. The clatter which followed, magnified by the stillness of the night, woke the whole family. Doreen and I, much too terrified to open our eyes, buried our heads well under the sheets. Papa, after a moment's pause, knew exactly what had happened. Mama, of course, had to get out of bed to investigate thoroughly, and having satisfied herself that there were no mutineers or *chors* about, re-erected her 'defences' and got back to bed.

We could not get away from the 'alarms,' they followed us even when we slept out-of-doors. A barrage of empty cans, pots, pans and kettles tied together was placed round our beds, and what fun it was when the dogs, startled by either a stray cat or hyena, would rush from under our beds only to get entangled. This would send Doreen and me into hysterical laughter which had to be stifled before Mama got too angry. Papa, losing his sleep, was naturally grumpy, and with a "Really, Jane, you are completely mad," would turn over and try to sleep again.

Fun we had in plenty, Granny providing a good deal, mostly unwittingly, especially when she and Moti Bai would get involved in an argument about some incident that had occurred years ago. They would get cross with each other, and at this stage were the only two not enjoying themselves! Laughing heartily, the bearer would encourage them to continue, and Papa hearing the commotion would say, "Don't those two old dears know the Mutiny ended over fifty years ago!" When Moti Bai died, Granny insisted upon paying for the wood for her pyre, Papa chuckled, "I bet that gives our old lady a lot of satisfaction."

We had now reached the age when the soldier boys visiting our house were at last able to persuade my parents to allow us to attend the garrison dances. I was sixteen now, and Doreen a year younger, but Mama accompanied us. What fun we had getting ready, and we always abided by the 'hard and fast' rule of a rest after *tiffin*, in a well darkened room. We would slip between cool sheets, and try desperately hard to sleep, we wanted, to look fresh. "We must not look like old hags," Doreen would say seriously, but sleep generally evaded us as we were too excited.

After tea at four p.m. our dresses would be taken by the bearer to the *dhoby*, for pressing. I remember one day returning from Mrs. Morgan's school to find my darling Mama looking very pleased. She took us into our bedrooms and pointed to the wall. There, on pegs, hung two new dresses, a complete surprise. They were made from new white army mosquito nets given to her by our kind-hearted 'Tommy' friends. However, they were beautiful in our eyes. Narrow frills from the waist to the ankles fell over a starched underskirt of cheap muslin. Mama had made a red silk rosette to match the red ribbon forming the waist band for Doreen, I had the same in pink. "Oh, Mama, Lovely! Lovely!" we cried, skipping round her, kissing and hugging her with joy.

Our baths on dance nights were ordered for seven p.m.; we never had to be rushed in that heat or the results could have been disastrous, powder running down in streaks showing patches of dark skin, the very things we went to great lengths to hide! It seems strange to me when I see my sixteen-year-old daughter sunbathing on the lawn in our back garden. In a swimming costume and smothered in some suntan lotion or other, she is trying desperately to change her pale skin to a nutty brown!

Rivalry amongst the various families was most pronounced at these dances. Daughters of snob families would prefer to dance with officers if they got the chance, or sergeants as the next best choice. The underlying idea was matrimony. We knew a large family of girls called Marrowful, who spent a good deal of money on clothes and beauty aids all to this end, and busy tongues would whisper, "Their poor father, my dear, he's terribly in debt," or "Must they be so snobbish, they've got nothing in their heads, only on their heads." This family of girls certainly worked hard. Getting all dressed up and ready to kill, they would wander down to cantonments walking past the Officers' Club, getting up concerts, never missing a parade service. As a result in these cantonments the bridegrooms were usually army men, and the brides Anglo-Indians or Eurasians. To please the men, two or three officers usually attended these dances, the married ones accompanied by their wives.

One evening, to our great joy, we were able to outwit the 'Marrows.' A soldier came up and asked me to keep the next dance for Major Williams, who had sent him. Not to be missed the girls always stood directly under the gas lamps. So when the dance was announced and Major Williams crossed the room, passing them to bow to little *me*, they were mad! I danced very badly; I think the 'Marrows' watching put a *hoodoo* on my feet. So I was more than surprised when a little later Major Williams himself came and asked me to dance again! "Glory, glory! Those 'vegetables' are mashed now," said Doreen.

Papa caught influenza in 1918, and was left with a bad persistent cough. Until this serious worldwide epidemic he had been quite healthy, and we often teased him about his red face which made his eyes a lovely deep blue. He was very straight, of medium height, and had light brown hair, with a 'Macmillan' moustache which, when he was agitated or in deep thought, he would twist. Sometimes, lost in reverie, we would see him twisting and turning it and staring into space. Mama would call, "Come on, Harold, let's have it, what's worrying you?"

"Worrying me, Jane, why nothing!"

"Oh, no, you can't hide it, you've been sitting there twisting that old moustache of yours without speaking for half an hour. Now tell!" demanded Mama with a smile.

"You see, Papa, we know your funny old habits," Doreen added.

"You women don't give a fellow any peace. As a master of fact, I'm thinking of a peculiar application I had from a *babu*. He wrote asking for a job as guard and said:

"I know all about the van, I know all about the safety of passengers, I know all about the signals, I know all about the red and green flags—in fact, Honourable Sir, I know damn all."

"Now, what do you girls make of that?"

Papa loved his work, his home, his garden, and was quite happy when in our company. To make the home life more sociable, he arranged for us to have piano lessons, promising to buy us a second-hand piano just as soon as he had saved some money, or heard of one being sold in cantonments. A regiment leaving the station would sell up cheaply. Usually, the merchants from the bazaar got in first and grabbed up everything, to sell later to the new arrivals at a profit.

One day, through his spies, Papa heard of a piano lying in a *godown*, stacked against firewood, old furniture end other junk. He contacted the *Sete* and was told that it was given in exchange for an unpaid bill. "It does not sound up to much, but I'll go and have a look," he told us. He returned in great excitement and told us that it was a bargain at the price, and that the *Sete* was quite willing to accept one hundred *rupees* for it. It was a German table grand, a lovely instrument neglected. One of its legs had woodworm; this was replaced, and though stained and varnished several times, never matched the others, giving the piano rather an odd lop-sided look. Very soon we were playing, "Won't you buy my pretty flowers?" and "The Blue Bells of Scotland."

After a few months we improved and advanced to "Handel's Largo," "The Maiden's Prayer," and "Rendezvous." After his day's work was done, nothing gave Papa greater pleasure than being able to sit with Mama—a glass of beer at hand—and listen to our playing. They were thrilled when we advanced enough to be able to accompany our guests—the two or three soldier boys—in singing the popular songs, "Cosy Corner," "Rose of No Man's Land," or "I'm for ever Blowing Bubbles." We had taught Papa many nice songs, but his favourites were "Little Brown Jug" and "Drinking, Drinking, Drinking."

Unfortunately, he could never sing for long before his cough started troubling him. This complaint grew worse, and he caught pneumonia. In those days this was serious, as the modern drugs were unknown. There were no oxygen cylinders at hand either, and in Neemuch there was only the Mission Hospital to which he could have been taken. This Papa refused to consider. "What?" he said in horror, "To have those little girls fussing round me, no fear!" He was referring to the Indian nurses. So Mama, with a little help from us and the servants, nursed him at home, using linseed poultices, (messy stuff to handle), and inhalations. Though he recovered he was never the same man.

Whilst he was convalescing he sent for a *mandoline* from Bombay and taught us to play it. Now we had duets. Papa told us he had also played the banjo as a young man, and promised he would get one just as soon as all the bills caused by his illness had been paid. "Then we'll teach your Mama the drums and form a band!"

Mama took a great deal of trouble over our food now, seeing to it that all we ate was nourishing. A coal range was bought and fixed up on the back verandah, and a young servant girl engaged to scrub the pots and pans whilst Mama did the actual cooking. All through the winter we had calves foot jelly and jellied soups; not the sort out of packets, but the good old homemade kind. I remember with nostalgia the delicious cow-heel curries! I can still see the huge barrel with pickling tongues, rounds of beef and gorgeous humps. And here I must tell a story against myself.

When we settled in England in 1950, and I had to get down to cooking and shopping seriously for the first time in my life, I went to the butcher's in a busy street in St. Albans. Besides the weekend joint and stewing meat I asked for a hump.

"A *HUMP?*" repeated the butcher, startled, "What's that?"

"Well, you should know."

"No, that's a new one on me, what animal supplies it?"

"A cow. . . . . no, I mean a bull or a bullock, a cow doesn't have one."

I was now most confused.

"Ah," murmured the butcher, cupping his chin in his hand, resting it on the table and giving me a malicious grin. "Can you tell me which part of the bull provides this strange cut?"

I was now beginning to feel foolish as all the other housewives were staring at me and waiting for this strange story to continue, "Yes, here . . . . . ." and I placed my hands between my shoulder blades. Then suddenly I remembered and said, "Of course! In England the bulls don't have humps!"

Now even the assistants had stopped to listen, and so to an interested audience I had to explain that in India the hallmark of the Brahmini breed of bull, or the gelded bullock, is a mound of flesh which grows in the position, just where the neck ends and the back of the animal begins. The 'holy cows' of India are really majestic Brahmini bulls, which stroll the streets with impudence, often bringing traffic to a standstill. In the bazaars they eat anything they fancy, helping themselves from the open stalls. In the hottest part of the day they walk on the shady pavements and push the frightened pedestrians on to the road. "*Maharaj* Lord Brahma, allow me to pass," will plead a timid Hindu gently, touching the beast on the flank and then touching his own forehead, but '*Maharaj*' strolls on unconcerned. Those lethargic pampered beasts are fully aware of the protection they enjoy as sacred animals, and take full advantage. The less fortunate bullock is the beast of burden, and is yoked to furnish the motive power for the primitive plough and carts still used all over India. The story told, the butcher offered me the next best thing; a beef tongue. Now the women looked kindly on me. Before this I think they thought I had escaped from the local mental hospital.

About six months after my earrings had been delivered, we could see Granny would not be with us much longer. She was slowly dying from old age, and one morning did not awaken. So, neither of us wore those earrings. Mama, not approving of jewellery on young girls, sold my pair and bought us some clothes instead. On the way to the cemetery, we passed the old fort in which Granny had been besieged. In the cemetery the graves, black with age and crowded together, were a grim witness of the Mutiny. On our return from the funeral, we sat on the platform talking about Granny, and Papa said, "I think it's a strange coincidence. The old lady must have travelled hundreds of miles round India since the Mutiny over sixty years ago, yet, at the last she returns here to join her companions of the fort in this cemetery."

Relations between Mama and Aunt Alice were "not very warm", as Mama put it in her simple way, when we were sitting on the verandah with our good friend Mrs. Pearce a few days after the funeral. "She has always been envious, ever since your Papa and I married. I think she resented me, a widow with children, getting a white man, whilst she, a young woman, had to be content with an elderly coloured man, even though he had money." Then turning to Mrs. Pearce Mama continued, "For many years now she has not shown any love for my children, her envy reaches down to them. My girls are prettier than hers, you see," she ended in a naive way.

At this Doreen and I shouted with laughter, I rushed from my chair to hug Mama, whilst Doreen called, "Hear! Hear! Mama, Bravo!" Mrs. Pearce looked at us in her sweet understanding way and smiled. She knew what Mama was trying to say, as we were often hurt by Aunt Alice and her family; we could not be sure if it was deliberately done, or merely thoughtlessness.

When we were again transferred to Mhow, they would call at our house on the way back from the bazaar, bringing their parcels from the *tonga,* to open and show us the new dress lengths—expensive georgette and *crepe-de-chine*—materials they knew very well we could not afford. "Look, Jane, isn't it lovely. My girls must have new dresses for the dance next week. Another time it was hats; one of these was placed on my head. They grouped round staring at me, Aunt Alice said, "It suits her, makes her look quite pretty."

"Oh, *please* make her leave it there," I prayed, silently, and with my eyes I implored her—but in vain. Mama, standing by quietly so far, must have guessed how I felt, she said, "But, Alice, don't you think she looks just as pretty without it?" And not waiting for a reply, she turned away.

Papa looked worried one morning after the postman's visit. He waited until breakfast was over and we had left for Mrs. Morgan's school before informing Mama that Grandma had written to say Uncle had lost his job in the South, and they were very worried. Would Papa visit them to help sort things out, and she requested Mama should accompany him. Mama refused this invitation for the second time, but said that Doreen and I could go. So, once again, I went down South, and feeling an old seasoned traveller, was able to point out various objects of interest on the journey to my younger sister. After we had been in Secunderabad a day or two, Papa took us to see his school—The Protestant Orphanage and Brigade School to which he went after his father's death.

On our return to Neemuch, Mama told us that Grandma, Uncle Tom and both aunts were coming up North to settle. Mama seemed quite calm and confident as she spoke, so we were not as dismayed as we might have been. Grandma had now met both of us, and knew what to expect, and we guessed Papa had warned them that he was not going to have Mama upset on any account. The idea was for them to stay in the *dak* bungalow for a month or two, actually Papa had permission for them to use the railway rest house, which stood close to us, till Uncle Tom got fixed up in the telegraph department.

Uncle Tom was what they termed a white Madrassi—an Anglo-Indian, born of one European parent, the other being mixed—born in the South with some Tamil blood in his veins. These white Madrassis have the added peculiarity, apart from the 'sing-song' style so well known amongst Eurasians and the Welsh, of dropping their 'h's' *and* adding them where they should not. I was to meet a number of these girls in St. George's Hospital, and in the Lady Lytton Club for Nurses in Calcutta and except for this unfortunate way of speaking, they would have passed for Europeans anywhere, with blue eyes and natural blond hair to help. The day Grandma and family arrived we were at school with Mrs. Morgan, and so were spared the meeting between them and Mama, though I am quite sure at the crucial moment Mama was serene. She did her best to make them happy, sending over meals and helping in any way she could. Mama knew they were miserable at leaving the South. Central India, with its different language, was a strange barbaric country to them. It was only with them about that we made the startling discovery that our bearer understood and could speak English! Up to now it had suited him to put on 'an act!'

After a while, Uncle Tom was fixed up with a job in the telegraph department, and they moved to Agra, but not before Mama had made a firm friend of Aunt Anne, the unmarried one and the darker of the two. She had had a hard time, and told Mama a curious story. Uncle Tom, it appeared, had visited them for two years, paying court to both girls without favour. At times it seemed as if one was singled out, then the situation would be thrown into confusion by, say, a bunch of flowers or a packet of sweets being presented to the other. This situation became intolerable, and Grandma tackled him one evening, "Thomas, may I know what your intentions are towards my daughters, and to which?" In other words, he was given the choice of 'shades'. Cornered, he had to declare himself; need I say he chose the fairer girl. Aunt Anne did find her man after they moved to Agra, and she had a very happy married life.

Soon after Grandma and family moved to Agra, we heard rumours that Papa was being sent to Mhow as stationmaster. This seemed too good to be true, and Mama warned us not to depend on it. We had lived in Mhow during the first two years of the war, and still had many friends there. Apart from this, Mhow boasted two cinemas, and the clubs and institutes were gay places. "Pity we can't pack this home and garden into the wagons and take them with us, Mama," I said. We had a lovely garden now, the best we had ever had, and the home was comfortable. We had actually had four happy peaceful years at Neemuch, the longest time we had spent in one place so far.

"Well, we'll have to start all over again to make a nice home and garden in Mhow. And we can go to the convent for piano lessons, and learn dressmaking, and lots of other things," said Doreen. "Oh, and Mama, what about bicycles? You did say we'd have these one day—can we have them there?"

"Yes, but slowly, one thing at a time, Doreen," replied Mama.

She looked sad as Papa's cough never seemed to leave him now in spite of all the treatment he had been given. We spent Christmas 1922 in Neemuch, and as we were leaving for Mhow in January, our friends tried to make it a happy one for us. A young fellow called Du Caen—he was a mixture of French-Anglo and Indian, probably his people were from Chandernagore, the French settlement in the Hooghly district of Bengal, was posted to Neemuch just before Christmas. He was a junior in the senior grade, and for some reason our friends decided to make a match between this unfortunate young man and myself. At parties we were thrown together, and playing 'forfeits' they saw to it that we were paired. He stood it remarkably well and I, having required a liking for older men and wishing he came in this category, bore it as well as I could. Christmas came and went by in a rush, as we were busy preparing to move. Early in the New Year we left Neemuch.

CHAPTER 7

Return to Mhow

Build a little fence of Trust around, today,
Fill the space with loving words and therein stay,
Look not through the sheltering bars upon tomorrow,
God will help thee bear what comes of joy or sorrow.

(Anon.)

As we knew Mhow, it was like seeing an old friend again, and we were very happy. Neither the house nor the garden was as good as that left in Neemuch. "The house is your job, girls," said Papa to us three, "I'll see what I can do with the garden—given time!"

Doreen and I were very excited getting the house in order because in the first week we had been here, we had received an invitation to a badminton party at the Condwicks', and this seemed to us a good inauguration! Mr. Condwick was in the senior grade—he was a white Anglo-Indian, she was coffee-coloured, but the use of a large powder puff, used heavily, made her appear a lighter shade. She was a good-looking woman, about thirty to thirty-five, always well-dressed. Highly educated, and she also played the piano and sang well. Mrs. Condwick seemed to like young people around her, especially the young men, and saw to it that she was the centre of attraction.

Parties at her house were attended by assistant surgeons (I.M.S.) and sergeants, nothing under this rank being allowed near her. Reciprocation came by way of homage paid at dances, 'At-Homes' or tennis tournaments. The men clustered round her like moths to a light and she lapped this up! Not having any children, this sort of life suited her but Mama often said, "I wonder if her husband is as happy as he should be, I have my doubts!"

We were never left out of her parties, and my mother expressed gratitude to her for taking us under her wing, as Papa had not been too well since we had moved, Doreen and I were Mrs. Condwick's greatest admirers and thought she could do no wrong until we got to know her better, then the spiteful little jabs and pinpricks were felt, without saying anything we could really object to she let us feel we were two little ignorant innocents. Well we knew we were, but why should she dislike us? We could never outshine her or even compete with her, the idea was ridiculous, and being something we could not understand, did not let it bother us,—but we did have a joke now and then. At table, *apropos* of nothing, Doreen would suddenly adopt an affected 'haw-haw' voice, and turning to me would say, "You poor little ignorant child, watch how I pour out and LEARN!" Then a pantomime would start. Clapping her hands she would call, "Boy, fetch me some hot water!" and "*Chaprassi*, that!" in the meantime using her hands in an exaggerated dainty way—pointing her little finger.

On our arrival in Mhow, Mama had taken on a station *coolie* to train as bearer, as the servants coming to fill this vacancy had asked for a higher wage than we could afford. "Gulab" was a very humble man and she had hopes of training him well. But, when addressed suddenly by Doreen in English in this 'haw-haw' manner, he got frightfully agitated, and would dash to the sideboard to pick up anything to offer her, she took advantage of this, and helped herself to a second portion of pudding or fruit. At my indignant "Oh!" she would merely look supercilious, we knew whom she was mimicking, and would howl with laughter, adding to the bearer's confusion. We joined the institute and met the same crowd there, in fact, a clique was formed—Mrs. Condwick assuming leadership. Mama wanted us to be happy and had some new dresses made.

"No more 'cast-offs' from our dear cousins. Hurrah!" said Doreen.

"I hope not," said Mama, but she shivered, "You'd better have some new things. I have spoken to Mrs. Condwick and she will chaperone you, as I do not want to leave your Papa until he is better,"

I imagine, like most mothers, she wanted to see us married, and thought, "Well, they are in the right set, anyway,—that's a good start."

Aunt Alice and family came over paying court after we had settled down; a son-in-law of hers was guard under Papa, and this was diplomacy. They gushed honey and syrup now. At dances it was fun. Mrs. Condwick leading, her retinue following, Doreen and I close on her heels, with the assistant surgeons and sergeants bringing up the rear.

By common consent, the seats at the top of the hall were reserved for the senior staff, and our leader made straight for these, and here we were joined by other senior families. We had a naughty thrill to see Aunt Alice and family sitting along the side of the hall. Attending these dances with Mrs. Condwick, we got to know the Pintos. He was a retired *medico*, and they were on the fringe of the Condwick set. There were two girls in the family who were always getting up concerts in aid of charities. The Institute Hall was hired for this purpose. A 'play' was put on once in which both girls, a Mr. Boodrie (Eurasian) and two 'Tommies' took part. It was considered quite spicy for Mhow because of a love scene. The hall was packed out for the three nights the show ran. Doreen and I were asked to play something in between two of the acts, and I feel nauseated now when I think of our choice—a duet 'Home, Sweet, Home'—Gooey in the extreme. Doreen at the piano, I playing the *mandoline* sitting well forward facing the audience. And it speaks highly for the discipline of the British Army that not a tomato was hurled and, bless their hearts, they even clapped.

In Mhow for the first time we saw the strange sight of two pretty girls dressed in frilly dresses, riding up the Mall, down the Supply and Transport slope, and on to the railway colony. The prettier girl was coloured. Her friend was white. One had long brown ringlets, the other bobbed hair. Both wore large stiff organdie bows; undoubtedly these young ladies wished to be seen! Those poor horses! Noble creatures to be so misused. "Doped they must surely be or they'd kick and throw them," said my kind little sister. It was indeed an incongruous sight, and I wonder what the 'Tommies' thought! Apparently they were two more hopefuls out to trap officers for husbands. Sad to relate, they failed! In those days the social barriers were high. You had to be in the official category to be allowed to join *The* Club. Coloured people, no matter *how* wealthy were absolutely TABOO.

At times Papa seemed to be better and his bed, which had been brought into the sitting-room to give him more air, was moved back into the bedroom. Once the sitting room had been cleared, my sister and I would rush round changing the curtains, pushing the furniture into new positions, filling the vases, playing jerky little frivolous pieces on the pianos and madly planning all the parties we were going to have. We were so very young. Again Papa would have a relapse, coughing horribly, a cough that seared our hearts; it, would rack him so loud, dry and hollow. We tried every remedy that was recommended to us, but nothing gave him relief, and for nights he would get no sleep. The doctors seemed so helpless. They told Mama it was 'heart,' but he never showed any signs of heart trouble. Were the doctors right? What did they really tell Mama? Was she told it was hopeless, and did she keep this from us—sparing us, thinking we were too young. Allowing us to have all the pleasure we could get in those last few months. These thoughts tortured me for years after he had died, and the pain receded only slowly, after I got to St. George's Hospital and was able, in a small way, to alleviate some of the suffering I met there.

Vi came home about this time. She had been advised to give up her job and take a long holiday, as she was getting malaria rather badly. Papa, thinking a change would do us all good, asked for permission to occupy the rest house at Kala Khund, a picturesque spot in the tree-clad hills not far from Mhow, and noted for its waterfalls. Soon after leaving Mhow, the train would start to climb the steep gradient up into the hills. Round the spur of a hill with a solid rock on one side, and a precipice on the other, over the viaducts, through tunnels with a glimpse of waterfalls in between, and then a repetition of the scene. It was all very beautiful. The *dhak* Butea Frondosa, with its broad, silvery leaves and fiery velvet flowers, grew thickly in this area.

On arrival at the rest house we were met by the *Pani-Wallah* or 'Mr. Gunga Din,' as Doreen called the old man, who was to be our servant during the visit. He brought us water in his *mussack* from the station below, A sweeper-woman came up at intervals as well, and she boiled our bath water in pails on the back verandah. She had an enormous bosom and great swaying hips, so was immediately named "Mrs. Mae West."

Mama did the cooking on two portable braziers on the verandah. We kept everything very simple. Helping ourselves, we would sit on the verandah steps with plates balanced on our knees. It was pleasant to look down the hill over the *dhak* tree tops whilst eating. Parakeets would suddenly appear swooping down the hillside to rest for a while in the *dhak*. Their bright green bodies showed up well against the silver leaves and red flowers, and their excited chatter could be heard far and near. Our dogs did not approve of this invasion and to frighten the birds off, they would rush down barking furiously.

Most nights we had community singing, and this is where the *mandoline* came in useful. Mama would always ask us to finish with an evening hymn, and 'Abide with Me', an old favourite, sounded so beautiful on that lonely hilltop bathed in moonlight. Apart from the station down below, with its one or two huts for the Indian staff snuggling alongside, our house standing on that hill was the only building in Kala Khund. and it was rather eerier especially on moonlit nights. We would lie awake to listen to the nightjar strike its metallic notes, two high, two low, then the pi-dog down at the station would answer back, howling mournfully. As soon as Papa felt better, he started fretting to get back to work, so after a month we returned. It had been a happy holiday, and a little later we were glad of the memories.

"Mrs. Boodrie has been quarrelling with her servants again, Harold," my mother informed Papa one evening, soon after we arrived back from Kala Khund. "She came over to tell me about it, and though I felt sorry for her I also wanted to laugh."

"Well, what was it about this time, Jane?"

"Mrs. B. told her husband their cook had been 'fiddling' the bazaar accounts. I expect he was making a little, but don't they all. Anyway, Boodrie struck Kassem in the argument that followed."

"He should not do that, it's wrong," and Papa started twirling his moustache in anger. We were sitting on the platform having a light meal of iced-mango fool with cream cracker biscuits, and Mama had taken this opportunity of allowing the servants a free evening to visit the *hat*, a travelling funfair and market.

"Oh, do go on, Mama, tell us about Mrs. B. What was it she said that made you want to laugh?" Doreen asked impatiently.

"'Oh, man! The *ayah* was veree cheekee to me!'" (and Mama spoke in the high-pitched sing-song Mrs. B. used), "'My *ayah* called me a *Kerani* and said I was onlee *ek pau*'. Here Mrs. Boodrie burst into tears," concluded Mama.

"What does *Kerani* mean? and *ek pau?*" Doreen and I wanted to know, we had never heard those expressions before.

"*Ek pau* is a weight meaning a quarter. *Kerani* is half-caste; the *ayah* was telling Mrs. B. she is only a quarter white—actually I think she is much less than that!" explained Mama.

"Well! I do think it dreadful of the *ayah* to say a thing like that; after all, she is their servant," and Doreen rose to help herself to more fool.

"I'm glad we don't have quarrels with our servants, Mama," I said, getting up to join Doreen at the serving table.

"Don't take it all—leave some for the parents," I was told as she walked away. This made me angry as she had given herself a good large second helping! Mama starting about Mrs. Boodrie again silenced our argument.

"The trouble is that she cannot decide what she really is—an Eurasian now she is married to Boodrie and, we hope, a Christian, or still a Madrassi and a Hindu!" We saw Mama smiling at some secret recollection and listened with interest. "I expect the poor thing is being torn between her loyalties. She has all the instincts and tastes of her old life. I know she chews *pan* secretly, and takes marigolds out to the yellow-daubed rocks under the *pipul* tree at the side of their house, and eats all the food with her fingers when Boodrie is on line. Yet he is determined to turn her into an Eurasian! He has even made her buy a pair of corsets!" The thought of that poor fat perspiring female squeezing herself into these was too much for us—we howled with laughter and Papa chuckled.

Then a sudden crash of thunder got us to our feet, and grabbing up trays, crockery, table and chairs we flew indoors. The monsoon had broken in some districts, but it was too early for us in Central India, and although we were sheltering, we knew we would have to wait patiently for a week or two before the rains came. We went to see the Pinto's the next day as Papa thought that Pinto being a relation of the Boodries, should know of these quarrels. It was not nice in our community for servants to be provoked into being insolent, to shout out things we would sooner not hear! The Pinto's lived in a very large double-storied building which had been converted, into flats. These were mostly occupied by Anglo-Indians and Parsees. Doctor Pinto had graduated from the Medical College Hospital at Calcutta, and after many years service with the I.M.S. had retired to Mhow. Being a Goanese he had a natural flair for cooking, which he had put to good use by opening a restaurant on Station Road. Here the 'Tommies' had their evening meal, and on Sundays there was always a big midday meal.

Mrs. Pinto was a white woman from an orphanage. Many of these children were the results of soldiers 'having an affair' with Eurasians or Indians, and were left with the Roman Catholic nuns. Although not all the children found in these institutions had the misfortune of being born 'outside-the-blanket.' Very often the 'Tommies' married an Eurasian 'off the strength'. They would then have to live outside the regimental married quarters, and wait for a family to go 'Home' before accommodation was available. The regiment was only allowed a certain number of married men officially, and until one of the quota had left, the man who married locally could not obtain married quarters with the privilege of rations and other amenities. The children of these marriages were often left in the orphanages to save them the constant travelling round which army life entailed. Then again some children were orphans in the true sense of the word.

In these institutions the nuns were doing an excellent job, under trying conditions. Financially they were on uncertain ground depending mostly on charity, so when a wealthy man, white or coloured, came along looking for a wife, providing he was of their faith and recommended by the local priest, the girls were persuaded to marry, and being eager to break the bonds of convent life, this way of escape was often welcomed. Mrs. Pinto told Mama she was glad to leave the convent, and had always been happy with 'Doc,' as she called her husband. They had three children, now grownup.

We never met their eldest. He was the black sheep of the family in more ways than one, not being content with taking after his father in colour, he sinned again by marrying an Indian Christian nurse from the Mission Hospital at Ajmer. Mary came next, she was a near-white, and was now being courted by a sergeant—this made the Pintos very happy. Papa Pinto being especially flattered! Their youngest child Susan was coffee-coloured—about my age. She intended to join the J.J. Hospital in Bombay to train as a nurse. As she and I were friends we planned to go together.

The desire to take up nursing had not died, rather it was fed and kept alive by hearing my father cough, and being unable to help. Doreen knew of my secret ambition, but only laughed at me. "You'll never do it, you'll faint at the sight of blood—think of the gory operations," and she looked down into the large red juicy pomegranate she was eating. I was about to start on mine, but now had to put it aside. Then she went on, "Besides you need a sixth standard education, at least. We never went to a proper school after the second or third! They'll never accept you."

"You are encouraging," I replied, getting up in disgust.

Returning one evening from tennis, where Susie and I had been discussing nursing, I decided the time was ripe to let my parents know how I felt, so I broached the subject. Papa's reply was brief and shattering, "Not whilst I am alive."

IRENE AGED SEVENTEEN

"But why not, Papa?" I asked, surprised.

"Nurses have a bad name, I do not know whether this is deserved or not, probably not, nevertheless I do not want my daughter getting mixed up with them!"

"You are old-fashioned, Papa, you want me to stop at home and marry some guard or driver, and have *ek pau, do pau* or *tin pau* children," I stressed, nearly in tears.

"Now that will do, miss," said Mama, looking very stern. "I suppose because you have taken after your father in colour you are now giving yourself airs, and I have tried so hard to keep you free from that."

We were not aware of impending disaster as the months of January to June, 1923 passed by. We discussed and argued, played tennis, badminton, danced and were happy. Du Caen came in from Neemuch. He called at our home once or twice, and I met him in the presence of the family. He was often at the Condwick's; but I never met him alone, and gave him very little thought, so I was naturally surprised when one evening on returning from tennis I was met by Mama who said, "Your father has heard from Du Caen, and we want to talk to you, come inside." I went in feeling apprehensive, as I did not like her tone. They then told me he had written to ask if he could marry me.

"Have you been seeing him alone, Irene?" This from Mama.

"Have you been encouraging him, Irene?" asked Papa.

"No. You ought to know I don't like young men, besides I have told you I *am* going to nurse: and now can I go or Doreen will finish all the mango-fool."

Then as I walked out I saw Papa reach for his writing pad whilst unconsciously twirling his moustache, and I guessed he was already composing a terse reply.

There were one or two fellows showing a slight interest in us about this time. A doctor in the I.M.S. seemed to be attracted to Doreen, and this little *madame* was having a flirtation with him on the tennis courts, much to the amusement of the other members of the Condwick clique. A fellow called Billy Adams—lately arrived from Ajmere, in a good position, about thirty-five, tall and dark with the pepper-and-salt appeal, seemed to hover between another girl and myself. She had all the advantages, bar one—she was very pretty, young and white, but there was something peculiar about her family. Her mother was never seen, not even in the compound, and gossip had it that she had run away from her soldier husband, and was living with a man who worked on the railway, letting the servants think she was his wife. We felt sorry for the girl, who never went anywhere and did not seem to have any friends—except Adams—who was seen to talk to her on one or two occasions over the fence. In the colony it only needed a simple thing like that to get tongues wagging. He was also seen walking home with me after tennis, and on one occasion he bought me sweets. As Doreen put it, "That about evens it up between you—I wonder who will win?" She knew I had lost my heart, just a very little bit.

It was hot, very hot, the storm clouds were gathering, but the "rains" still kept off. The brain-fever bird kept calling day after day with its maddening repetitive call, which was translated as You're ill! You're ill! You're ill! Ending up in a long drawn out piercing shriek enough to upset anybody when continued most of the day and into moonlit nights. The monsoons had broken in Bombay, and we expected it our way any day. Looking at the Flame-in-the-Forest with their bunches of fiery red flowers made one feel hotter than ever.

None of us was sleeping too well, the heat and Papa's cough kept us awake. We were all worried about him. Even Doreen and I realised now he was seriously ill. Mama was up, night after night, trying to help him. Looking at him one morning I was shocked at his condition, he was so thin and white, and suddenly I was very frightened. Hearing him cough one night, hour after hour, I could stand it no longer, and getting out of bed I went over trying to comfort him. I stroked his hand. "Papa, the monsoons will be here soon—it will be cooler then, and you'll be better." He didn't reply. He insisted, on going to work, daily dragging himself there, trying to keep upright, to look smart in his white drills.

Towards the end of June Vi and Doreen had gone to tennis, I had been delayed over something, then rushing towards our back gate hoping to catch them up, I was brought to a halt. Coming towards me was my father being helped home by two of his clerks—he looked dreadful. Calling Mama I rushed in and helped pull his bed into the sitting room. We were only able to put him on the bed and pull off his boots. Mama left me for a minute, to get some brandy and to send for the doctor. The sudden violent shaking of the bed, startled me. Looking down I screamed, "Papa, darling Papa," I grabbed his hand, his head turned sideways, and he was gone. With him went our childhood and carefree happy life.

CHAPTER 8

Hard Times

After the funeral Mama was asked what help she needed. "Somewhere to live in the railway colony, and a job for my daughter Vi." Vi was taken on as an assistant in the stores on a very small salary, and we were allowed a flat in the railway quarters behind the loco shed, This was a ghastly place in which to live. Apart from the noise and smoke we only had three rooms, one 12' by 12', the second half that size, the third smaller still—this was the bathroom-cum-lavatory. There was the usual front and back verandah, divided from the neighbours by a wooden partition. My mother cooked on the back verandah—all our servants had been dismissed. The servicer of a sweeper we shared with two or three other families. Our neighbours were mostly Indian Christians, Hindus and Moslems—all railway servants. They were kind, but not of our community—and we were lost and very unhappy.

Most of our furniture had to be sold—these rooms would accommodate little more than beds. We were so upset at the thought of our piano being sold, that Mama had permission to board up one of the arches on the verandah and the piano was housed there. We covered it with tarpaulins, but standing out there during the monsoons did it no good. The unkindest cut came from people who were supposed to be our friends. The Condwick crowd just dropped us. As far as they were concerned we existed no longer. The young men who showed signs of interest before now melted away. I expect they thought—"If I marry one, I marry the family," and this frightened them.

Looking back on this period years later we often discussed our escape, and were grateful to those young men for running away. Otherwise feeling lost, homeless and desperately poor we might have been tempted to take the easy way. However, at that, time Doreen and I were confused by the fickleness of human nature.

My mother, who had been widowed before, was not, and rolling up her sleeves, she explained things to us. She warned us that nothing would ever be the same again—how right she was. Often in the following days we were to recall Papa's talks to us on how to cope with problems that might beset us. As a young man, Papa had worked in the South of India helping his widowed mother; searching for better conditions he moved up North, settling in Agra. He met my mother in the boarding house she ran; then he joined the B.B. & C.I. Railway, and served this company for eighteen years. Promotion came very slowly, and it was only in the last four to six years when he was in the senior grade, that the salary increased appreciably. Consequently when he died the Provident Fund did not amount to much. We had to be very careful now, and Mama tried her hand at many things; with Doreen and me as willing assistants.

Catering for the dances; cooking meals to be packed and taken away; or buying old clothes from the officers' wives to resell. I was at that time helping Mama make hats for sale, which she would create out of georgette, silks or muslin. Large shady hats for garden parties or weddings, toques made from velvet or woollen materiel for winter. I discovered I had quite an artistic flair. Pulling a real flower to bits I would study the various parts and copy these in scraps of material which Mama discarded. For economy I would, use turmeric as a dye for yellow, and inks, red, green and blue for other colours. All the rice water from the kitchen was saved—this was used as a stiffening agent. After decorating the hats I would make sufficient sprays to fill a tray or two, and send then up the Mall to the officers' houses for sale, I was told more than once, "You ought to be on Bond street." Situated as we were, Utopia, Bond street or the Mall were all the same—far away and inaccessible.

Doreen on being told this exclaimed, "Bond Street? It would suit me fine, if we could get off this to *any* other street in Mhow, never mind Bond street."

Our sorrow being too fresh that first Christmas after Papa's death, and in that cramped accommodation we had no inclination for anything festive, and were prepared to face it as an ordinary day. Though kindness and a little cheer came our way from a complete stranger. Captain Busby, a retired sapper and a Roman Catholic, had heard about us through the priest. My mother had been to her *padre* to ask his help in advertising her catering efforts. The captain, who was a regular customer of the railway stores, bought three boxes of chocolates on Christmas Eve and handed them back over the counter to Vi to take home. This kind gesture, coming just then, touched us considerably, giving us encouragement and hope. Those chocolates were not supposed to be touched until Christmas morning, but the temptation was too great. Waiting until Mama and Vi were asleep, Doreen and I hopped out of bed and had a midnight feast, and they tasted so good that way.

We had been in the railway flats, about nine months when we heard of a vacant house in cantonments at a low rent. It was really the nursery wing to a big house but detached, standing well apart in the same large compound. A senior army officer occupied the big house and we were asked to give an undertaking not to be noisy or be annoying in any way, we were so thankful for the chance to move to a cleaner locality that we would gladly have promised anything. Having a couple of rooms to spare, we took in a family of three who were in poor circumstances. This helped them, and it also helped us to find the rent, we soon had the place looking like home, though we were badly off for furniture, we had to manage with *moprahs*, locally made bamboo chairs and cane tables, for the sitting room. Mama's rag bag provided us with enough material to make gay cushions and these, with Papa's paintings and sprays of flowers on coloured, tiles, made the place look cheerful.

When he was a guard, my father spent his free time painting in oils: he used any material handy, sheets of glass, roast dishes and earthenware jars picked up cheaply from the bazaars. Tiles and textiles were also used. On there he would paint scenes from the Bible with a verse or prayer added. Heads of animals, tropical birds and flowers were also a favourite theme. These were sold, easily, his pot-boilers he called them, but Mama always collected the money. It was whilst we were unpacking and settling in No. 56—the nursery wing—that I came across his case of oils, and thought that if I had any talent we might get rich that way. Laboriously I copied 'Monarch of the Glen,' much to the admiration of the family, but unfortunately it was unsaleable, and I had to admit that painting was not in my line, so my thoughts turned again to nursing.

Every now and again I would ask Mama to let me take this up— but she we against this. So I struggled along with my flowers, but my dream never faded. Now that we had a home again, Mama advertised

IRENE AS A YOUNG WOMAN

a meal service. The food she gave was so good and her prices so reasonable that soon we had plenty of customers, unfortunately she was much too reasonable and the business did not show a profit. We tried to get Mama to alter her prices, this she would not do. It made her so happy to see her food enjoyed that she lost sight of the real objective. It was through this activity that we were introduced to Captain Busby, that same kind old gentleman who had sent us the chocolates. Captain Busby had gone out to India as a 'band boy' in the army, and had worked his way up to a commission. He married into a respectable Anglo-Indian family, and when he retired he had a house built in Mhow. When we first met him he was a widower with two boys, the elder sixteen, his brother a few years younger. These boys were boarders in St. Joseph's College in Nainital, and it was when they were on holiday that Mama's good meals were required.

When we first met him, although in his sixties Captain Busby was still a good tennis player; his sons took after him, and finding out that we were keen on this game, he persuaded Mama to let us take it up again. We had lived very quietly so far, indeed, there was no alternative. Now we went on an occasional picnic with the Busbys, as they had a car. This was a treat for us. I need hardly say it was not long before Doreen had the elder boy a willing slave.

One day Captain Busby came to us with news that a very large house was vacant in the Mall, next to the Church-of-England called Champak House, which had a nursery wing joined to the main building by a covered verandah. He proposed to occupy this wing, as he was getting too old to control servants. And did not want the bother of housekeeping, The rest of the house he told Mama she would easily fill with guests. So it came about that we moved again, taking our three P.G.'s with us. It was nice being close to the church, which had poignant memories for us. It had its disadvantages, however. If we were sleeping outside on a Sunday morning, and heard the band coming down the Mall, we would have to rush indoors. Mama did not think it fair for the British Army to see a long line of sleeping figures, when they had to be up at crack-of-dawn to march to church.

We soon filled the spare rooms with guests, mostly teachers and nurses from Bombay, on holiday to be near their boyfriends in the army. We continued with the hat-making business, and the buying and reselling of old clothes, but for all this it was a struggle. Whether it was because Mama was too generous by nature, or was not charging enough we were not sure. Sometimes we had suspicions that she was let down by some of her guests who left without paying their bills; others who pleaded poverty would be let off free. We were never told these things, but knowing her kind heart we had doubts concerning her business acumen.

It was seeing her in near rags—not that we were much better off ourselves—that upset us. We never got anything new, but had to re-make from the second-hand clothes. I remember once wearing a really old pair of shoes at a tennis dance, and my heel kept slipping out of my shoe. Mrs. Condwick was there, and I saw her look at my shoes and smile. She caught my eye, then looking at my shoes, she laughed again. All my good resolutions were forgotten and I hated her. All this worried me end I was certain Mama was finding things difficult when the merchants from the bazaar or the old *Sete*, our landlord, came round at the end of the month expecting to be paid and were met by the servant, who had been instructed to say *Memsahib bahar gaye*—*Madame* is out. Vi could do no more, her paypacket was brought home unopened and handed to Mama; I felt it was up to me.

I begged her to let me train as a nurse. She was against this, though with Vi's help and encouragement, I wore her down and finally had. permission to write to the Sir Jamsetjee Jejeebhoy Jee Hospital—and the European General or St. George's, as it was also called, for their application forms. For weeks after this Mama went round saying, "If anything happens to you, I shall never forgive Vi."

My reply, "For goodness sake, Mama, I am nineteen now, and can look after myself," did not comfort her. Poor Vi, I thought, I shall certainly have to be careful or you are going to get into trouble.

One day going into the kitchen I caught my mother crying, and asked her what was wrong. "It's you leaving us—after a long time we have a happy home, and now you are spoiling everything."

I tried to reason with her, telling her I was wasting my time in Mhow. "I know you want us to marry, you do not want us to work—but darling—that is an old-fashioned idea. More and more girls are working these days." Then to please her I added, "I may marry some day, Mama, but I must get my training done first. You see, I will not marry just to have someone to keep me."

"Why don't you give God the chance to do something for you: I have prayed for the right partners to turn up for you girls. If the Lord looked after me in the Kamptoe Convent, I am sure He will look after my children." And then she reminded me of her early life. I had heard all this before, but never tired of having it repeated. When her father, the Portuguese farrier died, their mother went out to work as a nanny, and the two children—Mama and Aunt Alice, were left in the convent. Mama was happy there but for one thing, being a big-made girl with a healthy appetite she never had enough to eat. "I used to pray," she said, "Please God make Sister Agnes give me more bread; and do you know, Irene, most mornings after serving everyone sister would come round to me and say, 'Here, fatty, this is over, you can finish it.'

"Then another time God very clearly answered a child's prayer was when a party of us were taken by nuns for a walk to an old neglected garden. As no one worked there any longer, the jungle was rapidly taking over, but for a few fruit trees still fighting for survival. We were allowed to walk about on our own and I walked amongst the fruit trees, mostly bare except for a few dried leaves still hanging on, and I longed for a custard-apple—you know how fond I am of these—and I prayed, 'Please Jesus, let me find just *one*.' I wandered about looking from tree to tree, then—I could hardly believe my eyes: there in front of me, on a tree almost stripped bare, hung a large ripe custard-apple. So you see even a little girl's very materialistic prayers had been answered." Mama stopped now, smiling at the recollection, and I waited quietly for her to continue. "I feel, Irene, you ought to leave it to God."

"Listen, Mama, don't you think if I am *not* to nurse, obstacles will present themselves. I have three big hurdles to get over. My education is very poor, I may not be accepted at any hospital on that account. Then the work is hard, and you are always saying I am not strong. Finally, at St. George's, where the work is lighter than at the J.J., everyone says this hospital is only for Europeans: will they accept an Anglo-Indian? Now if everything goes smoothly and I get in somewhere, somehow, can't we take that as a sign?" and I hurried along, encouraged by a new look I saw in Mama's eyes. "All my life I have wanted to nurse, surely there is a reason in *that?* Please let me try."

"All right, Irene, have it your own way, but don't say I did not warn you, and now I must hurry through my morning's work, and visit the officers' wives to see if I can get any old white dresses for you," ended Mama on a mundane note.

The application, forms from Bombay arrived. Many people had told Mama about the work in the J.J. being hard and Doctor Pinto had advised her to get me into the E.G. if possible. "She will find it easier as she will only have Europeans to nurse," he told Mama. So I was only allowed to complete this one form, thereby feeling my chances had been reduced. I had to state that my father had been, an Englishman, my mother a Eurasian. About education, as I was on delicate ground, I was told to skirt this carefully. "Say as little as possible, mention that you were mostly educated at home—therefore can give no standards." Then adding references from our vicar, Captain Busby and our family doctor, this was posted, with a big prayer. I waited hopefully, hardly uncrossing my fingers for days at a time.

After an interval a reply came I was accepted and had a fortnight in which to get ready. It was all exciting now; Mama had managed to collect four white tennis dresses that an officer's wife had discarded, and these I altered. When they came back white and starched from the *dhoby*, I changed into one, then tying a tea-cloth round my head I went into the sitting room where Mama and the girls sat. "How do I look?"

Mama just gave a deep sigh, so Vi at once said: "You need not worry, Mama, she'll not nurse for long: she'll be married soon."

In this she was wrong—I spent many happy years nursing before I married.

Then dear little sister Doreen had to add, "And I wonder how many patients she'll kill before that happens."

Doctor Pinto and Captain Busby between them bought the watch and scissors I needed—and another friend, a coloured man on the railway, helped by taking me into Bombay; I travelled as his sister to save the fare! Mama said "Goodbye" to me at the house—I was glad of this—Captain Busby and Doreen went with me to the station, and passing our old home I thought of Papa's anger when I told him the first time I wanted to take up nursing.

I hoped now he would understand and forgive me.

CHAPTER 9

Trainee—Green Belt

When we arrived at St. George's by victoria, not in a taxi, and when my escort was seen, the raised eyebrows of the sister to whom I was taken on the mess verandah made me realise I had started on the wrong foot. Then I was summoned to matron's office, I would have liked my escort to accompany me, but he declined to go any further—perhaps he was being tactful. After many questions had been asked, matron told me my poor education was my weak point, but as my letter about our circumstances at home had been so candid, she had decided to give me a chance. She warned me that I would have to give a great deal of time to study to keep up with the other nurses. This I promised to do, and thanked her again; with my sincerity I made her realise how much this meant to me. I was then dismissed: and—"Whew",—was I glad to get out of that room.

To say I was nervous and shy is to put it mildly. I crept about passages for weeks hardly daring to lift my eyes from the floor—blushing when addressed. I hated myself for being so stupid. However, watching the new arrivals a week or two later, and seeing one or two of them behave in much the same manner, I was comforted. Fortunately I was sent to a ward for woman in the first month. The earliest jobs taught were disappointing. I expected to shake pillows, give medicines or soothe the fevered brows. Instead of which I was taught to scrub lockers, clean cupboards, "do" the doctor's table and collect stools. "And for goodness sake, nurse, don't go round collecting all the three or four legged stools you come across to bring to me," admonished staff nurse, "We have already had a silly fool to do that here." I muttered a prayer of thankfulness for that warning, because that is exactly what I *should* have done.

She saw I was puzzled, and thrusting a piece of paper and pencil into my hand explained, "There take these, just put down the bed numbers 1-12, then ask each patient how many stools she has had, write the answer against the number," and staff dismissed me impatiently. "Run along now—hurry. I have no time to tell you anymore." Goodness, I thought, they don't even have time to teach you in this place, Even the juniors I found could be cross if asked about anything twice; it was all very confusing.

Going up to my room that night, I found my roommate already in bed, reading. I introduced myself, and asked for her help. "You can tell me one or two things which have puzzled me— they were all too busy in the wards that I dare not ask any of them." She smiled and nodded; encouraged I asked, "Do you know what a stool is? I had to go round and ask the patients this. Some said one, some two, some none, and one said six. Can you tell me what they meant?"

She could and did.

"What you put your hand up for in school when you ask to leave the room."

All this time I had been undressing "You can put the light out, Green, as soon as you've finished. You must be tired." I confessed I was, then lifted the net and slid lazily between the sheets. I was soon startled to a frenzy. My foot rested on something that was cold, hard and smooth. I screamed and sprang out of bed and in my panic tore the net.

"There's something horrible in my bed, may I put the light on?"

Hetty could not answer she was trying to smother her laughter. I found the switch and she sat up not to miss a thing. Very cautiously I threw up the net, and slowly pulled away the top sheet. Where my feet had been rested sat a skull. "Oh, how could they?" I asked, between tears and laughter.

"You're lucky—it was a stinking appendix for me," was all the comfort I got.

The teasing did not stop at that. I had to endure it right through my training, though when it was done kindly I did not mind. It was the malicious spiteful sort that hurt. The nurses soon found my weak points, the unsophistication and shyness I was never able to conquer completely, and I was soon called "Mouse," and "Granny," by the kinder ones, and "The Villager," and "Greeny-Green," by the other kind. Sitting in the mess, waiting for a meal was where the baiting took place.

"Have you never seen a tram or a ship before?"

"My dear, she was terrified of the streets."

"Have you never seen a lift?"

She said, "I'd sooner take the stairs, please."

"Have you really never seen a man in pyjamas before?"—*Sotto voce*—"You'll soon see one without."

Peals of laughter, and little Irene getting redder and redder and feeling very foolish, "Where have you been brought up, my child, may I ask?" said a snooty, hoity-toity Bombayite.

I longed to have the courage to say, "I was taught simple good manners in a Christian home, which obviously you have missed." But I had not the nerve—more's the pity, or I may have been able to silence the bullies once and for all.

The brazen types would blatantly discuss subjects like sex, abortions, prostitutes and venereal diseases. In our home life these subjects were 'taboo.' If Mama had had to mention a prostitute, I have no doubt that she would have been called a "bad lady." Is it any wonder that now I sat feeling miserable and showing it, to their delight. Then ending with a few smutty jokes, and seeing me blush, they would laugh. "Look at Green, she does live up to her name." I was too dim at first to understand even this. Later when I did how I wished the name had been Brown, Smith or Jones. Though many years later I found it useful as my case was the only one never borrowed by the student midwives in Queen Charlottes. The initials I.M. before the Green saw to that!

I could not sleep that first night, in fact I slept little all through the first week. My feet were on fire, the pain reached to my knees. I must have looked a wreck because Home Sister asked me what was wrong. She advised me to soak my feet in hot water, adding salt to harden them. The hardening process took place in time, not however stopping at the feet, perhaps this was just as well as at first I used to get very upset when I saw a patient in pain or when a child died. It was a long time before I could get used to the *blasé* way in which some of the nurses broke the news that a patient was dying or dead. "The liver is going to Jesus," or "The heart has at last, kicked the bucket." Having delivered this cheerful bit of news they would, carry on gaily on their way whilst I went round with a lump in my throat for hours.

I would hate to look into a patient's eyes to see terror there. I saw this in a young girl's eyes in my first week. She was a good looking sportswoman involved in a street accident, and a leg had been badly fractured. She begged the surgeons to save her leg, and for weeks they battled—in the end her life was at stake, and amputation was ordered. On coming out of the anaesthetic she spoke of the tickling in her toes; in time sister had to tell her the truth—her cry of despair haunted me for weeks.

Though we had lots to laugh at also. The Indian staff consisted of ward boys who carried the stretchers, polished floors, brought the meals up from the kitchen and took the trays to the patients. These boys were found in the male and female wards. They wore white drill shorts and jackets with white *pugrees*. In the male wards *mathers*, untouchables, looked after the lavatories, and took the urinals and bedpans to the men. These attendants wore the white drill shorts and jackets also, but instead of *pugrees* wore a *fez*. In the wards for women *matheranis* looked after the lavatories and carried the bedpans round. They wore white cotton *saris*. It was one of these attendants who gave us a good laugh. She was the head *matherani* and had a commanding way about her, an absolute autocrat—in consequence she was called Victoria.

One day a new probationer made the mistake of calling her *matherani* as she was leaving the ward with a bedpan. Victoria's dignity was offended, slowly she turned to face the nurse with the bedpan stuck out at arm's length, and in loud clear tones, in perfect English said, "I am Victoria." This was the first time any of us had ever heard her use this language. Sister, standing at the duty room door, added, "and we are not amused." Victoria walked out with great dignity, the nurse retreated in confusion. After this I took good care to give the woman the full respect due to her. It is the Indians themselves who have given the untouchables these names: *mather* or *jemadar*. It is a cruel jest with a touch of irony. *Mather* is really a high Moslem title, e.g. the *Mather* of Chitral, a chief in the N.W.F.P. *jemadar* is an Indian Army rank.

A never failing source of fun was Fighting Flora. She was a large Cockney; what she was doing in Bombay, where she lived, or to whom she belonged, no one seemed to know. She visited all the big hotels, restaurants and hospitals in the big cities of India selling paper flowers; was nearly always drunk and could be very aggressive if you refused to buy her wares. She would call you many choice rude names; though few were brave enough to incur her wrath, and I have seen great big men dodge out of her way. On the other hand if you pleased her a whisky flavoured kiss was your reward. I had both and I do not know which was worse.

One evening she came into the word: this was always easy. Owing to the climate all the doors had to be left open. This time, apart from being drunk, she was dirty—going round she cracked jokes with the patients—sang a naughty verse or two, then threw each a flower, before presenting sister with the remainder. She knew all the doctors and sisters by name, and stood in awe of none. Sister called two of us aside, and asked us to take her and put her into a good hot bath. We had the *matherani* in to help us. At first Fighting Flora lived up to her name. She was like a tigress, but after a struggle we managed to get her into the bath. Defeated, she lay there calling us the vilest names. Seeing this had no effect, she stopped, exhausted.

Now whether she suddenly sobered up, or felt sorry, I do not know, but unexpectedly she stood up, naked, wet and unashamed, threw her arms about us and kissed each in turn. The *matherani* was not having any, and backing to the door she fled. We got her into a nightdress and marched her into bed, where she was given a good meal. "I'd not give her a meal, but a pint of castor-oil," said Rogers, who was annoyed and very wet after the struggle. Fighting Flora slept for hours; waking she demanded her clothes, dressed and walked out, talking cheerfully and promising to call again.

She was a well known character, loved by many, especially the prostitutes of Bombay. We came to know these ladies quite well, having them in as patients from time to time, She was disliked by a few, the few who could not see beneath her dirty drunken exterior—the heart of gold. To the prostitutes she was a friend, helper and adviser. To us nurses a source of kindly comic relief. Often when the hours seemed long in passing, or the wards gloomy and depressing after a death, the sound of her Cockney voice, her bawdy jokes, or drunken songs would revive us, and we were glad of Fighting Flora. Her untimely and tragic death brought sorrow to many. She was found drowned in one of the tanks on the Maidan in Calcutta. It was never explained how she came to be so far off the beaten track.

After I had been in "Womens'" for a month to six weeks I was sent to "Eyes," and as I was not called to matron's office, when transferred I took it for granted that I had been given a good report. So I started in "Eyes" with no misgivings. I worked just as hard here as in

"Womens'"—the training meant too much to me to try and slack in any way. Off duty I studied every minute I could, refusing all invitations to parties from patients and nurses in that first year. The piano in the mess was a temptation, but even this pleasure I denied myself. We had a club in the grounds, and the nurses used to collect there to dance or play games. I was often asked to join; excusing myself I would rush away upstairs to my books. Some of the nurses thought me a blue stocking, I do not think I was popular with many on this account, especially when it happened that at lectures I was able to supply the answers where the others failed. Then I collected some dirty looks. They did not know that I was starting handicapped, and had to put in the extra study.

In "Eyes" I appeared gauche and awkward because I used to get flustered when watched by Sister Crabbott on a job—she had this effect on me. My fingers turned to thumbs and would let me down. I dropped a kidney dish I was holdings containing dirty swabs, at a dressing. In the quiet ward this made a terrible noise making us all jump. The surgeon frowned, and sister turned on me. I was called an ass, and ordered out of her sight. I prayed for the ground to open and swallow me. After this—I tried to make myself invisible when she was about. This whilst irritating her also gave her a feeling of power over me, which she used without mercy. She bullied me for a month: nothing I did was right. My little mistakes were magnified. She would have me 'on the mat' before all the staff making me feel a worm.

One afternoon in my rush I failed to change my apron before she came on duty. Another time I had forgotten to empty the washing up bowl. These mistakes which seemed so trivial and were to be expected from a "trainee" were to her the sure signs that I would never make a good nurse. Her report at the end of the month left no doubt concerning this. I suppose, however, the poor frustrated lovelorn woman was to be pitied really. She had fallen badly for the visiting eye specialist, who was a married man, which somewhat complicated matters. I seemed to be the one on whom her venom was vented.

One morning my name appeared on matron's list. Walking to matron's office I wished I had not eaten such a hearty breakfast. After scolding me well, matron read me a line from sister's report, which said, "She has not the making of a nurse." That sounded like the end of a little dream and I wept. How could I explain that the little confidence I had gained in "Womens'" had ebbed away under this red-haired, pale-faced, wishy-washy, blue-eyed sister's cold look of unfriendliness? "Well," said matron, "After a report like that I should really send you home." I then begged and implored to be given another chance. I told her again why I had to get this training: I had to help my mother. She understood. This tall, good-looking Scotswoman, Miss MacFarlane, R.R.C. had a heart of gold. I was then informed I was due for a transfer, and it was hoped that the next report would be a good one. Leaving the office pardoned I breathed again. This time I was sent to a ward for men on the first floor.

They were a friendly lot. We had European shop-assistants; Russian taxi-drivers; Japanese sailors; Chinese cooks; and Eurasians of every shade and walk in life—in short a mixed bunch of all nationalities. I was shy at first seeing the men strolling about in nothing but pyjamas. Then one day I was called to assist a senior in giving an operation case a urine bottle; her manner taught me something; I realised then these were not just men but our patients, whose comfort and well-being were in our hands, and from that moment my shyness was not as acute, and gradually my confidence returned. The first time I was told to give an enema to one of these men, I remembered the teasing I had received, and wished that nurse could see me now. The aplomb with which I carried out the job, I may say that a lot of this was assumed, as I wished above everything else to help my patient. Fortunately, I had been taught to administer these in "Womens'," so calling for screens I walked briskly up to the bed. "Now, Mr. Smith, pull down your pyjamas quickly and turn onto your left, side, quickly! Quickly! Knees up to your chin. I am in a terrific rush as I have two more of these to give." This was a lie but so comforting. And before poor Mr. Smith could collect his wits the job was done, and I was away.

Sister Bennett, with her laughing brown eyes, was a great help. She was younger than the one in "Eyes;" perhaps that made a difference. Her own training days with its difficulties, problems, joys and sorrows had not been forgotten. One morning sister called us to her duty-room and suggested as it was getting near Christmas we had better start collecting money for our ward decorations. The collection was made from the visitors, our personal friends, or anyone with a kind expression. Now I had the courage or temerity, I do not know which, to suggest I would do a bit of painting which we could raffle. Sister thought it was a good idea and a piece of black satin was bought; on this, against the usual wintry background, I painted a robin sitting on a holly branch. This ghastly effort actually made quite a good sum, and for a while I walked about with a halo.

Each ward chose a colour scheme. The shades were softly blended and the whole hospital tastefully decorated. A prize was given for the best dressed ward. The tin lamp-shades were removed, and crepe paper flower shapes took their place. The old brass *jardinière* with palm on the big glass table in the ward centre was thrown out temporarily, and garlands of paper flowers cascaded down in its place. The money left over was used to buy festive food. On Christmas Day the nurses were allowed to ask their boyfriends to tea, as no "off-duty" was allowed for anyone. Actually visitors and nurses' friends and relatives were in the hospital all that day, coming and going as they pleased. Each unit of two wards, had a big lounge built off the front verandah, mostly of glass to give a good view of the garden. On Christmas Day, this room with its cakes, fruit, nuts, and wine, patients and visitors, nurses and boyfriends was in a state of confusion.

Masses of mistletoe were hung from all the vantage points, and this was not by any means wasted. Even sister's duty-room was not neglected, a huge bunch was hung over her office table. We wondered if the houseman had dared! Carols and community singing were heard from all the wards. Everyone had a good time, except the very sick, these were screened, and we took it in turns to nurse them. Christmas Day always began with a church service. In one of the units one of the two private-rooms had been converted into a small chapel. On Sundays and festivals, this was used by the Church of England nursing staff and matron, and the walking or wheelchair patients. I used to enjoy these services, with matron and the sisters in the front pews, and the patients and nurses seated behind. The smell of iodoform, castor oil emulsion or Friar's balsam mixed with the scent of flowers on the alter though making the atmosphere rather incongruous did nothing to mar the beautiful communion service, the *padre* later visited the wards seeking out his flock from the different nationalities and creeds present.

St. George's, or the European General as it was also called, admitted Anglo-Indians; Eurasians; Indian Christians; Japanese; Chinese; and Jews—in fact anyone wearing European dress, and with a smattering of English. If it was originally meant only for Europeans, it certainly did not enforce the rule. The Sir Jamsetjee Jejeebhoy jee Hospital built by a rich benevolent Parsee—was for the Asians of Bombay. This was a well equipped, well run hospital, with nothing lacking; nevertheless many Indians dressed in European clothes came to the European General and demanded admission as Eurasians; their prestige being heightened, or so they imagined, by being in there. Anyway, who was to draw the line, and where? It was a tricky problem, and as long as there was a bed vacant—the patient was admitted. The sister of wards 5,6,7 on the ground floor often grumbled about the Indian cooks sent to her wearing their master's cast-off clothing, but she never made any difference in her treatment. She was as kind to them as she was to the poor whites.

The floor called the Nursing Home and the two wards on the 2nd Floor were definitely kept for whites. In the three years I was there no coloured patient was admitted to these, even wealth and influence being unable to achieve this. The nurses were mostly whites or near-whites; though I was surprised to find about five to ten coloured girls when I got there, as "Upcountry" every one spoke of the European General as being colour-conscious, yet I found not only coloured patients, but these few brown girls. Talking this over with a senior, I was told a point had been stretched to please the clergy and nuns, these girls being admitted from the orphanages or from very poor homes. On duty all worked well together, and were happy; though later I noticed when making up parties the colour-bar did crop up, even amongst these cheerful happy nurses.

Our uniform was white aprons worn over white short sleeved dresses with white shoes and stockings. The colour relief come from the belts and armbands. These bands worn on the left-arm by the senior and juniors were navy with the badge of St. George pinned above a small cross made of white metal. A navy blue belt was also worn. Probationers—for a three month period—wore green belts only, with non-regulation white dresses and aprons. All the nurses wore' butterfly' caps until the end of the second year—when "Sister-Doras" took their place. Matron and the sisters wore veils, matron was the only one who did not wear an apron. After the first three months, "Matron's Exams" had to be taken. On passing this, sufficient white material for the regulation style dresses and aprons was handed over.

A *dirzee* always haunted the mess to cadge for the orders, after paying him, the *dhoby* and tipping the room boy the poor first year trainee did not have much left for herself. We were of course fed and housed, but our monthly salary was by no means munificent.

Apart from the tips the "Salary" had to cover stationery and toilet requisites, also white shoes and stockings for the wards, and mufti. A few lucky ones had money sent from home. These were the poshly dressed ones who frequented the race course, and used taxis; no dingy victorias with rude ponies for them! They had money to spare for luxuries. A couple of these pampered beauties when on night duty had a standing order with one of the big hotels for a meal to be sent over. If Home Sister knew she turned a blind eye.

A unit consisted of two long wards of twenty to thirty beds, and the overflow was housed on the wide mosquito proofed verandah. There was also a surgery and two private rooms. This was run by a sister with a third year nurse who was called 'Staff.' Two second year nurses—called seniors, two first year nurses called juniors, and a probationer or 'Green-Belt.' From this number a senior and a junior covered the nightshift. On night duty carriers containing the midnight meal were placed on the mess verandah by the bearers. The junior nurse had to take one up, and it was her job at the right time to warm the meal to serve to her senior and herself. If you were on with one of the pampered rich, for your supper you were sure to get a tasty bit of something *à la Taj*: or the Majestic.

However, most of the nurses did manage on their salaries, or as I, had no alternative. After settling the *dirzee's* bill for my first lot of uniform, and buying my stationery and toilet requisites I put aside a scrap towards mufti and the annual holiday. This sum the first time amounted only to a few *annas*, but just starting this saving in an old "Cobra" polish tin was a sort of consolation. Home did not seem so far away. The following month I had no *dirzee's* bill, so after buying the necessary odds and ends, and adding to my savings I found I still had some money. So with wings on my heels I flew to the general post office just across the street to send Mama my first small help. At last I was doing something that really made me happy. Mama wrote back at once, thanking me though she asked me not to send any more, she felt I was depriving myself. I then had to write and assure her that I could manage very well. Then telling her of the pleasure I was getting at being able to help I begged to be allowed to continue.

For the first year, two students shared a room, after which the privacy of a single room was enjoyed. To me this was a great treat as at home Doreen and I always had to share. My *bête noir* was that 6 a.m. rising bell. Just in case we overslept, a quarter of an hour after the big bell a *chaprassi* came up to each floor ringing a little hand bell. The only way I could make myself get up was to roll out of bed on the first stroke of the bell, and make for a bath. We had two of these to each floor, and fixed a routine, some bathing in the morning, some in the afternoon, and the remainder at night. We had to be down at 7 a.m. for breakfast, after which a peculiar ceremony took place in the mess. Matron's *chaprassi* would appear in the doorway with a brass tray on which were two typewritten lists: One was marked "Transfers." The other more ominously "Matron's Office." Home Sister would rise to read these aloud and the nurses would stand with bated breath listening intently. A few moans usually followed when the first list was read. These however turned to groans after the second. My name had appeared on that list when the sister for "Eyes" had given me a bad report.

The most unpopular ward was O.B. (Obstetrics), called by the nurses "Oh, be joyful." This brand of nursing was not included in the curriculum for the three years and had to be taken after the General in a recognised Maternity Hospital—here we merely fetched and carried for the sisters, who 'took' all the cases. Many of the nurses found this boring, especially those who had no intention of taking the midwifery training at all. Another ward feared was 1 and 2 Top Floor—Men's. Sister Murray, who was hard of hearing, had a name for being fierce, exacting and a rigid disciplinarian—however if she found a nurse willing to work and who tried—she was kind. After breakfast at 8 a.m. we left for the wards, waiting across the garden, down a narrow covered path in a 'crocodile;' usually paired with our own particular friend.

We had three hours "off" daily; a meal was always taken in this time, occasionally a lecture had to be squeezed in also; though most of these were given in the daily visiting hour 5 to 6 p.m. We had a day off each month, and the most wonderful part of this was to hear that beastly bell ring, then be able to pull the sheet over one's head and sleep again. On Sundays half the staff worked mornings—the other half relieved after *tiffin*. An extra half-day was given each week at the convenience of the ward sister and she had the authority to stop this if you were in disgrace. This half-day the staff of each ward changed round to suit themselves. On the "day-off," "half-day," or when Sunday afternoon was free, we could stay out until 10 p.m. On request a late pass was granted till 12:30 a.m.; three were allowed monthly.

These late passes could be changed to "sleeping-out" on production of a letter from a relative or friend. Matron usually made searching enquiries before granting these.

On moonlight nights, the nurses on duty had a little break from monotony. Standing on the verandah they would watch the "late passes" drive up, and spy upon the fond farewells, the couples vainly trying to got behind the palms for privacy. The late girls would then report to night super: she had a list and after checking this would pick up a bunch of keys and march them away to be locked up in their different houses. No one coming in late had a hope of being able to sneak in unobserved, those keys remained in night super's possession. The late arrivals had their names added to that dreaded second list, "Matron's Office," next morning. The old excuse "the car broke down" was not accepted. A severe scolding was given with a warning that if this happened too frequently late passes would not be allowed. We had a fortnight's holiday each year: though most of us turned this into four weeks by sending in a sick note from the family doctor. However these extra two weeks had to be made up at the end of the training. The hospital gained this way; a trained nurse was available on a student's salary.

We had a month to six weeks day duty and a fortnight on nights, which most of us disliked. I did, as the ward, cheerful by day, seemed to turn unfriendly at night, familiar objects took on strange shapes and corners grew deep shadows. The one light had to be shaded by a navy or green cloth and this cast a horrible gloom over everything. The beds with their white mosquito nets would look like fat ghosts all lined up. One could neither see nor hear anyone coming round one of these, because of the white uniform and soft shoes. I would welcome the occasional visits from the night super; or a senior, providing we met on the verandah, as coming unexpectedly upon either in the ward around a mosquito net I was apt to jump out of my skin.

Matron, who was very tall and slim, slept in one of the lounges in the hospital, and before going to bed late at night did a final round in her long white nightdress worn under her overall. She was one of the permanent perambulating ghosts. The *mather* taking a bottle to a patient, padding round in his bare feet, would give me the worst shivers; all I was able to see when almost on top of him was his white jacket, *fez* and white shorts; the rest of him had dissolved in the darkness. Then a patient dying at night was uncanny, especially a coloured man with the glossy whites of his eyes. This scene I found eerie enough by day, but much worse by night when I was alone.

We were never allowed to leave the dying: if nothing further could be done we would have to sit near the bed, doing charts and reports or making bandages, surrounded of course by tall screens. In the first year or eighteen months I absolutely refused to be left alone with one of these cases, and would bribe the *mather* or *matherani* to stay with me, gladly sharing my supper or tea. They knew how to melt away when necessary. Apart from the mysterious shadows, the patients seemed to change at night. The men that were cheerful, normal and friendly by day, would moan and groan more, or make horrible whistling noises. One or two always had nightmares: a sudden shout in the quiet ward would make me jump; and the pen I was using would shoot across the chart spoiling it, or if sewing I would jab my finger.

A very old sweeper named Ganpat was on nights with me when I was still a very green "green-belt." He was fond of his *char* and let me know this. He had most of mine as I would bribe him this way into bringing his tattered *razai*—the patchwork quilt on which he sat or slept, to where I could see him. Usually he slept in the lavatory corridor under the row of bells. One night he squatted a few yards from me smoking a *biri*. They were not allowed to do this on duty but I pretended not to notice. He watched the unequal struggle I was having with a huge leg splint I had been left to pad. This, or making bandages or dressings was night 'homework' so to speak.

When night super came I left this to go round the ward with her; on my return Ganpat and splint were missing. When I saw him next I asked him where my splint was. "My son has a tailor's shop just outside the hospital gates. I have ordered him to stop all his other work and pad that horrible thing for you." Then seeing the startled expressions on my face he hurried on, "since before you were born, *baba* we have been handling these horrible things."

"Ganpat," I said, aghast. "You will have me dismissed, don't you know we are supposed to do them without help? Go and bring that splint back at once."

"Now don't you worry, it is all arranged; you will have it back in less than an hour's time; and in the morning when you take that horrible thing to Matron *Sahib* for inspection she will think you very clever."

I begged him between tears and rage to go down and bring it

back, telling him I should be cheating if I did not do it myself. "As to that," he replied with a wave of his hand, impatiently brushing my plea aside. "It is a trifle, if no one knows, no one will be hurt, but you will be much hurt by Matron *Sahib's* tongue if you do it yourself." With this warning I weakened, remembering with a shudder my first visit 'on-the-mat'.

I could imagine the little shop down the road, the tailor squatting under a swinging oil lamp surrounded by a small group of curious *pan* chewing, or *biri* smoking friends. I felt guilty carrying that splint across the garden to matron's office, and I should not have been surprised to hear matron say, "Mph. . . .Yes, the tailor has made a good job of it." However the splint was examined critically, but no comment passed. Trying to sleep that day I kept on dreaming of an old, fat little untouchable who was chasing me round the ward with a huge splint. On duty that night, I met him just as I was putting the kettle on for tea, his old wrinkled face was wreathed in smiles. "You have not brought that horrible thing back with you, so I know it has been passed, *Ram-Ram*, tonight Ganpat will drink much *char Misses Baba*," said he, producing a large battered mug from under his jacket. "*Char*, you won't get *char*, you old *Shaitan*,"—devil. "What you deserve is liquid quinine."

CHAPTER 9

"The Mouse" and Pamela

Next morning, off duty, we found a bunch of new girls in the mess, and had breakfast together. There were five of them, and as two were to live in my block, Home Sister asked me to show them their rooms. This is how I met Pamela from Poona, as I shall call her in this story. She was a good looking white girl with blue eyes and golden hair: after a while I was let into the secret: this was pseudo, and I was asked to bleach it. Her parents were divorced, and she lived with her father and aunt, She was very spoilt; money was frequently sent to her, most of this went on clothes and the races. She was one of the best dressed. No *dirzee*-mades for her. Her clothes came from those expensive little shops run by the hard-faced women who made frequent trips to England, buying off-the-pegs during the sales, and taking these out to sell as 'models.' My friend Pamela was keen on the opposite sex and this was to be her undoing. She was a good dancer, witty and vivacious.

No two girls could have been more different, in appearance or character; when together we were referred to as 'the Star and the Mouse' by the other nurses. Yet from our first meeting we became friends and this lasted for many years. As she was sent to my wards I looked forward to day duty again. Then we had lots of fun. Most mornings Pamela and I walked to the hospital together, and she would tell me about her current boyfriend, how she had spent the previous evening or how much money she had lost at the races. Climbing the wide stone stairs together, she would keep pouring out her troubles into my sympathetic ear, allowing me to get ahead of her, suddenly my ankle would be grabbed and I would go down on my knee with a most painful bang. That little so-and-so thought this fun!

Then on returning from a lecture she would meet me on top of the stairs to say, "Sister wants you in her office, she is mad with you over something." I would be about to enter with my heart thumping wondering what I had done wrong when she would grab me back by the apron and laugh. She has even come to me on an afternoon shift on the rare occasion when we were not very busy and said, "Lyon wants you to give No. 8 an enema." I have got the thing ready and called for screens. The poor man looking panic-stricken would ask, "Nurse, is *that* for *me?*" And then before I could proceed Pamela would come round the screens and say, "So sorry I've made a mistake, it's for No. 8 in the next ward."

Looking at her on the verandah my suspicions would be aroused. "Is this one of your mad jokes?" Confessing, she would double up with laughter, but I would be really cross. "If you cannot find anything to do it's a pity you don't take up a book—It will help your mind." However, meeting later we would eye each other and smile.

She was always on the lookout for the good looking patient, and when we were on opposite shifts her first question on coming on duty would be, "Anyone exciting admitted?" One day I was able to tell her that No. 12 was a good looking Italian, we went into the ward together, ostensibly handing and taking over, strolling to talk to one or two, to give a cursory glance at an oxygen cylinder standing ready or at a saline drip, before ending at No. 12. "Here is your night nurse," I said "by way of introduction. Poor chappy he fell at sight, they married a year later, and he was the first of a succession—but that is her story. Many of the nurses met their future husbands as patients. Some left before completing their training—having no alternative. The wiser ones, however, got their diplomas and then married.

The nurses addressed each other by their surnames, so one afternoon washing an elderly Eurasian, a chronic dysentery who had been admitted a day or two earlier, I was not surprised when he said, "So you are Nurse Green." I admitted I was—he then seemed to go into a daydream and stuttered, "No, that would be too strange, yet the name is the same—I wonder?"

"What do you wonder, perhaps I can help?" I asked.

"Many years ago I know a chap called Harold Green. Are you his daughter?"

"Do you mean Albert Harold Green—if you do, I am his daughter."

Ignatious was delighted with this reply, though he was upset when

I told him my father had been dead about two years. After this I gave him as much time as I could, it made him happy and we talked of my father.

A week or two later a dreadful thing happened involving him, and I am ashamed to say I was to blame. Just before the first break at 11 a.m. we discovered a mix-up in the duty arrangements. All the nurses except myself were booked for a lecture that evening; and it happened to be sister's 'evening off,' the only free evening she had in the week. As it, was too late for any alterations to be made, sister had to give up her evening and she and I had to manage—which meant it was really up to me. As the nurses rushed away to the lectures I was inundated with long lists of jobs that had to be done. There were several No. 1 (Fluid) diet in Medical. I was not at all familiar with these as I was in Surgical at the time, but I knew I had to manage it somehow. I started doing the simple ones first, strained orange juice, milk and barley and soups; then I got on to the more complicated, ones. After a while I was pleased to find I had managed them all and the other jobs as well before sister came round to where the feed-table stood on the back verandah.

She asked me how I was getting on, and we discussed the diets. Going into details, she enquired if Ignatious had been given his Bengers. I replied that he had.

"I suppose you knew how to prepare it, nurse, you did give it the second boiling?"

"Sister," I exclaimed, aghast, "I forgot to reboil it in my rush. Oh, what have I done?"

"That was very naughty of you, nurse," and sister looked really cross. I was speechless with despair, imagining I had made a fatal error. Sister was saying something, but I could not take it in, then looking at me she said, "What is the matter, nurse? You look quite ill."

"Sister, he must *not* die. Oh, *please* tell me he won't die," I pleaded, I then told her of the friendship many years ago between this man and my father.

She now understood my extreme unhappiness and warning me to be more careful in future told me, "Your lapse makes no difference, he never had a chance. He was too far gone when he was brought in here; we told his friends the other day he would not recover, it's an unfortunate experience for you, but don't worry too much, Nurse Green." After this I watched the old man very carefully. I could not do enough for him, and each day he lived I breathed a sigh of relief; and was thankful to see him still there though gradually getting weaker.

I was transferred a few weeks later, but before I left this ward I had an embarrassing experience. In Surgical we had a carbuncle case, a middle-aged fat white man. A cook off one of the ships. In spite of the daily hot saline bath he was ordered he still smelt of stale grease. When sitting up in bed he looked really repulsive. The black curly hair on his chest did not quite hide his pendulous bosoms, which any woman would have been proud to possess. Being skinny and flat-chested myself, I secretly envied him. He had daily dressings which staff and I did together behind screens. She would leave me to finish off the bandaging—which had to be taken across his chest, over his shoulder and round the back, so I came in close contact with him, and as bandaging was the subject of lectures that week, I tried to make a neat job of it, doing it slowly and carefully. Then the silly old fellow got amorous one day, and to my astonishment he kissed me. I was very angry, and wanted to report him to sister.

"Don't do that," warned Pamela, "or you will be transferred—you are about due for one now, just try and dodge the old fool—tell him off yourself, Irene."

The bandaging now was hectic, I abandoned neatness for speed and dexterity. Flinging the bandage over his shoulder, I hurried along clumsily, trying to keep my distance. This had an adverse effect, he sensed I was nervous and I did not want a scene, so he tried again. I was furious and turned on him, "I'll tell Sister and you will be reported to your chief; don't you dare try that again." The silly old man now turned sour, he sulked. And with all the nurses. They discussed this in the duty room one day wondering what was wrong; Pamela catching my eye winked.

One morning hearing Home Sister read from the 'Transfer List' I was astonished and dismayed to hear I was transferred to work in matron's office as 'Office Boy.' Of all people me to matron's office, "I shall surely be thrown out now," was my miserable thought as I watched the long file of laughing chattering nurses walking to the hospital. Reluctantly I turned in the opposite direction towards the block in which matron's office was situated. A nurse was always on duty here to answer the 'phone, see visitors when matron was on her rounds or at meetings.

On her office staff matron also had an Eurasian clerk called D'Souza.

He was a dear old man and worked in an adjoining room. When I got to the office I was happy to find only the nurse I was relieving there. I begged her to give me all the tips she could. When told amongst other things, "You answer the 'phone when matron is out, I nearly died.

"I have never used one of those, I don't know how."

"You just pick it up and answer," she said nonchalantly, a smart, sophisticated Bombay-ite, not an upcountry yokel, so she could not understand my agitation. Then handing me long lists to copy she went merrily on her way leaving me to my gloomy thoughts: the sight of matron coming towards me in the wards frightened me, yet here I was to be right under her eye all day. She'll see what a fool I am right away and I will be sent packing: Oh, why did I have to be sent here? And before an answer could come from anywhere—in walked matron.

I jumped to my feet and was rewarded with a charming smile, feeling a little happier I settled again to my lists after she sat down. Then! The 'phone rang, and it rang and rang. Now, I had understood that answering this was one of my jobs if matron was out, so as she was here I thought it was none of my business, I felt it might be misinterpreted if I made a dash for it. So it went on ringing, matron now appeared to be deaf and by this time I was too frightened to do anything. Then a movement made me look up, there at the door was old man D'Souza looking puzzled; suddenly grasping the situation, he motioned me to pick up the receiver and answer.

Now I was thoroughly flustered and creeping up to the instrument picked it up. I made the same mistake as most people hearing a faint far away voice in the ear-piece for the first time. I yelled for all I was worth so that he would be able to hear me, "You'll be here at 3.30? No. I beg your pardon 4.30? Today? Tomorrow?"

This was too much for matron, she sailed across and grabbed the received from me to get the message straight. After replacing the receiver gently she whirled round on me and in a trembling rage said, "Don't you dare shout in my office again." And she could say no more.

I swallowed hard, trying to speak: there was so much I wanted to explain, so much I wanted to tell her but I could not utter a word, my mouth was dry, I wanted her to know that I had never even seen one of these instruments before, and in any case office routine was unknown to me, but I could see from the gleam in her eyes that I was through. She had decided that no savage from darkest Africa could be more stupid. She sat down at her desk, and when I could speak again, in a very small voice I said, "Sorry, Matron"....... to an expanse of fluttering white voile.

The next, time the THING rang (that is how I felt about it) I was alone and flew to D'Souza for help and he took the message. Then the kind old men patiently taught me how to pick it up and answer calmly and quietly—also how to call a number. In time I must have conquered my nervousness and stupidity—because matron gave me her stockings to mend, and the hem of her black evening gown. I took this for a sign that I had been forgiven. When the week or ten days were over, I was actually sorry to leave the office—though how matron felt—I leave it to you to guess.

By this time my first holiday was due, and I had saved enough money to get two mufti frocks for the occasion which the mess *dirzee* made. By Pamela's standards they were terrible. But to me they were grand. One was a two piece of flowered material: small bunches of orange and peach coloured flowers on a white background. I wore a white blouse with this. The second was a dance or party dress—white taffeta with a full skirt, and white rosettes of the same material encircling the hem. This was actually a copy of one of Pamela's models only she did not know.

For my family, I bought a quantity of the famous Bombay *hulva*, a lovely sweetmeat rather like Turkish delight, with masses of nuts—whole almonds, pistachio and cashews. I also took home a basket of mangos. Mama came to the station to meet me. I was glad she was alone, as we had the long drive home together, and it was nice being cuddled by her again and hearing all the news. She had not told Captain Busby I was arriving that day; she wanted me to surprise him; though when she ordered a *tonga*, she had to offer an explanation, as they usually shared these to halve the expense. "I am going to see the buffalo I am thinking of buying: you'll be bored so I shall go alone," was what she told him. "But, Irene you have grown so fat it's almost true! You are like a buffalo," and we laughed.

I had towards the end of my first year put on weight rapidly, a number of nurses had commented on this making me happy, as I had been too skinny and flat-chested. After leaving matron's office I had been sent to Obstetrics, where we had a large pail of buffalo's milk sent daily. After making cocoa for the mothers there was plenty over for the staff and I took full advantage of this. Mama was delighted at my appearance. None of my family or friends thought I would be able to stand more than a month or two of the hard work in the hospital, as I had never been too strong. Yet here I was back again, after a year, "like a buffalo." What they did not realise was that I was happy; at last doing what I had been fretting to do for years. The girls thought I looked very smart in my suit. They and Mama were now pleased I had taken this step. Their love and praise meant much to me.

In that first week Mama gave me my favourite meal twice. Ball curry with coconut rice, I could eat this forever. Minced beef, onion, garlic, chilli and coriander leaves forced into small balls and cooked slowly in a curry gravy. The rice is cooked in thick milk extracted from *freshly* grated coconut, coloured and flavoured with turmeric and spices. Mama and the girls wanted to give a party for me, but I was not keen, I liked having them just to myself; having dinner out-of-doors and going to bed early to lie and chat for hours under the stars; knowing there would be no horrible bell to wake me in the morning. I had found sleeping indoors in the stuffy atmosphere of Bombay very trying; in this the town-bred girls had the advantage. Being forced to use a mosquito net made it worse. Night super made an occasional surprise visit; walking on the verandah to switch her torch into the rooms, and if you were caught outride your net—you were reported to matron.

The mornings I spent visiting friends. In the afternoon there would be tennis with Doreen. She had a boyfriend in the S. & T. (Supply and Transport), and we were now members of this club, socially we were on the 'Up-grade.' One night I heard that amongst the P.G.'s that year there had been a couple of nurses from Bombay. Mama was delighted when she discovered one was from St. George's, she at once asked, "Have you met my daughter Irene, how is she? Is she well and happy?"

The tactless reply was, "I don't think she has been too happy: she has been seen in tears more than once."

This naturally upset Mama very much. She wanted to write and tell me to come home. Vi begged her not to do this. "We must not do anything to break her spirit—if it gets too much for her, she will leave of her own accord." I was glad Vi had said this, because I should have worried if I had thought Mama was unhappy and I should have been upset if I had had to abandon my training.

This I heard and other bits and pieces of gossip lying out in the fresh air, heavily scented by the *Champak* flowers (*Michelis champaca*) after which our house was named. Condwick, at last getting tired of the 'haw-haw' had left her for another married women. He had adopted the latter's twin babies, and one of his own was soon added, Gone were the posh parties; the invasion of doctors; sergeants; other adoring young men, and the clever rendering of 'Parted'—rather ironical that—it was her favourite song. Instead, the screaming of the children now made music; and he was happy. Then as another tit-bit I was told Aunt Alice had managed to get two more of her daughters married off to soldiers and was going about "all puffed up, like a broody hen," to quote Mama.

From my side Mama was glad to hear I thought I had got over the worst bit—the first year when my shyness had been an added impediment: making me appear extremely gauche and awkward. What I did not tell them was my anxiety and worry about the approaching exams. I confided in Doctor Pinto and he gave me some books Susie had left behind when she went to nurse in Calcutta, I told him that physiology and anatomy, familiar subjects to most of the nurses in my set—were unknown to me: my education had never reached those heights, I wondered how I was going to cope. "I shall have to study and study and study until my head bursts," I told Doctor Pinto.

"I do not think that will be necessary, Irene, you have besides the will much of your father's character—determination and fighting spirit—those will see you through."

"Oh, dear, I hope you are right," said I, sighing.

Anyway, I returned to face my second year quite happy, and my mother having seen me look so well, was content to let me go. I had hoped to take Doreen back with me but the tactless nurse's remarks had put paid to that.

CHAPTER 11

The Second Year

When I started my second year I was posted to Wards 1 and 2. These were for men in the 'top' class, senior officers from the ships and '*box-wallahs*.' This was a name scathingly given by the services for all Europeans in commerce, as *box-wallahs* are Indian pedlars who carry boxes on their heads containing merchandise for sale. However it is the "*box-wallahs*" who have had the last laugh, whilst their numbers have increased in the independent India and Pakistan, Europeans in the services are nonexistent. Only Europeans were admitted to these expensive wards. The four corner beds were unofficially reserved for those in extra good positions, and we were never allowed to put patients into these except under orders from sister. V.I.P.'s were put into the two private rooms and were given the full red-carpet treatment.

In these wards the sister was deaf: fortunately for me on one occasion. In the evening during visiting hours the junior nurse was expected to make some sort of savoury to be served as an extra—a touch of luxury these patients received in addition to the ordinary full diet which came up from the kitchen. The commonest and easiest was chopped tomato and onion fried and served on toast, scrambled egg and sardines were used as alternatives. These were repeated over and over again by the nurses with no imagination or inclination to try something new. None of us were cooks—in that country with all the servants about, it was not considered necessary for one to learn.

My mother had been taught good cooking by the French nuns. The result was a most useful person emerging from that convent. Then having the misfortune to be widowed twice she had been able to turn this knowledge to good use; she loved cooking, to her it was an art, and she tried to instil this love into us. Long before I started nursing, she would call us into the kitchen and show us meat in the large round basket the butcher had carried on his head from the bazaar, going from house to house selling in this way. She would teach us how to distinguish between beef and mutton, pork and veal, and name the various cuts. Though as our chances of ever having to cook were remote we were not as interested as we should have been. This Mama found disappointing and sometimes got cross with us.

Occasionally she would call us to her side and give us a lecture, or demonstration on whatever it was she was preparing at the time. It was a sketchy sort of training, but. I have had cause to be grateful for even that. Many years later I found it most useful, I think cooking must have been in my blood, because whereas the other nurses thought the little we had to do in Wards 1 and 2 a bore I revelled in it. Not being content with just savoury making, I would ask sister not to return the leftovers to the kitchen and from these I would concoct fresh dishes for the following meals.

I well remember a '*corner-wallah*', he was the age my father would have been had he lived. He loved his food and that was a bond between us. After cooking I was vain enough to ask the men if they had enjoyed my dish. Teasing me some of them gave rude replies, but as my savouries were always eaten, I was content. The ward 'boys' brought the meals up from the kitchen and placed them on the food table on the verandah; here sister, staff and one or two nurses stood to serve out. The trays were carried to the patient by the 'boys' but if they were slow, the nurses helped. It was in this way that I started taking the savoury that I had cooked to my '*corner-wallah*'. Sometimes he would ask me to repeat something he fancied, and if it was possible I would do this. Then encouraged by his friendliness, his interests I fell for his charm, and spent my spare time I had talking to him. The nurses were surprised by this, as I was known for my shyness: I suppose that made it more conspicuous; because after a few days I was warned by a senior to be careful. After that I took his tray as usual but hurried away.

He told me he understood the situation and before leaving made a suggestion that shocked me, I was offered a holiday up in the hills. He had been advised to get away into a cooler climate for a month or so—and asked me to go with him. He promised me a marvellous time and assured me that no one need know, Deliberately misunderstanding I suggested he wanted a cook, not a nurse, and laughing left him on a light note. After this I was careful and avoided fussing middle-aged '*corner-wallahs*'.

Most nights Pamela and I visited each other's rooms to exchange the days gossip.

"Well, Mouse, how is your pepper-and-salt Romeo," she would ask.

"My *corner-wallah*, do you mean?"

"Yes, that's right."

That night I told her about the free holiday.

"You are an ass to turn it down, why didn't you accept. He'd have given you a heck of a good time."

"He wasn't taking me just to cook his savouries, you know," I informed her.

"I know that, but do you intend remaining a virgin all your life?" and a curious smile played about her lips, it was almost a sneer.

I did not like this and bridled, "Oh, I hope not . . ." then I deliberately paused: she looked at me with interest now, then blandly I continued, "only just till I am married," and it was my turn to smile. I had tried to sound worldly, but like a fool I could feel myself blush. I had not yet accustomed myself to the frank way most of the nurses discussed these things.

"Well, I wish you luck," she said, with an unmistakable sneer. What had come over her? I wondered unhappily. She paused as she searched in her bag for her cigarette case—feeling the tension in the room I lay very still—the one chair in the room was occupied by the visitor—whilst the hostess occupied the bed. Lighting a cigarette she puffed once or twice, then spoke quietly. "Well, Mouse, here's a shock for you—I am leaving soon—going to marry Italiano, as you call him."

"Pamela, you can't," I gasped, sitting up. "You must finish your training first—think of all the plans we have made. Oh, of course you will wait," And I slumped down again.

"No, you little Muggins—I can't finish—you don't understand—do you?" She leaned forward and whispered, "I have to marry as soon as everything can be fixed." The whisper and the old-fashioned look made it clear.

After a while I was able to say rather limply, "I shall miss you terribly."

In a musing sort of way she continued, "I wish I could have finished, mother always said, 'It's good to have a profession in hand,' You know, Irene, she suffered a great deal after her divorce—but it's too

103

late for me to think of that now," And the sardonic laugh that followed startled me—not the sort of laugh one expected from a bride-to-be, "I'll miss you too," she said, rising. "Now promise me, Mouse, you will keep in touch? Promise! Promise!" And she sounded almost hysterical. Going to bed that night I was unhappy and bewildered, and wished I could help Pamela.

One evening on cooking? duty I decided to be adventurous: looking over the 'leftovers' in the *doolie*, the wire-covered food storage box, I found some cold chicken; taking this out I told staff who was passing, "I am going to make chicken patties from this as my mother did."

As an encouragement she replied, "Sister will be pleased."

Preparing the 'filling' was easy: I added hard-boiled egg and a thick white sauce to the chopped up chicken. Mixing the pastry was a different matter, I had only a hazy idea how to go about this: for ingredients I knew flour, fat, salt and water were necessary—but in what quantities? Guessing, I threw the lot together in a bowl and kneaded it. As this was such hard work, I guessed that something was wrong; then trying to roll the dough—I beg your pardon, I mean rubber, I *knew* something was definitely wrong, but I had to continue, as finding we had no flour in the store cupboard, I had been to sister to sign a special order for this: and of course she expected results.

Matron on her evening round looked into the pantry and smiled when she saw I was using an empty beer bottle for a roller; the back of a large tray for a pastry board. My pastry cases when baked looked quite good, and quickly filling these I passed them to sister to serve. She looked at me with approbation, and I swelled with pride—which goes before a fall, it is said. The walking cases in the dining room started singing. Staff and I looked at each other in horror as we listened to "Nearer my God to Thee," sister—who was able to hear only faintly asked, "What are they saying Nurse? Are those men singing?"

Staff, kicking me on the ankle answered after a moment's pause, "Oh, they are just happy, Sister—they like Green's savoury," but she swallowed hard. Later meeting me on the verandah she said, "In future you stick to the ordinary stuff—no more of your inventions, please."

The work in the second year I found even more interesting. Now instead of rubbing backs; filling ice-caps; making beds; taking temperatures and collecting stools, I was taught to pour medicines, apply poultices, fomentations and leeches, those horrible slimy fat black worm-like things, which were used in those days to suck septic matter from inflammations. I was particularly interested in preparing patients for the theatre and taking them there. As this was not a medical college we had no students, so were not crowded out round the table when our surgeon superintendent Major P. K. Gilroy gave a running commentary whilst operating. The nurses did all, except the very serious dressings. I was now taught to do these, and loved the surgery work: getting the bins packed for sterilization, boiling the bowls, kidney dishes and forceps, and getting the trolley cleaned and restocked.

As we did not have an outdoor department in those days, these patients came daily to the ward surgery for dressings. After the last 'outdoors' had gone, and the trolley cleaned again, I would wheel this into the ward and, feeling very important, walk to the "Doctor's table," which a little green-belt had laid out that morning with clean water, a bowl of disinfectant, a boiled brush, sterilised towel and gloves. Remembering sister's warning;, "Get under the nails," I would wash and scrub thoroughly. No fancy long nails were allowed. Going on duty the first morning a new probationer would be told to cut her nails as short as she could, and to keep them that way until she left. Having got ready I would begin my first dressing. This was a proud moment. I was now gaining confidence and felt accepted as a nurse, and could relax a little, so when Pamela asked me to make up the odd one in her party for a dance at the Taj, I surprised her by saying "Yes" instead of the usual "No".

CHAPTER 12

Breaking Out

Thus my debut into the social life of Bombay was effected. However I was not a success. In a crowd I was all right, it was when the crowd split into couples and the lovemaking began that I felt uncomfortable. Pamela was angry with me about this. "You are too old-fashioned. For goodness sake THAW, Granny. You won't have a baby by a little harmless kissing and cuddling, silly."

"It's not that, Pamela," I objected, "But I felt such a fool being kissed, I want to giggle, I did once and a fellow got, cross, he thought I was laughing at him—anyway he did have a bald head and was rather fat, so it served him right."

But Pamela was not amused although I did 'thaw'—just a little. One day I was brave enough to accept an invitation from a grateful patient after he was discharged. As I felt he had been in the ward a long time I felt I knew him; besides I had fallen for the 'pepper-and-salt' look. We went to the *The Dansant* at the Taj, I wore my white taffeta with a posy of yellow and apricot flowers at the waist—which in those days was down at the hip line, then the skirt ending just below the knee made it a hideous fashion. Two or three of the nurses were there, and the next day I was teased: "Mouse. I was surprised to see you out alone with a fellow. Growing up, are you? Who is the boy friend?"

Then one smiling kindly added, "Anyway, you looked nice."

This last remark pleased me and I smiled whilst murmuring, "Thank you." Then a catty one spoilt it by saying, "So our little Puritan has at last broken out, eh?" This with a sneer made me glad she would never know about the scene which took place in the taxi as we returned front the Taj. Carl put his arm around me but when I froze he withdrew it as if he had been stung.

Looking surprised he said, "You are a peculiar little thing," and as he had been so nice and I did want him to ask me out again I felt ashamed and tried to apologise and explain.

I started by telling him a little of my background, the strict training I had received from a mother who was almost a Quaker in outlook. "This is the first time I have been out alone with a man, I am sorry to seem such a prude but it's the way I have been brought up," I added with a nervous laugh. "You'll have to blame my old fashioned Mother."

"Don't worry, little one, don't apologise. You'll change, more's the pity; you see, I like you as you are." And with that he kissed me on the forehead, which is more than I deserved.

We saw each other often after that and spent many evenings on Pali Hill. It was pleasant to sit in the cool darkness and watch the fire-flies moving up from the valley in their thousands. Then with the bright stars overhead and the delicate scent of the cork flowers to enhance the setting we would sit in the little two-seater, which had been parked just off the road with its hood folded down, to eat chicken sandwiches, washed down with beer and tomato juice. After which Cupid took a hand. When he learnt that I had never been to Juhu, Carl fixed a picnic there. In those days this sandy beach near Bombay was not as crowded, or commercialised at it is today. There were no shacks, stalls or ghastly loud music—just courting couples or the odd picnic party.

As there were to be four men in the party, I was asked to bring three girls, Pamela was consulted about this as I knew she had often arranged parties and knew which girls were free and likely to accept. I wanted the right type; the kind to make a party 'go' and none from the 'mouse' tribe. She suggested three girls I might ask. This is where I noticed the colour-bar. For these parties only the white, or near-white were asked. The few coloured girls we had amused themselves by going to the pictures or arranging bathing and picnic parties amongst themselves and coloured men. In those days no coloured nurses were asked to the Yacht Club; Taj; or Green's Restaurant, The first time I was taken to Breach Candy and saw the tablet on the wall above the entrance which read, "For Europeans only—for all time." Or words to that effect. I was shaken and thought—"Thank goodness I am no browner," as I was very fond of swimming.

For our picnic we had a full moon. The coconut palms which grew thickly, fringing the shore, provided the *kala jaggas* the courting couples wanted. The sea was lovely, calm and cool: we had fun rushing in and out playing games and dancing with the wet sand sticking to our toes, A gramophone provided the music. The bearers had arranged supper on a carpet. We had lobster mayonnaise, cold chicken and ham. Then smell melons (*zardas*) scooped out and filled with chopped pineapple, mango and lichees, which were eaten with ice-cream. To wash all this down and to suit all tastes we had beer, whisky, fruit juices, wines and tomato juice. Time just flew by after supper, and soon we were packed into cars and on the way back to the hospital.

Carl took me to the pictures once or twice but unfortunately we hit on the sad films *If winter Comes* and *Beau Geste*, and though I tried to hide the fact that I cried, he knew and said, "I will not take you to the pictures if they make you cry; in future we will cut them out." But there was no future as he was transferred to Calcutta. I was unhappy for a while, then number two boyfriend came along. Just as Juhu, lobster and stuffed melons are linked in my memory with Carl, so caviar and the Taj, recall Peter Whyte. It was at a crowded chummery party, the abode of bachelors, that I met him and caviar for the first time. This delicacy was served on hot buttered toast spread over with sliced uncooked onion, and in my ignorance I thought it was marvellous. To start a conversation and not to appear quite dumb I remarked on this to the young men seated beside me. He was quite cross.

"Don't agree with you, this delectable stuff has been completely ruined, these fellows don't know how to serve it—do you like it this way?" he demanded.

I truthfully admitted I knew no other way, adding, "You have probably had it many times and are spoilt."

"I don't know about that," he replied, "But I am keen on food: good cooking and the correct serving of it."

Now we were on common ground and soon our heads were together and we chattered away, at least I did, I told him about the parties my mother used to cater for when she was left a widow for the first time.

Mama would say, "Oyster parties, Irene. I've kept oysters in huge zinc baths and we fed them on bran until required. Then I've arranged 'sitting and standing' suppers." This was probably Mama's definition of a cocktail party—"with hot game pies, venison, cold chicken, tongues in aspic, roast suckling pigs and. . . ."

"Oh, stop. Stop. Mama." I would cry. "You are making my mouth water."

All this I remembered and told Peter, he was interested and before we parted asked me to dine with him at the Taj. He said, "I'll arrange to give you a slap up dinner and show you how caviar should be served. I'll write to you when I've seen the headwaiter."

After we were locked in that night Pamela came to say room and remarked, "I noticed you and Peter Whyte clicked—he's in a good job, I'm glad you've made a hit; whatever were you jabbering about by-the-way?"

"If you must know we were talking about food."

"WHAT? FOOD? Couldn't you think of a more romantic subject? After all I've told you—you really are incorrigible, I give up—Goodnight."

"Goodnight," I replied with a chuckle; after all I had a dinner date up my sleeve.

Alas she was never to know about this date, as her mother suddenly arrived in Bombay to take her away, but before they left I was asked to tea at their hotel, and Mrs. Harrison asked me my plans, when I told her how I was going to miss Pamela. "Well, one day after I've saved enough money I would like to go to London to Queen Charlotte's to take my midder."

"Isn't she ambitious, Mother? No Bombay midwifery for our mouse, she aims high."

"I'm aiming high but I don't suppose it will ever come to any-thing—just a pipe dream."

"You go along with your dreams, and may they come true," said kindly Mrs. Harrison.

"And after your midder, what then?" demanded Pamela.

"Then—no, I'd better not tell you—you'll laugh."

"No, we won't, do tell," said mother and daughter.

"Well, it's a BIG dream. I'd like to be in charge of a hospital or nursing home, I think I would be able to run it successfully—I should have plenty of ideas. . ." then I stopped, suddenly feeling confused and foolish for having aired my secret ambition,

A week after Pamela left, Peter Whyte wrote and fixed up the dinner date, my education was taken in hand and I was taught to eat caviar the correct way. One minute quantity was placed on a little dish which rested in a large basket made entirely from ice. We had first been served a paper thin pancake each, the caviar was now placed in the centre of this which was then folded and eaten straight, neat and unadulterated.

We also had a tiny bird, "Ah, quail!" said I knowingly.

"So you know that one."

I told him about my childhood in Nasirabad, and the villagers coming round with game of all sorts—including peahen. He had to admit he had not eaten this. I was then able to interest him by talking of life in an Indian village; especially drawing a picture of the *Jalsas* the *Setes* put on for my father—and their marvellous 'spreads.' I was now beginning to realise that a girl had not only to know how to look after herself, dress and look well; but manners, a knowledge of food and drink, and above all repartee, were necessary—so I determined to keep my eyes and ears open and LEARN. A knowledge of books was also an asset. Here I got full marks by being able to quote passages or sentences from the good books my mother had read and discussed with us. Second hand knowledge no doubt, but useful.

Monthly dances ware hold in our club in the hospital grounds, and each nurse was allowed to ask her boyfriend. Matron received the guests. The clubhouse was surrounded by lawns, palm-trees and tropical flowering shrubs—hibiscus, bougainvillea and oleanders. Chairs and tables were arranged amongst these, and a pretty effect was gained by the coloured electric bulbs swinging between the palms. It was compulsory in those days to wear evening dress. Some clubs insisted on 'tails' for Saturday nights. Only once during my training was a fancy dress arranged. I sent an S.O.S. to Doreen for a costume. We had many of these at home, out of necessity making them from bits and pieces, improvising all the way, yet because my mother was so clever we nearly always won a prize.

In those days the Persian lady outfit I wore was considered shocking—full tulle trousers worn over very short tight panties. The nurses were startled—so out of character with the 'mouse' they knew, still for my cheek I won the prize, and matron handing it to me looked just as surprised. It was a lovely silver and glass powder bowl; which the other day I saw again after some years. It had been put away in a chest and forgotten. My daughter had been rummaging about in this and coming across it had taken it out and polished it and placed it on her dressing table. Going round the house with a duster at my daily chores I saw this. What a flood of memories it brought back; holding it in my hands I saw palm-trees, dim lights and a smiling twenty year old girl. I imagined sweet music: then an unfortunate glance into the, looking-glass shattered my dream, now I saw: but why elaborate? The insistent whirr of the Hoover was the only music audible, and a long handled feather duster the nearest approach to a palm-tree.

My next transfer was to Mental, which like Infections was a separate small building away from the main hospital. There were three rooms in Mental, the centre one padded, and the verandah was enclosed with expanded metal all the way round. Here I was to spend the next fortnight in the company of two mentally sick people; an Eurasian woman and a young good-looking Englishman who was discovered one morning in the office tearing up the office post, scattering it to the winds and raving the while. He was brought to us until arrangements could be completed to send him to England. As the army would say he had the "Deolali Tap" or was "Round the Bend." I had an occasional comforting visit from our Anglo-Indian hospital orderly Jones, who was always cheerful. "Still all-in-one-piece nurse?" he would ask, grinning. The Indian staff also came over for certain jobs. I was always glad to see my visitors, as it was not pleasant being shut away all day with these two sad cases.

The night nurse had warned me the first morning I took over from her to be careful of the woman, whose main aim was to beat up the nurses. For this purpose she used the enamel dinner plate as a weapon. One of her tricks was to crouch below the table and draw the cloth down, then hiding behind this she would call in a wheedling voice, "Nurse, darling nurse, I want you," then plaintively, "Nursey my head is paining."

Smith said, "You be careful, Green, or it will be your head that will pain. She once hid behind the door with the dinner plate at the ready to bring down on my head, and it was only the *matherani's* cry of warning that saved me." Picking up her case to go she concluded, "Don't let her fool you."

"I I'm. . . . . she sounds a nice friendly little thing," I replied, rolling up my sleeves. Thwarted of her favourite pastime and becoming bored our Mrs. Brown would scream for hours, using bad language. Then rude notes from the nurses in Infections and the hospital would arrive, asking me to control my patient as theirs could not rest.

I think the Englishman was even more tragic. He was very quiet spoken and gentle, but spent his day saying the vilest, obscene, filthy things. He would repeat these over and over again, looking at us in a cold, sneering way, trying to hurt. Smith said, "I'm sure for some reason he hates nurses."

Even Jones was disgusted—and he was a tough man. Fortunately he was with me when this poor man pushed the door open, which was on a latch, to wander into the padded cell. He went round, feeling the wall and repeating, "They've brought us into a padded cell." We tried to get him out but he resisted, so leaving the door open we told him he was free to come out just when he wanted. We stood talking quietly, but watched him. Soon he reached the door, having been all round, then Jones guided him back to his room. I was glad when he was taken away, and hoped sending him home would cure him. I was not sorry when my turn of duty came to an end. This is one branch of nursing nothing on earth would induce me to take up. I salute the brave ones that do. Leaving Mental I prayed I would never see it again; in this I was unlucky, I was to nurse there again—but not for a long time.

CHAPTER 13

Ward Life and Death

Going back to face my third year I resolved not to go out as much as I had done in the second, as the finals had to be faced in September. A few interesting cases stood out in that last year: a Japanese officer from one of the ships was admitted with suspected hydrophobia; which was confirmed. I need hardly say he was segregated and a nurse was detailed to special him. Nurse Jackson wore a gown with long sleeves, a cap to cover her hair completely, gloves and glasses. We were allowed to peer through the glass pane and it was most ghastly to see this poor man's struggles. He could not drink, trying to swallow caused horrible spasms. His mouth remained open and saliva poured out all the time. His eyes rolled and he was restless, throwing his arms and legs about he banged the bed and bruised himself. Unable to speak he made guttural noises instead. It was the kindest thing when he died.

Malaria was a common complaint in Medical. Quinine T.D.S. was the routine treatment and the houseman gave I.V.Q.s. Then the violent reaction had to be waited for and dealt with, rigors and a mounting temperature. All cases with temperatures of 103° F had to be ice-capped, over this, tepid sponging, higher still, cold sponging. The final stage was the application of ice-packs, sheets wrung out of ice cold water would be draped over the patient, and lumps of ice slipped in here and there. Two fans were placed to blow directly on to him. What the poor patient felt like no one knew, burning up inside, head on fire, and being frozen from without; fortunately he would be unconscious at this stage. With this gentle treatment in mind when pouring out doses of quinine for the children, I always swallowed some myself. Then taking up a trayful of small glasses I would go from bed to bed, saying sternly, "Open your mouth," to pour this bitter liquid down their poor little throats. To be gentle meant having to deal with tears or refusals, and we had no time for that.

Our pneumonias were treated with camphor-in-oil injections, and anti-phlogiston jackets, whilst oxygen cylinders stood at hand. I mistrusted these things, expecting them to blow up at any time, and one day something happened that did not help my nervousness. I was at the far end of the ward pouring out medicines when a sudden loud explosion caused me to jump and turn round. Nurse Mullins giving oxygen had found a leak in the bend of a glass connection, she took a candle to it trying to get the melting wax to drip on to the hole. Poor dear, she paid for her mistake, and was cut about her arms and legs. The patient was either too far gone, or very brave, he looked the calmer of the two. Matron on her afternoon round on the floor below heard the explosion and hurried upstairs. She took Mullins off to the nurses' ward. That evening at lecture we were told what NOT to do when a leak was discovered, unless we wanted to blow ourselves and the hospital sky-high.

We did not know it then, but the poor old hospital was to be blown nearly sky-high during the Second World War, when a ship in the docks behind the hospital, carrying explosives, blew up and damaged the hospital and parts of Bombay. This was pointed out to me in 1954 by the English matron who spoke of herself as being the last of the Mohicans. She was due to retire shortly and thought she would be replaced by an Indian. It was a weird experience going round that day; I *knew* I was in St. George's because the building and wards were the same, but the brown faced nurses in *saris* and aprons and the brown faced patients made it seem unreal. I was filled with nostalgia and asked if any of the Indian staff I had known were still there. That old rascal Ganpat—the untouchable—must have died years ago; and I hoped that as he had been Hindu by religion, which believes in reincarnation, he was back on earth as a high-caste Brahmin with plenty of *char* at his disposal—I think he deserved this for once trying to help a very 'green' green-belt. I asked after Victoria.

"Victoria? Who was she?"

"The queen of the *matheranis*." I answered sadly; no one knew of her. Then on going down to the kitchen we found the cook who used to be a *misalchi* or cook's mate when I was a student nurse. He well remembered Miss MacFarlane and Major Gilroy who used to inspect the kitchen daily, Major Gilroy, a brilliant surgeon, died from a brain-tumour sometime after I had finished my training. A tablet in the entrance hall today records his good work for the hospital. Unable to sleep that night I realised this return sentimental visit had been a mistake.

Then I remember what I called at the time "The week of the worms." We had nearly finished a week of heavy 'nights' and the 'night-duty' feeling was well established: this was once described to me as "a persistent very bad hangover." Never having experienced one of these I cannot say if this is an apt description. The night-duty feeling being bad enough, I have no wish to sample the other. One morning, not being able to face my *chota hazri* which was usually tea and toast served by the ward 'boy' at about 4 a.m., I left this to go and find out the cause of a commotion in the ward. I was greeted with a cry "Nurse. Come quickly, see what Billy has sicked up." A group of children who should still have been sleeping soundly were gathered round a locker gazing into a kidney dish; Bill, who was six, was kneeling up in bed looking very proud.

"What is it?" I asked, joining them. In the kidney dish I saw two long round pink worms swimming in bile.

Then two or three mornings later a girl of ten had used the bedpan. The *matherani* called me over, just as the 'boy' appeared with my *chota* tray. Going round the screen I was met with hysterical cries from the little patient. "Nurse, take it out. Take it out." Sticking out of her anus I saw a fat wiggling worm. Silently I invited the *matherani* to remove it. Just as silently she declined—so it was up to me.

The coughing and spitting of the T.B.'s; the dirty dressings to be changed; the tongues and mouths of the typhoids, dysenteries and pneumonias to be cleaned were all early morning duties, tasks not easily faced after being up all night, tired and hungry. It was being able to stand up to moments like these that made nursing a vocation. We were discussing this once in the mess and a visitor who was a typist and a cousin of one of the nurses sat comparing her free life and large salary with ours. She said, "You don't know it—but all of you are mental." She could not understand our wanting to do this work. "The bullying and strict discipline, the small pay and long hours—then being locked up at 10 o'clock like a lot of criminals: why its degrading. You *must* be mad," she concluded.

"Well, if everyone felt as you, who would nurse the sick?"

She had no answer to this. Then someone warming up added,

"When you get sick, Merle, don't come in here, remember the lunatics."

She could not realise the interest we found, the feeling of usefulness, the joy it gave turning a pillow to make a patient comfortable, offering a drink or a hot water bottle, or finding time for a smile and a kind word: then hearing the softly spoken "Thank you, nurse," or if this was too much, seeing the gratitude in a patient's eyes. These amounted to much for some of us, and we were amply repaid. A few had made a mistake and nursing should never have been chosen, mostly the patients suffered. I have seen this many times and felt sorry for both patient and nurses. My friend Pamela was one of these. I realised she was the hard type when I followed her on night duty. Taking early morning temperatures I was told by several patients more or less the same thing. "You are different from our last night-nurse," or "You have the gentle touch," or "Your approach is more pleasing nurse." I asked for an explanation.

Apparently Pamela woke them roughly, pulling up the net to say, "Come on, I've got to hurry," or "I'm in a rush," and pushing the thermometer into their mouths she would wait impatiently, pull it out, make her note and rush away to the next bed without a word. One of the patients continued, "You wake us with a 'Good morning' and a smile, and always say 'Thank you' before you leave." I must admit I felt very flattered and hoped I would not get a swollen head. There must have been some truth in all this because the patients talked it over between themselves as I went from bed to bed. Whilst I tried to find excuses for Pamela, I was silently thanking God for blessing me with the 'gentle touch.' Apart from the mundane round, occasionally an interesting case arrived.

Whilst on night duty a very bad cholera case was admitted. She should really have gone to the Infectious Hospital in the city but had been brought to us by mistake, and being so ill the M.O. would not risk sending her on another journey. She was an Englishwoman—a railway official's wife, if I remember rightly, and I was detailed to 'special' her. We segregated her as best we could on a verandah where there were no other patients. Then began a hopeless fight to try and save her. Intravenous saline into both arms and sips of iced-water and brandy, at least wetting her lips with these was all I could do, as she was unable to retain a drop. When she died at crack-of-dawn I was given an injection, an 'anti' of some sort, I suppose. This case and one of *Kala-Azar* just before the medical oral made such an impact on my memory that Colonel Vazifdar, I.M.S. of the J.J. Hospital, the examiner complimented me. I remember his exact words, "My own student could not have done better." This was one of my 'proud' moments.

Now it was my turn to be a patient. I had tonsillitis, and was warded. The nurses' ward was a delightful place, Just six beds, the decorations ware blue, white and silver, with cane basket chairs and gay cushions. No shortage of flowers here, the visiting boyfriends saw to that. I was advised to have my tonsils out, and, having absolute confidence in Major Gilroy I agreed. As I did not wish to worry Mama, I waited until it was over and I was convalescing before I wrote home. I enjoyed my convalescence, we had Edna Newman in at the time, She was a tall, jolly girl with a fund of naughty stories which she told to keep us laughing all day. In due course I was discharged and posted to the theatre as junior nurse.

The sister here had a name for being fierce although I never found her so. I may have been lucky. Making a few small mistakes I was scolded but it did not amount to much; though I remember that horrible day I held up the suturing because I could not find a used swab. The beastly thing had got tucked up somewhere and it was only after a second or third recount that it was discovered. Everyone breathed a sigh of relief, and I said a silent prayer of thankfulness. Catching sister's eye, I got an angry look and slunk away with the dirty swabs. Another day we had a leg amputation. Most of the leg, wrapped in cotton wool and bandage, was very heavy and being the junior nurse it was my job to hold on to this whilst the surgeon sawed through the femur. I was so interested watching the saw going through that when the leg suddenly came away in my hand I was thrown off balance, and would have fallen but for the senior nurse's restraining hand; this, of course, made her 'dirty,' and sister was cross.

The theatre was the one place dreaded by all the timid nurses, as one had to work directly under the eyes of the surgeons. So when the senior nurse was transferred and I moved up to her place I was nervous at first and had to steal myself, after getting 'cleaned-and-gowned,' to walk calmly in and stand before sister's table when she was off duty to officiate in her place. However, once the operation started I was soon absorbed and everything but the work in hand was forgotten. As time went on I came to realise that this branch of nursing for me held the most interest. I should like more experience in surgery, I thought, so took a step that six months earlier I would not have even considered.

Apart from my new-found interest—I had managed to pass my Junior successfully—getting through the finals was going to be more difficult. I wanted more time to swot, so went to see matron and asked to be allowed to sit in March of the following year, instead of September. This meant that apart from the six weeks accumulated against me for taking an extra two weeks holiday each year, I should be doing an extra four and a half months on trainees' pay to the benefit of the hospital. I was asked my reasons for this and explained them. I was grateful when permission was granted,

Sometime after my tonsillectomy I was in a large party at the Taj. There was a good cabaret and we had a table on the floor. It was Christmas week, and the decorations were beautiful. As I had not been out much in my third year I was enjoying this to the full, especially as I was wearing the prettiest frock I had possessed so far it had frills from the waist to the hem line, each frill wider than the last in red spotted white taffeta. The bodice had a sweetheart neck line. I wore a spray of artificial holly pinned to my hair. The current boyfriend told me I looked pretty.

"Are you feeling Christmas-sy, Peter?"

"Christmas-sy?"

"Yes, you know—Good will and spreading a little good cheer, and all that."

"No, I mean it, Mouse-all-dressed-up," said he, touching the spray of holly.

I laughed, "Anyway, I love you Peter for saying it—true or untrue: you're nice."

Then the waltz ending we joined our party sitting round the table. I had noticed a fellow staring at me in a puzzled way with a 'where-have-I-seen-you-before' look. Then when he found me beside him he said, "Now that I can get a good look at you, I know where I have seen you before."

"Where?"

"In nurses' ward, the day your tonsils came out, I was visiting Joyce. You did give everyone a good fright, didn't you?" This startled me, and noticing my bewilderment, he asked, "Don't you remember? No, of course you couldn't, you were hardly conscious."

I now turned to Joyce, "Whatever is he talking about?" I asked.

"You haemorrhaged very badly, Greeny, and we were asked not to tell you. Reg has now spilt the beans." Then she added, "You were quite bad for a time."

"Jolly," was all I could find to say, but my thoughts flew to my mother. Then suddenly that party was lovelier than ever; the decorations of snow-scenes, icicles end soft blue, grey and white crepe paper sky seemed to take on an added beauty, and Peter getting his hand squeezed under the table wondered what it was all about.

My wide grin could not have told him that suddenly it was wonderful to be alive, healthy and happy. Before the end of the evening we were asking each other what, if any, New Year resolutions we were making. My reply, "No more parties until the end of the finals in March," made Peter groan. "I shall have to swot like mad from now onwards and you had better look around for another girl friend," was all the comfort he got.

On Saturday, March 2nd, 1929, at 10 a.m. we had the written medical. This paper was set by Colonel Vazifdar. That afternoon at 2 p.m. we had the written surgical set by Major Gilroy. It is not because of a good memory that I am able to give dates and time; I have these question papers still and looking at them I shudder. Today I would not be able to answer a single question, Fighting Flora visited us just before the exams, and made a good thing out of our nervousness. "If we don't buy her wretched flowers, she'll put a Cockney curse on us and we will fail," said someone. Going for the written paper transported in the ambulance, several girls revealed their lucky mascots. Not a few were hideous paper roses rolled into the top of their stockings.

I cannot remember much now about the exams: except the oral medical, and Colonel Vazifdar's kind remarks. Major Gilroy took us for the surgical. I had been warned shout the nurse who through nervousness kept allowing the bandage to slip from her fingers—this lost her many marks! and I was determined this would not happen with me, so when the major wanted to take the bandage from me to demonstrate where I had gone wrong, he was surprised at the vice-like grip I had on it. His raised eyebrows drew the explanation, "I don't want it to slip from my fingers and lose marks," this made him laugh. He passed me. I can only surmise about the written exams that as I have an atrocious handwriting, they gave me the benefit of the doubt.

Before I left Bombay I was asked to a wonderful picnic, given by some fellows for their girls sitting this exam. They confessed they were previous in celebrating, but it was a good excuse. I was lucky to be asked to this as Peter had taken me at my word, he was now taking out the 'blonde-bombshell from Barrackpore!' She was the new probationer who had replaced Pamela, and was very hoity-toity and sophisticated. We had bets on whether her hair was really that colour or bleached, her roommate promised to let us know in time.

"Hell's Bells, Mouse, she's a fast worker, she only met Peter for a few minutes when he came with Reg to collect me for the party you turned down and they clicked!" Joyce looked bewildered.

"Oh well, she'll be taught to eat caviar the correct way now," I said with a sigh.

"That *Houri*-from-Puri doesn't require any teaching," muttered Joyce. Reg overheard this and went "Meaow-meaow."

"Anyway you'll come to the picnic, won't you, Greeny? The exams are over now so you have no excuse for going into *purdah* again."

As this picnic was to be an all night affair It was arranged for Joyce's mother to write a sleeping out letter for me. I had never been to one of these before and was looking forward to it. At last the day came, and how the time dragged. Fortunately 'Fighting Flora' visited us in the late afternoon, and her cheerful voice and jokes sped the remaining hours. Eight o'clock arrived and we were able to rush off duty to change into mufti and pile into the waiting cars for the long drive out to Juhu. Some of the party were already there. These were the office workers and shop assistants. They had been there all afternoon supervising the servants. Pressure lamps had been fixed to poles between coconut palms, carpets were spread out under these and plenty of cushions for comfort. The wisp of smoke and tantalising smell of food coming from behind large packing cases told as the bearers were at work warming up the meal.

While this was being done, the men unloaded the drinks and a bar was soon in operation. It was a marvellous meal in perfect surroundings; for decor we had the sea, coconut palms and stars. For music the lapping of the waves competed with the gramophone. Before I sat down I was told by the eldest girl acting hostess that the fellow on my right was my partner. I took one look at him and fell for the fellow on my left. He apparently took one look at the girl on his left and decided he preferred the one on his right! So there we sat and talked getting dirty looks which we pretended not to see! I wonder where he is now? Dusting our little library the other day I came across the two leather bound volumes of Kipling which he gave me in Peshawar a year or two later; on the fly-leaf he had written, "To Irene with love, Llew." Meeting him the picnic became more interesting. We shared a cushion balancing our plates on this.

We ate, drank; swam; played games; danced and flirted the night through, and how the hours flew! Round about three o'clock, the bearers produced ice-cream, which they had made out there. Two or three hours later these wizards produced breakfast, bacon and eggs, and as an alternative fish, caught that very moment by men fishing just along the beach. That fish eaten in those surroundings and so very fresh was something out-of-this-world! While the bearers had been preparing breakfast we had our last bit of community singing ending with "Auld Lang Syne," as a number of nurses had got jobs in various parts of India and were leaving Bombay in the next day or two. Back at St. George's we just had time to rush upstairs, change into uniform and be down in the mess for roll-call. Today, writing this I wonder how on earth I got through that day, but then—I was young!

CHAPTER 14

Frontier Nurse

Packing up to go home I must confess I was sad. The work had been hard, the hours long, the discipline harsh, the pay small: but the reward for all this had been the tremendous happiness I had shared with the other students. Nurses all over the world will agree with this sentiment. I had no plans for my future, not even a clue as to where or how to start looking for a future. Most of the nurses passing out with me seemed to have everything cut and dried, jobs arranged, or a father, uncle or cousin in an influential position ready to help, or they, being city-bred, knew the ropes. Anyway I was not worrying. Just then all I could think of was Mama and home! I enjoyed the rest for the first fortnight and then began to get restive. Vi suggested I scan the situations vacant column in the *Times of India*. This I did and one day saw that the Lady Harding Hospital in Delhi wanted a nursing sister. Plucking up courage I applied. Having only just graduated I never expected more than a polite refusal.

I should have been happy now or at least restful if I had not been getting little twinges in my right side. I could not decide if they were real or imagined. It had been the fashion in the last six months for the nurses to go down with appendicitis—was I now one of these? I wondered if I should go back to St. George's and let Major Gilroy pommel my tummy. Then a reply came from Delhi; the post had been filled but my application had been forwarded to the matron of the Lady Reading Hospital in Peshawar, and I was informed that I would hear from them in due course.

Now I was on the horns of a dilemma. Should I go to Bombay and have the appendix out, or wait and see what the answer was from Peshawar, or would that be wasting time? Should I keep it in—or have it out? Then one evening at the pictures a good twinge decided me. Next day I left for Bombay.

As I was not now on the staff I could not be sent to the nurses' ward, but was admitted to the little annexe to "Eyes." Now again I contacted Sister Crabbitt—this time as a patient, and I must say right away that she was very kind. I was not at all frightened and when Major Gilroy asked me why I had returned to Bombay for the operation I was able to answer truthfully, "Because I wanted you to open me up and no one else." By this time I was quite certain it was appendicitis, in fact as each hour passed, in my imagination it got worse, until finally it was on the point of bursting: so when questioned end examined I assured the surgeon that it *was* appendicitis. They operated and removed a perfectly healthy appendix!

Four days after the operation Mama forwarded a letter from Miss Creighton, the matron in Peshawar, who was willing to accept me and offered a five-year contract with a good salary. I was to be a civil servant with all the amenities and privileges enjoyed by them. She asked me to send her by return a photograph of myself. I could not think why she wanted this and asked the staff nurse.

"She wants to see if you are black," was the reply.

"I have not been photographed since I was a child, though I have a snapshot taken here during my training, will that be all right?"

"It could not be better as you are in uniform, send her that, and good luck, Green Mouse."

So I wrote and asked Mama to find this snap and post it to Peshawar. Now I wanted to get out of bed right away, to find my legs and gain strength, and decided to show Miss Creighton's letter to Major Gilroy and matron. "You see, Sir, I must get up soon—*please*. Getting this job means a lot to me."

The major understood and congratulated me; matron did this too, but looked surprised. I could not resist the temptation and showed Crabbitt the letter also; as I passed it over I remembered her biting remark on my report, "Has not the makings of a nurse." I suppose I was showing off, but being young then could be forgiven. Sister Crabbitt was more than surprised and asked me how I had wangled this. I told her I had not. "I have no one to pull strings for me, Sister, it was all taken out of my hands, and just happened." This was the truth.

When I was ready for discharge two or three of the nurses very kindly volunteered to take me to the station; they made all the necessary arrangements for my journey to Mhow. Walking up the platform of Victoria terminus one of the girls pointed to the name of the train, "The Peshawar Express." "You will be on this train again very soon, Green. I think you will board it at some point 'upcountry.'"

That is how I came to be on this train going up to Peshawar a fortnight later, got to Lahore at night instead of the morning, and took eighteen hours longer on the journey then was necessary. When I got home I found trouble waiting for me. Mama had not realised all this time that Peshawar was on the North-West Frontier, and of course our dear friends had to enlighten her when she went round telling them what a wonderful job her girl had been lucky enough to collect. Some of them managed to wipe the smile from her face by recalling the kidnapping of Molly Ellis from Kohat in 1923. While they were in spate she was told of the murders, the 'wars' and other atrocities. Mama now tried to oppose my going up there, and I had to work hard to win her round. It was the little glimmer of envy I caught now and again when speaking to some of the girls that made me more determined than ever that the Frontier was the one place in the world for me.

The Peshawar Express left Victoria terminus—Bombay at 9.30 p.m. I left Mhow at 7.40 the same night for Khandwar where I would make the connection. I arrived there at 1 a.m., and though very tired I dare not rest on the sofas provided, as these ware always infested with bugs. Reading and dozing the hours went by, and at 6 a.m. *chota hazri* arrived. After this I paced the platform waiting for the Express and met some people we had known years ago in Neemuch. They enquired after my mother and the girls and then asked where I was going. "Peshawar! The Frontier! It's a most dangerous place, don't, you know?" I caught the surreptitious looks then exchanged and was beginning to enjoy myself. Then they warmed up to it, telling me all the grim things I had already heard over and over again. "See the Pathans don't kidnap you," was the parting shot. This was getting so exciting I could hardly wait to get there.

The express soon roared into the station. The inspector now hurried up, and ordering the *coolie* to follow, led me to the Ladies' Second Class. My reservation had been made two days previously from Mhow. He found my name on the card outside the compartment and I clambered in quickly, followed by the *coolie* with my luggage; he only had time to dump the bedroll on the vacant upper berth before the train started. Most of that day I spent resting on my berth; only getting down for meals, I had decided to have all these brought to me from the refreshment car, instead of running along the platform at the meal stops, climbing in and out of the train and running the risk of being pushed around by the frenzied third class passengers. There were no corridor trains in India in those days.

At Jhansi, about 9 p.m. that night I got out with one of the women for company, and we stretched our legs for a few minutes on the station verandah where it was quieter, before boarding the train again. I slept well that night in spite of the terrific heat. Next morning about 7 a.m. we were at Delhi. Here two of the women left, but another two joined us.

It was nice having company all that day. One of the new passengers was a missionary going to Lahore, one was an army wife, the third an Anglo-Indian business girl. They were surprised to hear I was going up to the Frontier alone, and as I expected the grim stories were repeated. The missionary seemed to know more about these than the others. She gave us some of the details of the kidnapping of 1923. The occupants were leaving the train at various stops. The missionary would be the last to leave so unless another passenger got in at Lahore I should be travelling alone through the night. Though I was a little alarmed about this, I would not admit the fact. It was dreadfully hot that day—we had a large bowl of ice placed on the floor and had the two fans in the compartment playing on this at full speed. We also kept the lemonade *wallah* busy. Reading, dozing, having meals, the hours slipped away, Gradually it got cooler and gradually the carriage emptied. The missionary said "Goodbye" at her destination reminding me I still had time to turn back. I watched her retreating form with some misgivings.

Then suddenly a voice at my elbow made me jump. "Are you travelling alone, Miss?" I was asked by an Eurasian official, I told him I was. He then explained a railway or police rule;—"No white woman is allowed to leave Lahore by this train going to the Frontier without a special guard if she is alone in the Ladies Compartment—it isn't safe," he ended. I asked in alarm how much this "Special Guard" was going to cost as I had very little money. "You will not have to pay one *rupee*," he answered and hurried away. I was not feeling so good now. Soon he was back with an armed guard who wore a white drill uniform with a rifle slung over his shoulder, I was to see many of these in the

DAIMLER ARMOURED CARS

next five years; mostly khaki clad, but never again was I to have one all to myself.

Speaking in Urdu which is a flowery language, my guard informed me that from that moment until we got to Peshawar cantonments he would be responsible for my safety. He would lock both doors only to open them at Peshawar. Like a silly I asked him what he thought might happen to me if I travelled alone. "They would not bother to rob you, anyone can see you are poor; and they would not kill you— Pathans do not kill women if it can be avoided; you would be kidnapped, Miss. You are young and beautiful." As these Urdu speaking gentlemen have a flair for this sort of language, my head did not swell. He continued, "They would get much money from the British *raj* for your return—that is if they decided to return you!"

Then reading the alarm in my expression he hastened along. "Do not worry, I shall stay awake all night and guard you, at each stop I shall stand outside your door." By this time I was so frightened I nearly invited him to share my compartment but thinking better of it I resolved instead to keep awake all night. So some hours later, glancing through the shutters, I was glad to see the daybreak. A little later the train stopped and I heard someone in a foreign language— Pushtu—calling and knocking on my window, I guessed he wanted the window lowered; this I was determined not to do until I heard the more familiar Urdu, then lowering it I saw my smiling guard, and near him stood a tall Pathan bearer with *chota*. It was he who had been addressing me. After a sleepless night a pot of tea was very welcome, and I gladly reached for the tray—placing it by my side I noticed a strong smell. Pouring out a cup, I took a cautious sip, but soon put it down again; hastily I passed the tray out through the window. "What if that smell?" I asked.

My guard answered. "It is the milk of the camel, they use it here— very good for your stomach, Miss."

"That might be," I thought, "but what about one's nose?"

Seeing the Pathan's eyes were on me, I smiled weakly and said, "Perhaps I am too tired for tea this rooming," and covered the bill with a note.

Then we were off again, crossing the river Indus over the Attock bridge to Khairabad, We stopped at Nowshera, Peshawar City and finally at Peshawar cantonments at 11.30 a.m. This was now Tuesday and I had been travelling from Saturday 7.40 a.m. (1263 miles.) Here my guard opened the door with a flourish, his responsibility for my safety was now at an and. The matron—Miss Creighton—a slim, very attractive woman met me, and we had the long drive through cantonments, I felt I was being inspected and after a while she made a disquieting remark, "You do not look very strong, and you are much younger than I imagined." I heard disapproval in her voice and was alarmed.

I answered as best I could, "The long journey has tired me—coming so soon after my operation, but I am really quite strong." The only answer I could think of—off-hand to the second part of her remark was, "I may look young, but I am really very sensible. I was called 'Granny' by some of the nurses." This sounded lame even to my ears!

Then we got to the limits of cantonments and passed through a big gate that was always guarded, Now we were outside the safety of the perimeter. We crossed the railway and over the bridge the road forked. One branch led to the C.E.Z.M. Hospital and School: the other which we took led to "K" Supply and beyond, near the fort this branch forked again, and led to our hospital and the city. The fort and our hospital had been built on the site of the Bala Hissar, where a palace and beautiful garden once stood. These were destroyed by the Sikh invaders more than a hundred years ago, I was told this by Khan Bahadur Hakim Mullah Khan, our registrar, who also told me about the Pathans—how they lived and worked—their habits and customs. Listening to him they did not sound such a bad lot after all!

The Lady Reading Hospital had only been opened on April 12th, 1929, by Sir William Birdwood. It was sandwiched between the fort and city. One side of the fort ran parallel with our mess, and a huge green lawn with the doctor's bungalow at the end of this. We were separated from the fort by a *nullah* or dry moat. To hide the ugliness of the *nullah* and fort walls, along our low wire fence *chenar* and eucalyptus trees had been planted. They were saplings when I last saw them; now after thirty years they must be beautiful shady trees. It was comforting having the fort so near, one felt safe seeing the familiar khaki of the British Army, but it had its disadvantages, as we were to find out. One summer, in a moment of madness between the 'wars,' two or three of us decided to sleep out-of-doors; this, however, had to be abandoned when the wolf-whistles commenced.

Driving through the gate I was shown the police guard and was assured we were quite safe. The guardroom was built on to our mess which was hard by the gate. At the other end of the long drive were the doctors' bungalows—separated from ours by a lovely lawn and flower beds. Peshawar City sprawled just beyond the hospital walls.

CHAPTER 15

Burra Club, Kala Jugga and Band Nights

When our *tonga* halted, the biggest Pathan I have ever seen came out to remove my luggage. He was Kareem Bux, our bearer. On the verandah I was introduced to the senior sister, Mrs. Williams. She, like most of the others, was an ex-army nurse, in fact three of the five were ex-army.

Looking at them all at dinner that night, I realised why matron had made that remark about my age. In the five years I was there I was always the 'baby,' and was a good seven years younger than the next, and about ten, twelve and fourteen years younger than the others. I had been there just two or three days when matron gave a cocktail party, to which we sisters were invited. There were three or four men guests also. I sat quietly in a corner, my horrible shyness had returned in full strength. When the party was over, and the men rose to go, matron walked out on the verandah with them. When she returned she was smiling and Mrs. Williams asked her, "What is the joke, Miss Creighton—or is it private?"

"I have been asked who the little girl is," and she looked at me in a kind way.

Encouraged by this I said indignantly, "I hope you told him I am twenty-two!"

"I did, but as you look so much younger than that I am not sure that I was believed!"

Remembering her disapproving remark about my age in the *tonga*, I felt if I'd had a gun I might have shot the man! How I wished then I was thirty-two as I was so anxious to keep the job.

I had written home and promised to send Mama Rs100*l.*, about £7/10s. each month, "Darling, this will buy you some of the comforts, end especially the kippers you so love." Besides which, after paying my mess bill, buying clothes and other necessities I reckoned I should be able to save a little monthly towards my 'Mecca', the maternity training I hoped to take some day at Queen Charlotte's, London, I had not lost sight of that dream! Some time after I joined the L.R.H. a young Anglo-Indian nurse from Calcutta came to us—as she was about my age I was happy to see her; unfortunately she did not stay very long. Listening to them all at dinner that first night I was overawed and hardly spoke at all, as they were all 'haw-haw', but unlike Mrs. Condwick it was natural. I kept my mouth closed but my ears and eyes open and learnt quickly in the following months. "How-do-you-do" replaced "Pleased-to-meet-you," "Not-at-all" instead of "You're welcome," "Thank you" took the place of "Ta," "Goodbye" for "Cheerio" or "Chin-chin." And I learnt to bow slightly on being introduced after having my proffered hand ignored once or twice.

Before the first year was over I was speaking with the same accent; 'haw-haw' had replaced the old sing-song or 'chee-chee.' This was not a deliberate attempt to ape them, but living in that mess and hearing only that accent it was inevitable that I should acquire it, I remember once walking into the duty room and asking in the high pitched tone that had evolved, "Is the Mayjar he-ah?" I was not putting it on, but the young one from Calcutta who did not stay mimicked me and laughed. I was furious! When I went home on my first leave I was teased terribly by Doreen who firmly believed I was swanking, and I had a hard job to convince her that I was not.

"I am sure you are swanking," she said.

"Don't be silly," only it sounded like "Don't be silleh".

"There you go again Frontier nurse; you are being posh now."

Indignantly I replied, "I am *NOT*. You are very silly," only it came out 'vereh silleh' which made her roar; and me mad: so it went, but by the end of the fortnight she believed it was not put on as the accent never slipped. In fact even now, after thirty years, a slight 'haw-haw' exists, and often my nearly grown-up children tease me.

"Now we are being N.W.F.P." the girl will say, and the boy will add, "By Jove, Peshaw, Poonah! And all that, what! What!" I have tried to get them to understand that 'haw-haw' is to be preferred to 'chee-chee,' but as they fail to understand all that a 'chee-chee' implies the point is lost.

After I had been in the mess about a week, matron said one day at lunch, "I'll take you to the club, Miss Green, and get you fixed up as a member."

"Thank you," I said, though I had not a clue as to which club she meant and thought it wiser not to ask. That evening after tea, we set off in a *tonga*; it was a long but lovely drive. Up the Mall, lined with flowering trees, with the bungalows and gardens on either side. Arriving at the club and looking at the numerous tennis courts, the gravel patch at the side where the dining tables were being laid by *kitmughars* in white *chapkans* and well starched *pugrees* I realised this was the *Burra* Club, and had to fight down an exclamation! My feelings were mixed, pride and pleasure with fear. I was apprehensive about the questions I should be asked; however, I was asked none, as civil servants of official rank we, like the Q.A.'s, were automatically members. I felt rather bewildered at this stage, things seemed to be happening to me without a by-your-leave. Getting this job was not of my planning, I had tried for the post at Delhi and from the moment that the matron there had decided to send my application on to the Peshawar, and Miss Creighton to my surprise accepted me, a girl straight from a training school, everything had been taken out of my hands.

Now as they say in the N.W.F.P. "*Allah* knoweth best," I relaxed and settled to my new life; the hospital routine, the mess, and above all I had to try and keep fit in that heat. From April to July it was hot and dry, 117° to 120° F., and I have often seen the tar melt freely on the road. From July to September it was hot and damp, this was worse, as it brought a crop of prickly heat. To escape the heat in the summer the families went up the hills—Kashmir—Nathiagali—Abbotabad and Murree were chosen—but we had to stay and endure it. In a way we enjoyed the summer; being the only white women in the place—apart from the Q.A.'s and the missionaries—we were thoroughly spoilt. Invitations to the club—band nights with beer on the lawn. Swimming in the Government House pool. Golf, tennis and even riding. Two subalterns offered to teach me to ride, but I was too frightened of those huge animals and declined. When I told Doreen this on my first leave home she was disgusted. "You showed yourself up for a real softy then."

We were often asked out to dinner, not in a bunch but in separate parties. After dinner we would go to the pictures, or for a drive

LADY READING HOSPITAL SISTERS' MESS WITH GUESTS

along North Circular Road where we would see the guard patrolling the perimeter. Huge arc lights faced outwards—lighting up the aerodrome and the fields all around. Then on to South Circular and home. Those drives, especially on moonlight nights with the top of the car open were pleasant. Usually the car pulled up at some convenient *kala jugga* for a few minutes: All this helped us through those dreary summers. When in the autumn the families returned, we were neglected! We had blazing summers; and freezing winters when it rained and we had frosts. It snowed in some parts of the N.W.F.P. but I never saw any in Peshawar, though plenty was to be seen lying on the grey tops of the Hindu Kush.

A fire was a novelty to me, I used to love finding a cheerful blaze in my bedroom, with the copper scuttle all shiny and bright, I enjoyed the privacy of my room, having a bed room, a dressing room and bathroom all to myself, after having to share with Doreen and the nurses at St. George's it was a treat, I took a pride in my 'home' making it look pretty. We were allowed to pick flowers from the borders, and I smothered my room with them, much to the bearer's disgust. The *ghusul khanna* was a real luxury. There was a pull-the-chain instead, of a thunder box which was common except in places like Calcutta, Bombay or Delhi. This abomination was a square box with a lid, inside which was suspended an enamel 'top-hat,' which the *mather* or *jemadar* took away to clean. Then instead of the zinc bath we had English baths with hot and cold.

Once as I was about to turn on the water I saw a tiny black shiny snake in the bath. I called the bearer, who carefully picked it up between two sticks and slipped it into a jar I held. Over in the hospital I was told it was a baby cobra. Another luxury I enjoyed here which I had missed in my training days was *chota* in bed. Kareem Bux brought this in at about 6.30 to 7 o'clock, but actually we were awakened earlier by the unusual noises made by the gardeners. They were prisoners from the local jail. Each man wore heavy chains from his waist to his ankle. He was able to walk easily, but running away would have been difficult. To discourage such thoughts an armed guard strolled around with them. The clanking of those chains was our 'rising bell.'

It was strange while sitting in bed drinking tea to see a prisoner rattle past to water the palm pots on the verandah. I never knew what crime these men had committed and perhaps for my peace of mind it was better that way. Though to see them walking round in chains made us unhappy: it seemed too great an indignity to impose on any human being. The European staff consisted of the surgeon superintendent, the medical officer, matron and five nursing sisters. The Asian staff, headed by the registrar Khan Bahadur Hakim Mullah Khan—a darling old man who was looked up to and respected by all. Then came five to six surgeons and physicians—all brilliant men, next the male nursing orderlies and *dais*—the women orderlies. Lastly male and female sweepers—the untouchables.

The hospital consisted of the main block, a double storied building named after the Chief Commissioner Sir Norman Bolton. The ground floor was given up to the offices and store rooms. The floor above was divided into eight or ten single rooms with a duty room and labour room. A wide verandah went all round, in front it overlooked our mess, the big lawn and flower borders; with the fort in the background It was a pleasant spot. In summer the patients slept out here and entertained their visitors here in the cool of the evening. In Bolton Block Europeans, Anglo-Indians, Parsees, Pathans and Hindus were admitted: in fact, anyone prepared to pay the fee. Here each sister took a patient to 'special' as far as possible.

The rest of the hospital consisted of four one storied wards, for men, built on terraces behind Bolton. Medical and Surgical were on one side, with Eye and Medico-Legal on the other. Here I ought to explain that, as there were always so many cases of stab and gunshot wounds with policemen at the bedside waiting to take statements; and to see that the patient was not whisked away by relatives in the middle of the night; a special ward had to be set aside for them. We often had the strange experience of having the victim and aggressor on opposite sides of the ward, each with his attendant policeman. The Theatre Block was built right behind Bolton. All these buildings were detached, but connected to each other by corrugated roofed pathways, and it was hot walking under these in summer.

CHAPTER 16

Mummies, Feuds and Infidelity

A block of family quarters had been built for the women. These consisted of a room to accommodate two beds. A kitchen, lavatory and small walled in courtyard built on at the back for privacy—owing to the strict Moslem *purdah* system this was necessary. The numerous relatives who always accompanied each patient to the hospital used the open front verandah as a squatting place by day and a dormitory by night. The nursing in the Family Block was done by the *dais* supervised by us, we undertook any complicated treatment. A strange sight was the massage carried out by the relations. A child of ten or twelve would pace up and down a patient's leg pommelling all day long, holding on to the wall for support. We frowned on this, of course, and out of respect, with their tongues in cheek, the relations would wait for us to finish the round before resuming the treatment. For fun I have often pretended to walk away, and then run silently back to catch them out. I scolded—and they gathered round trying to look sorry— until I laughed. I would then have a crowd of hefty laughing Pathan women round me, thumping me on the back, stroking my cheek and arms. I was not 'sister' now but 'a' sister; I may not have been so useful this way, but I was more loved.

Another custom we discouraged, again with little success, was the swathing of the infant. Starting at the back of the neck with a bandage made of old rags sewn together, crossed over the chest and with the child's arms pinioned, this bandage was wound round, and round until in the end only the head was free; and the baby ended by looking like an Egyptian Mummy. These were not unwound more than strictly necessary. The women considered the baby felt safe this way, "And think," ended a Pathan woman to me one day when I told her

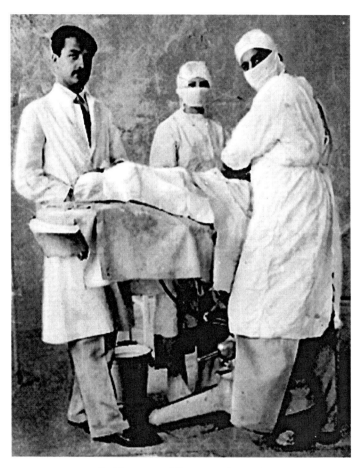

IN THEATRE (THEATRE SISTER)

how wrong it was to tie up her child, "Have you ever seen a round-shouldered Pathan?" She had something there—these people carry themselves superbly; they are tall, straight and proud.

Besides Family Block, away in a corner of the huge grounds we had four to six cottages. These were for the wealthy Asian patients, and I have often stood rooted to the spot in amazement to see the patient carried in on a *palanquin* or *charpoy*, followed by ten to twenty relatives—adults and children—followed in turn by goats, chickens and camels. It was hectic getting to the patient, dodging the playful children, picking one's way over sleeping babies abandoned anywhere on the floor of the verandah or room; being careful not to trip over the goats and chickens tied to each other to hinder escape. And lastly keeping clear of the camels' long legs and snapping jaws. I experienced many strange cases.

We had a Hindu girl of thirteen admitted. She had been in labour for two to three days being treated, or ill-treated, as you will agree, by the village *dai*. For the purpose of dilatation a length of sugar-cane had been used. She was in a poor way when we saw her. On palpation twins were discovered and a 'caesarean' had to be performed. Conjoined twins (at the sternum) were removed. I am happy to say the little mother recovered. We had many cut-noses and amputated breasts. The men away on feuds when returning rightly or wrongly suspecting infidelity would use the knife to savage purpose. A horrible case was that of a pregnant woman with her abdomen ripped open. Fortunately the knife had not gone low enough and the uterus had escaped. We patched her up, and a couple of days later she delivered her baby in the normal way. They were a tough lot!

There are many good books written by Englishmen who have spent their lives on the Frontier working and living with the Pathans, which tell of the family feuds and life in general as lived by these war-like yet fascinating people. Although I was given a pretty good picture of the Pathan way of life by our doctor and patients, it would be completely beyond me to do justice to their story, so I will rest content with telling you a little of the 'patching-up' we did.

It was a common occurrence to have a man brought in with his intestines on the outside wrapped in the skin of a chicken, their idea of asepsis. Picking out the shot, cleaning and suturing, the surgeons often had to do an end-to-end anastomosis—cutting away a portion of gut and joining the two ends together to form into a tube again, on 'eye' days we took out cataracts like shelling peas. Tumours which had been allowed to grow as big as footballs were removed from different parts of the anatomy. Abdominal stab wounds, mutilated arms and legs, all these came to our theatre regularly.

It was whilst I was taking my turn as theatre sister that we had a visit from the surgeon-general. He stood watching us at work, and then moved round speaking quietly to each taking part in the operation. He told me I was very lucky to have this experience: cases admitted here would not be met anywhere else in the world, he said.

Being 'Theatre' meant one was awakened at any time in the night for an emergency. At first walking across the dark garden I was nervous and wanted to run, even though I was accompanied by the orderly sent to fetch me. Then working alone for an hour or two with the Pathan staff I came to realise I had nothing to fear. Some nights they 'phoned for the surgeon superintendent, but as he had to come all the way from cantonments they did not do this unless it was absolutely necessary. He was always present at the serious operations.

Apart from taking turns in the Theatre and 'specialising' in Bolton we each had a ward to supervise. After the morning rounds we collected in the duty room in Bolton for coffee, for this we were joined by the surgeon superintendent and the medical officer.

At 11 a.m. the coffee session would break up. Two of the sisters going off duty to return at 2 p.m. until 8 p.m. The other two or three went off at 2 p.m. until the following morning. We did these shifts alternately. Night duty was only done when we had patients in Bolton Block. Often in the summer for long periods we were free. The winter with the families back in Peshawar was our busy time when we usually had from three to six maternity cases booked. These were the wives of the civilians—I.C.S., police, bank and railway. We also had one or two army officers' wives though they had their own hospital in cantonments, and I can remember at least one young subaltern being admitted, though how this was managed I do not know.

Tony Wakefield, of the Poona Horse, was in with typhoid, and was not allowed to read; all books and papers were withheld, but in his locker he found an unopened packet of a world-famous brand of toilet paper which has its virtues and replicas of gold medals won printed on the cover. One day I walked into his room unexpectedly and caught him studying this packet intently. He then held it up and exclaimed, "I know every word on this by heart, I have read it over a thousand times: aren't you sorry for me?"

"Come on, Tony, let's see if you really do know it," and I took the packet from him while he recited it word perfect. Yes Tony did know his 'Bromo-Blurb' and every time I see any of this particular flimsy I am reminded of him.

Another young man I helped nurse here was a good looking young Pathan, the son of a chief, who spoke excellent English. As he was lonely and I talked to him as I did his treatment—I asked him to tell me about the Pathans, and through him learnt a great deal about these people. Whether he mistook my interest I cannot say, but he shook me by suggesting I should turn Moslem and marry him. This was said in a flippant manner, but the look in his eyes warned me it was no joke. "If you refuse I can easily arrange to have you kidnapped!" he threatened.

I had the sense not to laugh, and said, "I don't think you'll find it's worth it; another kidnapping and the Frontier will get such a bad name that no one will want to come up here to nurse or teach; then your people will suffer." And I told him about the trouble I had to get Mama to agree to my joining the L.R.H. after she had been told about Molly Ellis being kidnapped. Thinking over my reply he must have decided I was not worth the risk. What I felt like telling him though was that I had no desire to spend the rest of my life in a *burqa* as a *purdah nashin*. However he was not the only Pathan to suggest I should turn Moslem and stay in the N.W.F.P. Just before my five years were up, I was talking to K.B. Hakim Mullah Khan, our darling old registrar. He quite seriously asked me not to leave, "Stay with us Sister Green, we like you. You can embrace Islam and I will arrange to marry you to a Pathan chief."

I thanked him for the great honour, but told him I had my mother's feelings to consider.

CHAPTER 17

Fairies in the Khyber

In the summer of 1929 I paid my first visit to the Khyber: in all I think I visited the Pass three times. This famous gateway connecting Afghanistan and what is now Pakistan is thirty-three miles long and in parts only fifteen feet wide. The first proper road through the Safed Koh mountains of the Hindu Kush range was made by the British, probably the work of the sappers, to connect India, as it was then, with Afghanistan. A railway from Jamrud on the Pakistan side to the Afghan Frontier (twenty-seven miles) was opened in November, 1925. One can get glimpses of this railway from the road before it gets lost in the fold of the mountains, or disappears into tunnels. Fort Jamrud at the entrance to the Pass looks almost like a battleship cast adrift on dry land. Then comes Landi Kotal and Landi Khanni, two more forts with Ali Masjid—a mosque—near Landi Khanni. The Masjid, a white building lying in s valley against the grey mountains with trees dotted about, stands out conspicuously. Driving through the Pass one sees, carved out of rock, badges of all those regiments that have served in this area. The Pathans' *khassadars*—tribal policemen—help to keep the peace. These gentlemen, in their baggy trousers and loose khaki shirts, with a bandoleer across the chest end carrying rifles, are on guard throughout the Pass.

The first time I went up I was alone with the fellow who was giving me this treat—I cannot remember his name, there was an embarrassing scene as I was not *au fait* with the polite, ambiguous jargon of the English language. Besides, having lived in the civilised district of Bombay this sort of situation had not arisen before. After driving for what seemed miles we suddenly pulled up by a wall of rock—I suppose we were in the Pass. "This is no *kala jugga*" I thought startled.

Noticing my surprise my escort said, "it's not what you think, but do you want to pick a daisy?"

I looked round wildly for flowers and seeing none said, "No, thank you," wondering where the catch lay.

He groaned, then tried again, "are you a fairy?"

Having said "No' I decided to try a change, and this time said, "Yes, I am!" I had heard girls referred to as fairies before and thought this quite the correct answer.

However, this too was wrong because he put his head in his hands and almost; wept! "You need shaking!" he wailed and getting out of the car pointed to a large rock and said, "I'm going for a walk behind that rock," then pointing to another in the opposite direction added, "that one is for you. Now has the penny dropped?"

I had not even heard this expression before but dare not risk more, so feeling both bothered and foolish I fled behind my appointed rock.

Another time I went up the Pass I was with three friends. I have a snapshot showing us standing at the barrier which marks the boundary between Afghanistan and India. I smiled at the armed guard on the Afghan side, then putting my foot over the border and touching the soil with my toe I exclaimed, "now I can say I have been in Afghanistan." A snapshot of another visit taken at Michin Khandoo looking down on Landi Khanni is dated February, 1930, and it must have been cold as we are in fur coats.

During the first summer I was there Miss Creighton suggested I should go around to pay my respects to the C.E.Z.M.S. folk. So I ordered visiting cards and was duly instructed in this rite of dropping bits of pasteboard into those little "Not-at-Home" boxes fixed on the gate posts. I thought, this was a waste of time and a waste of card, if nothing came of it, but if an invitation to tea or dinner followed this was another matter. Mrs. Cox, the senior lady, was kind and asked me to dinner. This really was my debut into Peshawar society. In the end I came to know the mission folk quite well and spent many happy hours there. Doctor and Mrs. Cox followed Doctor and Mrs. Starr who were responsible for going into tribal territory to bring back Molly Ellis after her kidnapping in 1923. I was told the Pathans had crept into the bungalow at Bannu one night whilst Major Ellis was playing bridge in the sitting room. After murdering Mrs. Ellis, Molly was kidnapped and held to ransom, but ultimately returned unharmed. It was at Cox's,

MICHIN KHANDOO LOOKING DOWN ON LANDI KHANNIS

for dinner, that I had the half of a tiny melon chilled with ginger and brown sugar for the first time, served as a *hors d'oeuvres*. In that heat it was refreshing.

One day I was able to visit the chapel in the mission compound. It was a dome shaped building, so Moslem in architecture that I wondered if originally it had been a mosque. I knew it, was once the Guide Cavalry Mess. In this mission apart from Doctor and Mrs. Cox, there were one or two sisters and the school staff. They were all hardworking good people. One of the teachers and I became friendly; as this was her first job we had such in common, and we were both fond of tennis. She was pretty with a pink and white skin and curly light-brown hair. We would have been very happy had she been a club member; then in the winter when we were lonely we could have arranged foursomes. I asked her often to the club for tennis, after which we would have cosy teas and chat for hours by the blazing coal fire in the 'snake-pit,' or *moorghi-khanni*, (the hen-house.)

Sometimes we were joined by a couple of 'lounge-lizards,' 'sofa-cobras' or 'poodle-fakers;' of course this made the evening more interesting. Celia asked me to try and get her in as a member. Before mentioning this in our mess, where somehow I felt I would not meet with much sympathy, I had a quiet word with Miss Bolton, our visiting lady doctor whom I knew was kind. She was sympathetic, but not hopeful. She pointed out that apart from the fact that Celia had been born in India, her parents were living in the district and she had relatives in Peshawar; none of whom were members. This would make things more difficult and we could hardly hope for success. While I was disappointed, and disgusted at the snobbery, I was made nervous of my position for the first time, and decided to confide in Miss Bolton. "Should I do something about it?" I asked, "Clear the air?"

"Leave well alone," was the reply.

One summer I received a command from Queen Boadicea of Stonehenge. The mission folk were giving a party, and everyone had to dress as an Ancient Briton. I was unable to borrow a skin, so decided, that a foreigner would pay her respects to the fearless British Queen; and from a sack and paper flowers I made a Hawaiian dress for myself. I expect in those early days—the islanders wore little besides the '*leis*' but out of respect to the mission folk, I added a skirt. The men, a weird looking lot, caused lots of fun: most of them were draped in skins and carried large soup bones. The party was held on the lawn. After paying homage to the queen, we had chariot races; as the queen was too heavy for her chariot someone picked me up, and I was given a ride in her place. It was a hectic party, and before the night was through the Church of England *padre* finished up in the *Mali's* pond (the gardeners' water supply). Though before this happened we went onto the club after visiting some other mission people in cantonments. The peaceful club members sitting on the lawn looked startled when a boisterous savage mob appeared in their midst. As a subaltern said to me later, "we wondered if the Afridis had arrived in a new guise."

If they were gay in the mission we were also gay in our mess, and had many happy dinner parties. Once we had a most lavish cold buffet spread on the verandah. Unless we were at 'war' with any of the tribes, or trouble was brewing in the city, we 'changed' into evening dress. As we were already six women, we only had men guests; if individually we had hospitality to return to any of the *memsahibs* we did this at the club. Our Goanese cook excelled at parties. We always had a five or six course meal, and he used his imagination to give us the unusual aubergines stuffed with crab and shrimps, pumpkins baked with minced beef and mushrooms; and I remember with nostalgia the saddle-of-mutton baked crisp. The *dhumbas* or fat tailed sheep peculiar to the Frontier supplied these. He had imagination all right and it was only at the end of the month, when bills were cleared, that we realised just what this meant in *rupees*.

As one of the sisters, put it, "He thinks we are ruddy *ranis!*"

After dinner we played games. Once it was rounders on the lawn, fun on a moonlight night with the fort in the background, and the eucalyptus and *chinar* trees like sentinels all round. Or we danced. If it, was too hot for anything strenuous we just sat on the lawn in a large circle, chatting and drinking beer. Portable electric fans were placed behind the chairs, and we would have the sweet scent of the flowers blown across to us from the borders. I was teased a good bit at these parties, as I was very unsophisticated; when *risqué* stories were told most of them passed over my head, but I laughed with the others, though not fooling the young subalterns who would say, "Little Audrey laughed and laughed and laughed!" We gave these parties to return the hospitality we received from the men who asked us to dine at Deane's Hotel or the club: after dinner we sat on the lawn in the summer to listen to the band, drink beer and eat chips. I quite enjoyed my glass of beer now; gone were the temperance days of orange and tomato juice; beer or a glass of sherry I had discovered made me a little less tongue-tied.

At the start of the season, my first winter there I was taken round by one of the sisters and we did our 'calling' together. We began by writing our names in the visitors' book at Government House. Then we called on the senior ladies of the station, the judicial commissioner's wife, the D.C.'s wife, the general's wife and other V.I.P.s. We also called on the wives of our medical men. A number of people we called on merely returned the cards and did nothing else. However some were kind enough to follow this up with an invitation—our medical wives always did this. They were the kind ones that understood we depended on the married women to take us under their wings. Conventions were strict in those pre-war days. The expense of entertaining was negligible, and the trouble non-existent with all the servants about; but some could not be bothered with us, they were too busy having a good time themselves! Still we had our revenge in the summer: we flirted wholesale then, married men and all.

There is quite a collection of cards in the 'Souvenir Casket' I started in those days and which has grown through the years, with the addition of photographs, foreign menus and newspaper cuttings. The card from Lady Fraser, wife of the judicial commissioner, reminds me that she was kind to all and I was asked to dinner on more than one occasion. Cards from the general's wife and one or two other senior army personnel did not lead to anything further. Very likely nothing under the status of a matron was recognised by these *burra memsahibs*. This card business did, however, lead to a long friendship with Ann Veryard, the wife of Captain P. Veryard of the R.A.F. Meteorological Service, a friendship which continued when we met again in England, and I was grateful for their kindness and hospitality.

The Parkers were another R.A.F. couple I remember with gratitude. Mrs. Parker tried to help Cupid on my behalf; I was often asked to their flat to find young men on the scene. However, the work was being undermined and from our mess. I was just beginning to realise that spiteful forces were at work in the background. I sensed the hints, or less strongly, the innuendos which were being dropped from some of the things the subalterns said to me, and the probes and feelers they put out. I guessed the idea could only have been put into their heads by one or two in our mess. One day Chris Grayrigge, *apropos* of nothing, picked up my hand and closely examined my finger nails; then he asked me to show him my gums; startled at so strange a request I obediently parted my lips. He looked for a moment than muttered to himself, ". . . . .No, not there."

"What's not there?" I demanded, "what are you looking for, Chris?"

Knocking my two front teeth with his thumb nail, he said, "You ought to have those tuskers out." He was just hedging and though I pestered him I did not get a straight answer. So, I decided to ask 'Uncle Jim Clark', my middle-aged lay preacher friend when I saw him next. He explained, after a slight hesitation which told me a great deal. "He was looking for the blue mark which covers the 'moon' on the nails, and the bluish tint that is found on the gums of persons of mixed blood." Possibly my blood is insufficiently mixed—I have neither. Uncle then said "Don't let this worry you or hurt you, child." I told him it could not as I always remembered Papa's advice on this subject.

Not all the sisters were 'catty' I hasten to say. Miss Snob was hard and cruel, as one the sisters told me, "she is terrified you'll marry before she does."

I did, but that has nothing to do with this story. Menelaus was definitely not catty, she and Miss Creighton several times had peculiar little scenes over me. One morning Miss Creighton came to breakfast and said, "I've had an awful night. I dreamt Mr. Paynter wanted to marry Miss Green, and I was most worried!"

I was dumbfounded, and thought what a queer thing to say! However, Menelaus took her up at once. "Why worried? Surely you should have been happy?"

With all our eyes fixed on her Miss Creighton looked as if she wished she had not spoken; rather lamely she replied, "Well, they are both so young."

By now I had recovered my wits and decided to speak for myself; very quietly I said, "there is no cause for alarm, Miss Creighton, Mr. Paynter's just one of my many friends—no more than any of the others—I have no 'steady.'"

My champion then said, "Well I don't see why you shouldn't have a 'steady' Green—you're bonny."

"Bonny? What do you mean by 'bonny,'" asked Miss Creighton, now trying to turn the tables on Menelaus.

"Just bonny," answered Menelaus with a smile. When Miss Creighton turned her attention to her bacon and eggs, Menelaus caught my eye and winked.

Another time my action caused disapproval—though not in a dream—was when a colonel, who was a mess visitor introduced by matron, made a fuss of me. Alas! He was a married man, more's the pity. I was ill and he sent me flowers, then followed this up by coming to see me. He then asked me to dinner and the pictures when I was well again; and as I knew no reason for refusing I accepted. If any would-be Casanova took me out, he only did that once. I had not had my mother's training for nothing. "The Gypsy's Warning" had been drummed into my head too thoroughly. Yet Another time was when Rai Sahib Mere Chand Khanna, an influential Hindu gentleman, who later when partition came in 1947, took office in the new Indian Government, asked me to dinner to meet his wife.

At dinner we discussed *purdah* and Rai Sahib suggested I could do some work in this field. "Get them out—get them emancipated—you can do it—you speak Urdu." After dinner, as I was young and he probably thought I would be bored spending the evening just talking to the two of them, Rai Sahib suggested we go along to the pictures. His wife being in *purdah* it meant just the two of us going; as he was such a respectable man I never hesitated for a moment.

Though at the pictures I wondered if I had been wise—as I got such curious cold glances from the people around. Feeling uncomfortable I hoped Rai Sahib had not noticed; to make matters worse he was the only Indian there! Again I thought of my father, here were the snobs he had mentioned. Some of these people were not capable of living up to their positions and so took refuge in petty tyranny, and always the women were the worst offenders with their superior airs.

Next morning at breakfast I was asked how the dinner party went, I thought it best to tell them everything and as I expected my going to the pictures was censured.

"But why not?" asked Menelaus, again coming to my defence. "You should be honoured if Rai Sahib asks one of your staff out—he is a very important man."

"Oh, yes, yes, I agree he is important, but . . . . ," and then there was a stony silence. Menelaus and I looked at each other and smiled.

In the hospital that morning I met the Khan Bahadur, that dear old orthodox, and in a teasing mood I told him about my new mission in life. "I am going to free the ladies from the *purdah*," I said gaily and mentioned Rai Sahib's suggestion.

"Leave well alone, Sister Green, or you might......"

"Be kidnapped?" I finished for him. "All right, Khan Sahib, I'll leave your Moslem ladies alone," I said, rushing away.

CHAPTER 18

Pasteboard Memories and Preparation

The 'Souvenir Casket' reveals that the most important thing that happened to me that first winter was shaking hands with His Excellency the Viceroy. I had an invitation to the Garden Party at Government House on the 7th April, 1930, "To have the honour of meeting His Excellency the Viceroy." However the second visit to Peshawar by the Viceroy and the Countess of Willingdon in April, 1932, stands out in my memory, as the countess visited our hospital. There was great excitement, preparation and the usual 'spit and polish' for weeks beforehand. The garden was especially groomed and along the covered pathway the *mali* put up hanging baskets of trailing purple flowers— a nice touch—as everyone knew Lady Willingdon's fondness for the colours purple and mauve.

All sorts of rumours went round concerning the colour scheme, and a naughty subaltern at our mess one night said, "even a purple padded you-know-what has been ordered for her *ghusl khanna*." A faded snapshot of Lady Willingdon with various members of the hospital staff makes that day come alive in my memory. The sisters were to be introduced to Her Excellency, and for weeks we chaffed each other as to who would make the best curtsy. With my door bolted and the curtains drawn I practised curtsying before my mirror for hours.

At last the great day arrived and Lady Willingdon went round the hospital: we were to be introduced to her wherever we happened to be working. Alas for me! I was on the verandah of Bolton Block with a ten day old baby in my arms when the party came round the corner. Lady Willingdon made straight for the baby to admire and tickle it

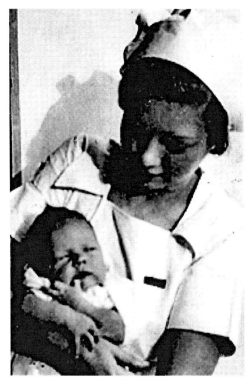

WITH BABY BORN IN THE L. R. HOSPITAL
(Wearing the ribbon of the Frontier Medal)

under the chin—starting it crying—before she turned with a laugh to speak to the mother who sat near at hand in a wheelchair. Gone was my moment, even I had the sense not to try a curtsy with a baby crying in my arms. However, I consoled myself with the thought that I would make the best curtsy at the 'At Home' being given by the chief commissioner and Lady Griffith at Government House on the 18th April. To my disappointment this was again out of the question as we were all pushed into a close tight queue. As we shuffled along and came abreast of the A.D.C., he took the card we held and announced our name, a quick handshake with Their Excellencies and it was all over. We now kept moving blindly one after the other like a lot of sheep, but I was happy to find myself suddenly before a heavily laden tea-table. This was indeed a consolation!

Government House stood on a knoll surrounded by beautiful gardens and lawns; after tea we strolled on the lawns listening to the band. So ended a proud day, and to me it seemed quite an achievement for a little Anglo-Indian born into a railway community.

For that garden party I had had a new dress made. For these State occasions they were worn down to our toes. I gave Kirpa Ram half my month's salary for a large picture hat. A snapshot that someone took as we were about to leave 'all dressed up' reminds me that we felt very posh. Another photograph of a large group taken under a spreading banyan tree in a garden shows me wearing a hat of a different type; looking over these photographs the other day I was joined by my nearly grownup daughter who laughed at my creations. "Mummy, how could you have worn those ridiculous hats? I wouldn't be seen dead in one of them." The young can be very cruel!

It was the pomp and pageantry of the balls at Government House that I enjoyed. After leaving our cloaks in the Ladies' Room which was downstairs we would join the throng moving slowly up the wide stairs.

To receive their guests, the governor and his wife stood on the landing with an A.D.C. standing by—he announced, our names: a handshake and we moved along. The ball was opened by the governor and his wife. The hall with its paintings of royalty; former governors; the military band playing on the stage; the women in their beautiful dresses whirling round to the Viennese waltzes; officers in their varied mess dress with the gold and silver trimmings and medals, all made it a scene of splendour.

I remember the little trees in pots with the gold coloured oranges which were used for decoration. Those trees were carefully placed by gardeners under instructions from a sympathetic A.D.C., no doubt, round a seat for two—the nearest one got to a *kala jugga* in that grand place. The first time I saw one of those little orange trees laden with its ripe fruit I could not believe they were real. A running buffet provided marvellous refreshments. These Government House balls stand out for pageantry, but for fun the ordinary Saturday night dance at the club could not be beaten, I remember sitting under the large table in the club library sharing a plate of bacon and eggs with my partner. We were trying to get away from the crowd in the dining-room. This was either at supper or the very early breakfast that was served when the dance did not break up until sunrise. We were nice and comfortable when another couple came in and spotted us and asked if they could join us. After a while yet another pair walked in and this time without asking crept under. Soon we were so crowded that a clumsy fellow knocked his kipper into a girl's lap. Then someone suggested a game of sardines. "Why play sardines," replied my partner crossly, "we are sardines."

One winter Peshawar had a visit from the Duchess of Dufferin and Ava, and that Saturday the club was crowded. Between the dances I decided my nose needed powdering, and I made for the Ladies' Room, At the door I took hold of the green curtain to pull it aside at the same instant as someone from the inside pulled it in the opposite direction. This resulted in an *impasse*, which after a second or two we ourselves sorted out, and coming face to face—laughed! She got out—I got in, and as I moved across to a large mirror the woman using it said, "That was the duchess you were struggling with."

"Oh, dear," I wailed, "I wish I had known—I should have looked at her more carefully. I shall never get so near a real live duchess again."

Another dance which I remember well was one given by the politicals in the grounds of 7, Commissioner Road. This was held in April and to make it unusual was held out of doors. Coloured electric bulbs were strung between the trees, and the flower beds were floodlit. In one corner of the garden the band played on a *dais*. The pretty dresses, colourful mess kit, and the stars shining brightly all helped, to make a beautiful scene. Then the Bachelors' Fancy Dress Ball was another highlight each year and many handsome costumes were worn. One year I had a striking Punjabi dress made. My Pathan women patients

IN PUNJABI DRESS

helped the *dais* to embroider it with gold tinsel and beads. I was hoping to wear this to the Bachelors' Ball, but was asked by Captain and Mrs. Parsons to accompany them to the Sergeants' Fancy Dress. I won first prize at the sergeants' dance.

This was a curious experience for me. In Neemuch or Mhow before my training I was just one of the girls from the railway colony draped round the walls with their Mamas, to watch with awe and respect the officers and their wives. We would go into hysterics—almost—if asked to dance with one of the officers. Now at this dance Mrs. Parsons and I were 'Stars' and once or twice catching the eye of a 'wall drape' I wanted to smile. Apart from carrying off the prize—our party had been joined by a couple of other S. & T. officers. We were well feted. It needed all my tact to refuse the dozens of drinks the sergeants wanted to buy me. It was most difficult trying to convince these men that one or two glasses of sherry was my limit.

Besides the dances the other events I enjoyed in the winter were the gymkhanas, 'At Homes' and point-to-point meetings. We would travel as far as possible in cars to the chosen places. Then walk across fields suitably dressed for the country. One year I determined to make a splash—and I did, I had a rough tweed leather trimmed suit from Scotland. This with a Kashmir shawl round my head and shoulders, and the shooting stick I carried made me feel right. I had an added confidence. The young man accompanying me said, "you fit the picture well."

"Thank you—so I should. It has cost six month's salary." Then with my head in the clouds I put my foot, in a hole and fell in the mud.

I enjoyed watching the competitions, but whilst admiring the women taking part, I did not envy them. It looked terribly dangerous. They would come down the steep banks on those huge horses with their spindly legs spread-eagled, but as there were few, if any, spills it was good horsemanship, even in my ignorance I recognised this. Tea was served buffet style, often in a green wheat field with blue irises growing wild, The sun shone out of a cloudless blue sky. The *kitmughars* in their starched white *chapkans* and *pugrees* flitted round amongst the couples sitting on mounds or groups sharing a rug, or even balancing on shooting sticks, and we had not a care in the world.

Between all this frivolity or in spite of this jollity we did our job. Menelaus and I engaged a *munshi* to teach us *Pushtu* to help us in our work. We now greeted our Pathan friends and patients with "*Starey-*

mah-shey!" And got the reply "*Khor mah shey!*" They were asked on the slightest pretext—often the opening gambit—"*Taze Yeh? Khusal Yeh? Jor Yeh?*" But whether they were fresh, happy or strong, or all three combined, we were not quite sure, but it did give us some practise in the language. A more sensible query; "*Durad, chartah deh?*" or "Where is the pain?" was useful in trying to discover what was the matter, asking then: "*Sta killi chartah deh?*" "Where is your village?" gave us the necessary information for our records. It was not very encouraging however to learn a language at our own expense when we knew that contracts expiring at the end of five years meant we would be leaving.

Discussing this with Menelaus one night I told her of my secret dream, the ambition to take my 'midder' in Queen Charlotte's. "I shall need plenty of money for that—it's no use wasting it on the *munshi* if I cannot stay after 1934. In any case I must leave then or I shall feel too old to start as a student again."

Then as her interest had waned for a reason only made clear months later, when she suddenly left us to go as matron to a hospital in one of the Indian States, we decided to drop the lessons.

Menelaus now went in for a car and I took, to reading really seriously. I selected books by the good authors from the club library and read these greedily. Hugh Walpole, Galsworthy, Deeping and Margaret Irwin were my favourites at that time. Although reading for enjoyment I realised this was a form of education—now when in company and books became the topic of conversation instead of being a tongue-tied little ignoramus, I was able to take part. I startled a crowd of them on one occasion by telling them that I had read Jew Suss in about two days. What I did not confess was that on my "day off" that month I read all through that day, and all night. Next morning getting up for work I felt so groggy that I never repeated the performance but rationed my reading hours instead.

After I had been in Peshawar nearly a year matron dropped a bombshell at breakfast one morning. She turned to me and said, "I had a letter from Sister Crabbitt of St. George's Hospital: do you know her, Miss Green?" Then matron paused to pick up and read from a letter she had carried in with her while I waited impatiently my heart thumping madly. At last putting the letter down she said, "She wants to come here to join our staff."

"What?" I shouted, almost leaping out of my chair, "Do I know her? I should think I do!" Then choking in my agitation, I could say no more until someone made me swallow some water, and someone else thumped me on the back. When I had recovered I said excitedly, "Oh, Matron you can't. It will be impossible. Hell's Bells, she hates me—it will be murder. But I'll be senior to her here! Won't that be fun!" and I ended by laughing hysterically.

Matron looked at me keenly for a while then said, "I'm not sure what you mean by all that, but I can see it won't work, so we'll forget it." I breathed a sigh of relief. Later in the duty room, I told Menelaus about Sister Crabbitt in "Eyes" and the rotten report she had given me. "Well, you've fixed her, Green. In spite of choking you had your own back," and she laughed.

"I did not mean to be spiteful but I was taken, by surprise and it all gushed out before I could think."

"Well, don't look so glum, it's probably all for the best; it might have caused unpleasantness in the mess had she come."

So that is how it came about that—unwittingly—well, I was never *very* sure of that point—the 'mouse' fixed the 'cat'.

CHAPTER 19

Politics and Piety

One morning soon after this I was told I could take my first leave, but before I went I felt a sense of unrest and trouble in the air. The political situation was getting worse. I heard about the Faquir of Ipi, that notorious British-hater. (Strangely enough, whilst writing this part of my story in the spring of 1960, it was given out on the news that he had died in that part of the world that we now call Pakistan.) I was shocked as I had been brought up in a country swarming with religious *faquirs* and *sadhus* whom I had been taught to respect as peace-loving pious men.

I was told about the Red Shirt army and one day saw them on parade; they wore uniforms but were unarmed. These Hindu or Moslem gentlemen under the leadership of Abdul Gaffur Khan fancied themselves as soldiers destined to liberate India, General A. G. K. had a brother Doctor Khan Sahib who had studied medicine in England and married an English woman. I cannot remember exactly when it was that Mrs. Khan Sahib was brought in as a patient but I think, it was after her husband and brother-in-law were jailed. Anyway she was given V.I.P. treatment in one of the private cottages and I was detailed to 'special' her—it was all to do with politics and I had to be on my toes as Congress leaders were in and out all the while, and they only wanted an excuse to make trouble, though fraught with danger this gave an added zest to our work.

Mrs. Khan Sahib had turned Moslem and she recited the Islamic Lord's prayer repeatedly. This I soon picked up and found I was sub-consciously intoning, "*Laillah il Allah Mohammed la rasul lllah*," and the rest of the prayer at odd moments. Her son John, who was at Oxford, was sent for. The first day he visited his mother I met a good-looking young man in a well cut English suit, who spoke very 'haw-haw' with his Oxford accent, and his manners were perfect.

A few days later, or it may even have been the very next day, the change was startling. Gone was the English suit—he now wore Pathan clothes. He spoke only Pushtu and squatted cross-legged on a *charpoy* to draw on a *hookah* while chatting with his friends, the Congress and Red Shirt *Wallahs*. The Kabul *coup* was also being discussed freely. Sometime previously Bach-i-Saque the son of a water carrier had ousted King Amanullah from the Afghanistan throne and the ex-king had departed into exile. Another gentleman, Nadir Khan, got support from some Mahsuds and Wazirs under pretence of regaining the throne for Amanullah, but when he succeeded, he retained the throne for himself.

The British were not too happy about all this, as the Mahsuds and Wazirs were Frontier tribes, and the idea might have got around that they were meddling in Afghan affairs. Above all they wanted a stable political situation in Afghanistan to counteract the possible trouble with the Frontier tribes and the trouble-mongers amongst the local Congress and Red Shirts. Some idea of the political issues is necessary to the story to show how we nurses became involved in the Frontier 'wars,' and how some of us were fortunate enough to get the 1930-31 Frontier Medal with its green and black ribbon and Fort Jamrud on the reverse.

Menelaus had two lucky breaks about this time. She went to Kabul to nurse the *burra memsahib* in the British Legation, and then later was flown to Chitral to nurse the political agent. This I believe was an appendix case as a surgeon went with her. If I had been in when they came for a sister for this case I might have had the chance of going, I was told, and was mad with myself for missing the opportunity.

In 1931 I came to know some missionaries. This party consisted of Mr. and Mrs. Barrington and their twin babies, Helen and John. With them was Mrs. Barrington's sister, Claire Trumpler. The women were French-Swiss. The Barringtons were on their way to Leh in Ladakh, where the Chinese have now infiltrated. At the time I met these people I was going through a phase. I was 'pi' as we used to say as student nurses—religious, attending Bible classes and prayer meetings. Through these I came to know a middle-aged man called Jim Clark—Uncle Jim as I came to call him later.

Mr. and Mrs. Barrington asked me to join their party to provide the medical side of the expedition: I would have some of the local girls to train as *dais* and was promised a free hand to get this side of things organised. This project appealed to me, I liked the chance of adventure and travel, apart from the fact that I should be doing a useful job. I wrote and put the whole thing to Mama, and though I badly wanted to go I was determined I would not make her unhappy. Her reply was what I half expected. She was very distressed, and a very reluctant but firm "No" had to be given.

This was not going to be a picnic; for anyone. The Barringtons would have to build a house on arrival, "Just a hut" I was told, as no accommodation was available. Tents and a certain amount of provisions were being carried, and when these ran out they were prepared to live off the country. Some called them inspired, some called them foolish. Apparently Miss Creighton had asked Mrs. Barrington what she would do if one of the twins developed appendicitis. "I would kneel down, pray and then operate myself," was the answer.

"Well! I think she would, and she would be successful," I said, and then the way they all stared at me made me wish I had not spoken. We were at breakfast whilst discussing this, so then I had to explain that I had raised one or two points like that when we were discussing the possibility of my joining them. I had told Mr. Barrington that to me the difficulties seemed unsurmountable, and he had quoted the passage from Corinthians including the words "..... *and though I have all faith so that I could remove mountains.*"

"I believe they will succeed," I said, "you see, I have been converted." I tried not to sound too smug. However they did not take me as seriously as I should have liked; some of them laughed. Mrs. Williams said, "you are too fond of the boys and dancing, my girl, to make a missionary," while Mrs. Breithaupt added, "you'll grow out of it. Green."

In March of that year Llew came up to Peshawar to see me for the second time. He was the fellow I had met on that all-night picnic at Juhu. He had been up the year before, and had brought me a small gift then as now, a leather bound volume of Kipling with the date and a little message written on the fly-leaf. He had to tour the North on business ending at Lahore, but each time kindly decided to look me up. It was while he was on this second visit that he noticed a change in me. "These people have influenced you," he said. We had a good time while he was there; we dined and danced at the club, played tennis and went to the pictures.

After this visit I was 'blue' until I met a fellow with a motorbike. I had never been on one of these before and enjoyed pillion-riding. At night we would ride round, the perimeter along North and South Circular Road, and I would urge him to go faster and faster! This must have blown away the cobwebs as I talked less now about being converted and gradually the pious air evaporated, and I returned wholeheartedly to flirting, dancing and enjoying everything that came my way; this was the girl Llew had known! The sisters were kind, they let me down lightly. I cannot remember a single "I told you so!"

It was on that first leave in 1930 that the name "Frontier Nurse" was given to me, and for years afterwards I was called this. My family and friends were never tired of asking about the N.W.F. and I had much to tell them, though on my second leave I had many more exciting tales to relate. When on holiday I hardly went out, I was glad to go to bed early and sleep late. Then to eat all my favourite meals which a doting Mama was pleased to supply. For the return journey I decided to take the Frontier Mail as this cut out twelve hours off the long journey going by the Peshawar Express *via* Khandwar and Jhansi.

I left Mhow at 1 a.m. on Saturday and arrived at Rutlam just in time to catch the Frontier Mail which rushed in from Bombay at 6.40 a.m. This only halted for about ten minutes and it was a nightmare trying to get into the Ladies' Compartment. We had to dodge the bearers carrying *chota hazri* trays to the upper class passengers, balancing a tray with teapot, milk, sugar, toast and crockery on each palm held shoulder high, whilst they cleverly dodged between frenzied third class passengers heavily laden with pots, pans, bundles and lengths of sugar cane, and passengers like myself who were being assisted to the right compartments by a platform inspector, followed by one or two *coolies* carrying the luggage.

All this took time, then getting up to the Ladies' Compartment more time was wasted, as these doors were usually found bolted at this hour in the morning against thieves, and the harassed inspector had to convince the occupants that he was a genuine railway employee before they would unbolt the doors.

By this time the guard of the crack India Express was waving his green flag and the inspector just about picked me up and threw me in, and my luggage after me. That night at 8 p.m. we were in Delhi

161

and Sunday morning at Lahore. Once again I found I was the only woman left in the Ladies' Compartment to complete the journey to the Frontier, so when the ticket collector came to inspect my ticket, I was prepared for him to mention my 'special guard'—when he did not I decided to ask about him. The ticket collector then explained that it was only when the journey; into the N.W.F.P. took place at night that a woman travelling alone in the Peshawar Express was given a guard. As I always took the Frontier Mail from then onwards, I never again saw my 'special guard.' The Frontier Mail arrived in Peshawar about 9 p.m.

CHAPTER 20

Frontier War

Arriving in the hospital grounds I was surprised to see the army in occupation, British and Indian troops were moving around, and mules stood about under the large *pipul* tree. "What's going on here?" I asked stepping on to the verandah, then two of the sisters came into my room to give me all the news as I unpacked. It was clear that the Bombay papers had given us very scanty news of the Peshawar riots, and I was glad of this, because Mama would have been most unhappy at my returning if she had known the whole truth.

On April 24th, 1930, the city had rioted and Congress Volunteers had taken over control with the aid of the Red Shirts. "*Inquilab Zindabad*"—"Up the Revolution"—was shouted loudly in defiance. That night after Sister Williams had tucked up her last patient for the night, and was settling down to a nice 'cuppa', the front door was suddenly flung open and Major Dimond rushed upstairs to tell her to get all her patients up and dressed again, as the situation was serious. A fleet of cars had been sent from Government House to evacuate the European patients and staff. Some went to Government House, others to Deane's Hotel, and two, a mother and daughter, went to their own home with Williams to nurse them.

"Jolly!" I said, after Williams had finished speaking, "I have missed a lot of excitement. Just like me to be away when things happen."

"You'll get your share of excitement, Green, it's not finished yet," I was promised. Then I was told, "The army are in Bolton: they have completely taken it over—we have no patients there now."

We had officers with British and Indian troops, mules, sandbags, guns, telephones, the lot—all over the place, and it did seem strange to me. The peaceful block I had left had entirely vanished. Getting into

Bolton was tricky now, one had to jump over sandbags and squeeze through a narrow opening between walls of sandbags built up before the door. Behind this defence work stood a burly Sikh Guard with his rifle chained to his body; all the doors leading into Bolton were so guarded. Most of the rooms upstairs were occupied by officers, the rooms downstairs were now taken over by B.O.R.s and I.O.R.s, and one was fitted up as an office with army telephones, charts and other necessities.

Where our Hindu clerks had been transferred I never knew, but doubtless the *babus* were glad to get away from those fierce looking armed Sikhs. Walking to the dining room that first morning I could hear shouts of laughter and men's voices. "What fun," I thought, then on our hat rack on the verandah I saw a strange looking object. Later I learnt this was a field telephone. Officers' caps and jackets occupied the pegs that usually received our veils. When I stepped inside Mrs. Williams introduced me as "The baby of our mess."

Whilst breakfasting I heard an unfamiliar sound, great '*BOOM-BOOMS.*' "Are those guns?" I asked, "they seem very close."

A silly ass of a sub thought I was nervous and replied soothingly, "they are guns, but they are really quite far away, and you are safe."

I turned on him indignantly and replied, "I am *not* frightened!"

Now each meal was a party. The officers brought us juicy bits of news from the city, and every now and again there would be great shouts of laughter. A curfew was ordered and one night some Hindus were found breaking this: the 'Tommies' tried to get them indoors peacefully, but they pretended not to understand the *boli* so a little gentle persuasion with a bayonet was found necessary. A fat *babu* getting this stuck in his rump moved quickly and a surprised Cockney was heard to exclaim, "Cor blimey, doesn't it go in easily!"

Each night a very senior political, I think the D.C., anyway he was Mr. O.K. Caroe, came and had coffee in our mess before going up with the officers to sleep in Bolton. His presence was necessary as his permission had to be given before the troops could fire. The following *Ruthless Rhymes* explains much better than I can some of the complications concerning polities, civil law and the task of the army at that time.

RUTHLESS RHYMES FOR FRONTIER FORCES

There was a large force in Peshawar
Who stood at their post by the hour.

The Pathans by surprise
Right under their eyes
Burnt the dump and went off with the flour.

There were also Waziristan Scouts,
Who left their remotest redoubts
To help a division
To gain a decision
In the requisite number of bouts.

The Afridis advancing by bounds
Were met by the rendering sounds
Of the roaring propellers
Of R.A.F. Fellers
Patrolling the aerodrome grounds.

The Lashkars remained in full view
For all of them very well knew
Our Political purity
Gave them security
From all that the Air Force could do.

The Civil was shocked to the core
At disturbances so much like war,
The Police were appalled,
The D.C. grew bald,
And the Hindus made tracks for Lahore.

If only the Powers that Be
Would see what the rest of us see,
That the stronger the hand
We display to this band,
How better for both it would be.

These words were given to me by a sub but I have forgotten by whom, and have no idea who wrote it. As we had the Essex, the K.O.Y.L.I., the H.L.I., 2nd/11th Sikhs, Signals and others in turn it may have been an officer from any of these. We had the troops stationed with us for four to six months, as the riots were followed by the Afridi 'war'. There was always a 'war' going on somewhere or other in the N.W.F.P. Some were gazetted, others, not. Even in 'peaceful' times the snipers were active, and some unfortunate unsuspecting Britisher would be killed or wounded unnecessarily.

It was when the 2nd/11th Sikhs were with us that it became necessary for us to leave our bungalow and sleep in Bolton, as a special guard could not be spared for us. After dinner each night we would pack our toothbrushes, a change of uniform and a few valuables into *attaché* cases, which the officers very kindly carried up for us. As I was the youngest, Major J. Smythe, V.C. picked up my case and when he did this for the first time, the subaltern I was following with whispered, "You should be honoured." I whispered in reply, "Of course I am honoured," and through the years I have been grateful for this memory—a 'proud' moment—you see in company with the subalterns I adored Jackie Smythe. I always had a weakness for the older man and here was one with a V.C. attached! He was kind, too, as I think it was this O.C. who ordered a subaltern to take me out. "Go to the pictures you two young ones, it will do you both good." It was all the encouragement we needed; though I did not fail to notice the sickly smile on Miss Snob's face, and the poison flowed more freely from then onwards.

In Bolton Menelaus and I shared a room, the sisters had to double up as accommodation was limited. We were lulled to sleep by the clanking of the chains of the guard; it was a comforting though unusual lullaby. One night after we had got to Bolton we younger ones collected in the duty room for a final nightcap. One of the fellows opened a bottle of beer by pulling off the crown cork over the bolt attachment on the door. This made a loud bang and the sub. was drenched in foaming beer. We shrieked with laughter, but soon stopped guiltily, when in the doorway we saw the D.C. in his pyjamas with his revolver in his hand. We apologised in chorus, he nodded and silently turned away; and we were left wondering if we would be reported, but he was a sport.

Then another time Menelaus and I got into trouble. Until she learnt to drive the car she had bought a Pathan driver was engaged, and the three of us were often out together. Abdul was friendly and jolly, but had a peculiar sense of humour; he enjoyed our embarrassment when with Menelaus at the wheel, suddenly the car would choke, cough, splutter and then die. It was terrible when this happened amongst a herd of goats, and worse still when we were leaving the Golf Club. The members sitting on the lawn, especially the men, would laugh and clap. Getting into the car I would beg Menelaus, "don't let it happen here, oh, *please* don't let it happen here." And invariably it did.

One Sunday we decided to drive to Kohat forty miles away through the Darrah Pass. We did not think it was necessary to inform anyone where we were going before we left the mess. On the way Abdul suggested a visit to the rifle factory in tribal territory where the Adam Khel Afridis made the local version of the Lee Enfield 303 rifles—he told us he had friends there and assured us we would be quite safe as his guests. Hospitality amongst the Pathans is sacred: and guests or enemies *asking* for shelter are unharmed. Once departed the feuds are resumed.

The factory was crude and rough—nothing like even the smallest factory in this country—and how those rifles were made there I could not imagine. They were kind enough to try and explain, then abandoning the attempt offered us sherbets and fruit—this was better. Here the little Pushtu we had acquired came in useful. Menelaus had her camera with her and was tempted to take a snapshot of the factory—but she was not sure whether they would approve, so kept the camera hidden—until we got out on the road again. At the fork of two roads stands a board marked "Tribal Territory." This was the demarcation line between proper provincial authority—and tribal areas where chiefs were paid for "keeping the peace."

When we got back to the mess at the next meal we mentioned this visit to the factory. The effect was startling—the officers nearly hit the ceiling! And we were severely scolded. Later, one of the subs remarked, "I don't know how you two dared, you are probably the only white women who have visited that factory unaccompanied." I explained that we had not gone out of bravado or to seek notoriety: it seemed a natural thing as we were near for Abdul to suggest we call on his friends. That drive was the last we were able to take going really far, as the situation had worsened.

About this time someone, a political 'high-up' no doubt, gave orders that the sisters had to take a police guard when they went to the golf course, which was outside the perimeter. On the Frontier to the normal hazards of the game was added the risk of attacks by some idle Pathan who wished to discover the reactions of the British to a bullet overhead. Mounted policemen or sentries unobtrusively patrolled the links until the last player had disappeared behind the shelter of the barbed wire. Even golf on the Frontier had an element of the heroic. So now going to golf or to the club—if we were without a European male escort—either singly or in pairs, the *tonga* had to pull up at our

167

police post by the hospital gate for a guard to jump in and sit beside the *tonga wallah*, who I am quite sure did not relish having a loaded rifle sticking into his ribs.

Once over the railway bridge at the cantonment gates the *tonga* stopped to allow the guard to jump out; he was left to chat and take a turn at the *hookah* with his friends the police on duty here, until out return. Going to tennis or golf in sport clothes with an armed guard escort seemed incongruous and I felt ridiculous. Even so I found this 'war' exciting and often whilst walking along the covered pathway between the wards I wanted to skip, and would have to pull myself up with the thought that this for a sister was unseemly behaviour.

One day at lunch I shocked the matron. The officers had just finished relating an exciting incident and I exclaimed without thinking, "Oh! I wish this war would go on forever." The men roared with laughter, but Miss Creighton rebuked me, "Miss Green I am shocked at you," whilst Chris Grayrigge (Signals) thumped me on the back and said, "Good old Daphne,"—this was his name for me.

When the officers were first billeted on us the subs asked me my name. "You heard when we were introduced, it's Green—Miss Green." As they were calling the other sisters Miss So-and-so and Mrs. So-and-so, I thought this the correct answer—but not they! So each one gave me a different name. I found this confusing but was told this served me right. I was "Jessie" to one that thought I looked like Jessie Mathews—I apologise to her. Another said, "As you are the youngest and least important you are "Tuppence." "Ever-Green-Eye" was one I did not like. The silliest one was "Baby-Face."

If we had our fun, excitement and jokes we also had our tragedies.

On May 31st or June 1st, at Kabuli Gate, a K.O.Y.L.I. sentry discharged his rifle accidentally killing two Sikh children and wounding their mother. They were in a *tonga*. The woman was brought into our hospital and taken to the theatre; very soon we had a howling mob of Sikhs round this building, they crowded onto the verandahs and even tried to get inside, and it took the strength and courage of our Pathan compounders to keep them out. She was nursed in one of the private cottages and was given V.I.P. treatment. We were told to nurse her as if our lives depended on it, which was probably true! Serious riots followed this unfortunate accident and a British despatch rider was killed, an armoured car after having petrol thrown over it was set alight; the crew (K.O.Y.L.I.) managed to escape. At about this time to add to the confusion and distress part of an Indian regiment mutinied, but this was quickly suppressed.

CHAPTER 21

Afridis—and Guest Nights

For some time now the authorities were getting anxious about the sisters being outside the safety of the perimeter; it was suggested we spend the nights in cantonments, returning in the mornings. We did not think much of this idea. However in the end we had to move, as early in August the R.A.F. reported a *lashkar* of Afridis estimated at 6,000 strong advancing on Peshawar. They had been told by Congress that the British regime was coming to an end: further encouragement was given by way of cash.

On the 9th August at 5 p.m. the first Afridi attack in 'K' supply depot, roughly northeast of our hospital took place. When someone came rushing into the ward where I was working and said, "Come along quickly, the Afridis are almost on our doorstep." I thought it was a joke! Then I was told that Major Dimond was at our bungalow with cars to evacuate us. We were barely given time to pack toothbrushes. I was pushed into the back of a car with one of the sisters, an officer sat with the driver. The car in front was packed the same way and off we went, trying to get into cantonments, as quickly as possible.

I can still remember the surprise and indignation I felt when just before we got to the bridge over the railway, I saw an Afridi bullet spatter the dust behind the car. I called attention to this and then told them of a conversation I had had only the day before with an old Afridi patient; he was telling us how grateful he was for the attention he had received.

"Then why do you want to kill us?" I asked.

"No, no, we will never kill the sisters! I have told my friends how kind you have been—you will not be harmed," he had promised.

The officer seemed sceptical. "I don't think much of your old Afridi boyfriend's promise, sister—I think we have got you out just in time!"

On arriving in cantonments we were taken straight to the Q.A. Mess where we were given tea. That night we slept in a large bare room—I cannot remember in which building this was, but British soldiers were on guard in the grounds. This was very comforting. We shared this dormitory with several Eurasian women and were surprised to see them as we had no idea there were so many in Peshawar. There they were huddled together whispering in their soft 'chee-chee' voices when we blew in from the Q.A.'s Mess, after a good dinner with drinks which had been added "to fortify your spirits," we were told, not that in my case it was needed: I was 'bubbly' enough. Thoroughly enjoying all the excitement. A rumour had gone round that all the nursing sisters and these women were to be evacuated by 'plane in the morning to Rawalpindi. I was looking forward to this, but alas, it was found to be unnecessary, as after a heavy defeat round the city the Afridis had withdrawn.

That night, the sherry taking effect, I slept so soundly that not even the firing that took place in the garden below awakened me. I was furious when I heard the women discussing this in the morning, "Oh, why didn't I wake—why didn't someone wake me?" I cried. Matron told me she thought it was more sleep I needed, not more excitement. Anyway I was consoled; that morning before leaving I was given an Afridi bullet that was picked up in the garden. A raider or two had actually managed to get into cantonments and had tried their favourite pastime of sniping but from trees and not from behind rocks for a change.

We had breakfast in Deane's Hotel that morning and then returned to the hospital. Leaving again for cantonments just before it got dark. We slept in the hotel now, this was grand as we had nice dinners, soft lights and sweet music at government expense. So I could never understand why the men felt sorry for us, I suppose they thought it was a tedious business, this travelling to and fro, and I noticed on occasions when a senior civil servant appeared, to impress him one or two of our sisters put on a serious expression. This I was unable to copy.

One day I was up in Family Block when an orderly came running to call me as the sisters had been ordered to leave for cantonments at once; this was hours before our usual evening flight. I have forgotten now what was wrong—fresh riots, or another Afridi visit but what upset me was the way the women patients got round me, clinging to me and begging me not to leave them. If they had been just Hindu I could have understood. The Afridis would have liked nothing better than to get hold of a Jewel-laden, fat, juicy Hindu *bebe*, but most of these had fled to Lahore at the outbreak of the riots which were started, anyway, as anti-British. Possibly the patients knew this might be an opportunity for old scores to be settled: or just for the fun of it—fresh feuds started. The state of emergency continued for a while, then with an improvement we were allowed to sleep in our bungalow again. The army came back to Bolton, and the officers used our mess again.

After dinner we sat outside and talked; sometimes we had our gramophone going. They were a new lot of men, and one of the subalterns was musical, strumming and singing to us on his banjo. One of the songs he chose was "The Ladies" by Kipling from *Barrack Room Ballads*; rather suggestive and hurtful to any Anglo-Indian. I am sure this was just an unfortunate choice. However, I had schooled myself pretty well by now, and never batted an eyelid when they discussed scathingly the 'chee-chee' or O.T.C.'s. Miss Snobb very often steered the conversation round this way, or would make a point of speaking of 'Home.' Often I would get involved, then she would say patronisingly, "sorry, Green, I've forgotten, you wouldn't know what we are talking about!" Smarting terribly on one of these occasions I vowed that as soon as my five years here were up I would go to England for that 'midder' even if I had to walk there. Then I would return and speak of 'Home.' Thus was my ambition fanned by a poor frustrated female.

Before leaving Bolton, when transferred, the officers or C.O. would come over to say "Goodbye," and to thank us for the use of our mess. One lot promised to have a Khattack dance arranged for us. I was pleased when I heard this as I had been told so much about it. However something went wrong with the plans and it never took place. Though we did have a Ladies' Guest Night laid on especially for us, by the 2nd/11th Sikhs, when Jackie Smythe was host. We had the band in attendance and all the trimmings. Masses of silver down the centre of the table which was bare. The sides were covered by two narrow tablecloths; and before dessert the Goanese steward did some sort of conjuring trick with these; we were told to watch very carefully whilst he stood at one end, whistled or muttered "*Abracadabra*" and the cloth swiftly folded up concertina fashion. Before dinner we were shown round the mess. There were masses of cups and shields on display, and in a glass cabinet all by itself was the silver book for their Roll-of-Honour. After dinner we danced. It was a lovely evening and I have been grateful all through the years for this happy memory.

Then we had a second guest night given us by the Essex. I do know we had them in Bolton and the officers used our mess, as I have an amusing pen and ink cartoon done on Essex notepaper and sent to me by 2nd Lieut. Paynter, who was one of their officers. This depicts what is alleged to have happened after the R.A.F. had reported a *lashkar* of Afridis on the Kajuri Plains, and a platoon or so of the Essex were ordered out. On arriving, taking up position and firing big guns all they found was a very frightened little shepherd boy with his *dhumbas*. Mind you I am not saying that this story is true! Those subs made an awful lot up as they went along.

This second guest night, given by the Essex is remembered by Sister Williams very clearly, I have recently been in contact with her and she has refreshed my memory. Apparently we had such a hectic evening that we never got back to the hospital until crack of dawn— we danced all night! "Don't you remember how foolish we felt in evening dress coming home at that hour in *tongas?*" I was asked. I have a pretty good suspicion that I must have been persuaded to have more than one glass of sherry because the memory of this guest night is blotted out—more's the pity! And what she went on to say confirmed this, "Don't you remember the lovely Christmas pudding and the glasses and glasses of champagne?" These she reminded me were supplied by the Duchess of York—now our Queen Mother—who is their Colonel-in-Chief. Those 'glasses and glasses of champagne' must have been the trouble: I probably spent most of the evening asleep on the verandah sofa after the final glass. At this point Mrs. Williams and I got into an argument; she says that it was at this dinner that the table-cloth trick was done by the steward. Now I can distinctly remember this being done at the 2nd/11th Sikh guest night. So which of us is right? I still do not know.

Now things at the hospital were back to normal. The army had left Bolton Block and we were on our own again. We felt that this was rather an anti-climax, or at least I did: then once again we had some excitement. This was at Christmas 1930. We had *tongas* ordered to take us to church on Christmas morning. When *chota*, was brought in by Kareem Bux he told me, "the *gora log*," (literally the 'white people,' the colloquial Indian name for British troops) "are back, and they have stopped the *tongas* from getting in, so you will not be going to church, Miss Sahib."

"Are the Afridis back—or have the riots started again, Kareem Bux?" I asked, sitting up. He could not tell me.

We finished breakfast quickly and got over to the hospital to get the news. The British had decided 'General' Abdul Guffar Khan and his brother Dr. Khan Sahib had gone far enough, and in the middle of the night our politicals had carted them off to jail. The timing was cute, taken by surprise the *coup* was peacefully effected. However, taking no chances, the authorities had troops placed around the city—just in case.

It was the strangest Christmas Day I have ever spent. We felt we were sitting on a volcano, and seeing the fully armed B.O.R.'s chewing turkey under the *pipul* trees by Bolton, whilst the patient heavy-laden signals mules stood around made an unusual though hardly 'peaceful' Christmas scene. The manoeuvre was called off fairly quickly. There were no incidents, at least we heard of none, and the city was quiet but sullen—this uneasy peace lasted until July 1932,

After Major Huban left, we had Captain Coldstream as our superintendent. He was thirty-two, kind and had very informal loveable ways. Whilst talking to a patient or a doctor he usually placed a hand upon the man's arm or shoulder. An orderly passing carrying *roti* tucked under his arm—most unhygienic, but a way they had—never went unnoticed. The captain would shoot out a hand and nip off a piece to eat as he went along on his round. Matron was shocked at this. "He really should not do that," she would say, but the Pathans loved it, one day when a blood donor was needed the captain was the first to volunteer, and his blood was used to save the life of a Hindu woman.

CHAPTER 22

Murder by the Stairs

That summer he was a dinner guest in our mess on two or three occasions. He reciprocated by taking us to dine at the club, or to play golf. This was a new craze of mine, so he gave me a lesson. One morning I did a round with him in the ward under my care, then parted with him before Medico-Legal; what happened there I heard later from the sister who was in charge. To his surprise and annoyance he found a Congress *wallah* holding forth haranguing the patients. Captain Coldstream asked this man whose permission he had obtained before entering and speaking. Then in the manner of most educated British-haters this *babu* became offensive and was summarily ordered out. When Captain Coldstream finished the round of the ward he went on to the next, and then to the theatre before making for the duty room and coffee. I met him again on the way there, we were the first two so I poured out. He asked me then if I was still keen on golf.

"Would you like another lesson this evening?"

"Oh, yes, please, as you are so kind and patient," was my reply. Then I left my coffee to see where Menelaus was, as she was due to go off duty at 11 and it was getting late.

Just outside the door leaning against the wall I saw a compounder, who was from the dispensary which was near the back gate that led to the city. He had a sheaf of papers in his hand. "Do you want the Captain *Sahib* to sign those, Abdul Rashid?" I asked, pointing to the forms.

"No, Sister *Sahib*—they can wait," and with that he moved away and ran downstairs, I went to the back door and looked out towards the wards, there I saw Menelaus talking to one of the doctors, so I turned back. At the top of the stairs I met the captain who had finished his coffee, and as he ran down he called out, "I'll collect you at 5 p.m. then," and he smiled and waved. I stood where I was until he disappeared behind a thick column at the bottom of the stairs, where he had to turn into the corridor that led to his office.

I had just about reached the duty room door, which was only about three paces from the top of the stairs, when a peculiar muffled noise reached me. Then there was shouting and the sound of running footsteps. More shouting came from outside Bolton. I knew something was wrong so ran out to the verandah and looked down; I saw three or four men running towards the gate: one was dressed in the white coat of a compounder. Then on hearing shouts of "Sister! Sister, come soon!" I turned back and ran to the top of the stairs. Looking down I saw two clerks carrying Captain Coldstream upstairs. There was blood all over his coat and it was spurting from his throat.

"What has happened?" I screamed.

"He has been beaten," replied one of the clerks in English.

The other then added correctly in Hindi, "he has been knifed."

They had got to the top now and I moved before them to fling open the door to a room vacant opposite the duty room. "Put him in here, and call matron—call Major Dimond, call them all," I said wildly in my distraction, as I could see he was dying rapidly from the ghastly wounds. Matron was the first to arrive, then Sister Williams and her theatre staff, soon the room and corridor seemed full of people. When this help had arrived I turned into the duty room and saw his coffee cup which was still warm. I picked it up and cupping it with both hands held it tightly then put it down. I now noticed my own cup half full, then moving into the lavatory I was sick. There I stayed crying and being sick alternately. After a while I decided I would look for Menelaus.

Outside by the backdoor that opened on to the pathway leading to the hospital, amongst a crowd of doctors, compounders, orderlies and policemen, I saw Abdul Rashid with an arm held out stiffly, and this was bleeding. Noticing this I stopped and asked sympathetically, "Have you been wounded too, Abdul Rashid?"

No one answered, and I was given some queer looks which I did not understand. Then I met Menelaus outside the theatre where they had taken Captain Coldstream. "He is dead," she whispered, and then I learnt that it was Abdul Rashid who was the assassin. I just could not believe I had heard correctly.

"I thought it was an unfriendly Afridi or a Congress *wallah*—someone from the city," I told her and added, "I thought Abdul Rashid had gone to his assistance and was wounded that way. He had hung about the duty room while the captain was there; I even spoke to him and asked him what he wanted!"

We were told later that after the incident in Medico-Legal between Captain Coldstream and the Congress agitator, someone had tipped this compounder *Rs*300/- to turn murderer. With this intention he had followed Captain Coldstream to the duty room, but my being in there stopped him—why, I do not know, unless he thought, "if she goes to his assistance I'll have to kill her as well," and he did not fancy killing a woman. After I questioned him he had run downstairs and hidden behind that thick pillar. As the captain turned round this he sprang out and drove a knife into his lungs. Captain Coldstream turned and grabbed his assailant's wrist, this is how the knife point pierced his arm. Abdul Rashid freed his hand and struck again, this time he severed the jugular vein and carotid artery. When the clerks reached him Captain Coldstream whispered, "take me upstairs—I am dying." So that evening instead of playing golf with him I attended his funeral, walking behind the coffin with the matron and sisters. At that moment I hated the N.W.F.P.—that violent yet fascinating country.

After the murder we were asked out frequently, the men were kind. They either called and took us out, or spent the evenings with us. I accepted all the invitations that came my way—I was out for good clean fun—and mostly that is how it was. Occasionally when the return expected was more than I was prepared to pay this association was swiftly ended. Sooner or later someone else came along; and in the meantime there was always 'Uncle Jim'. However, there was a young buck who fancied his chances; he was more persistent and blunt. One evening returning from the pictures I was asked outright if I was still a virgin. This shook me. "I want the truth," I was warned.

"The truth is simple. I am still a virgin, and mean to remain that way, and now shall we talk of something else, do you mind. I find this slightly embarrassing."

"I do mind," was the surprising reply. "You see, I want to make sure. I must be sure, as I have only your word for it."

This brought me sitting bolt upright. "Josh! How dare you? If we were not outside the perimeter, and if I was not frightened some

Pathan would get hold of me and find out what you would like to prove, I would make you stop the car and get out and walk!"

"Oh, don't be silly, Jessie—you know all nurses have a name for being 'hot stuff'"

"Thank you, but you are wrong. Not all, some of us *are* different."

Apropos of this there was a misunderstanding on another occasion which had its humorous angle. I asked one of the superintendents for an interview, which one it was I am not sure, as we had three or four in the five years I was there. "I want to see you alone—not in the duty room, or anywhere in the hospital where matron can come barging in."

"Yes, of course, Miss Green, come to my house," and a time was mentioned. I went along to lay my troubles before him.

Matron had been going for me lately, and on more than one occasion had hinted that my job was in jeopardy. It was not that I had done anything wrong, but she was cross with us all, and getting at the others through me. One cause of trouble was the evening report. She wanted us to come off duty and go to her private sitting room and stand and read this to her like the evening lesson. The sisters said this was wrong. If she wanted the report she should go to the duty room for it, in uniform. When we left the hospital and were in the bungalow we were off duty. Personally I did not mind the idea of going to her room, but the others told me I had to stand by them.

Then there was some trouble over our coal supplies. Matron said we were using it too freely in Bolton and the stock was low. She warned us that we might have to give up our own ration for the patients. This we refused to consider, we said the indent should have been made out properly. I found out from the others that they were not being told off as strongly as I was, and their jobs had not been threatened. How I resented this, especially when for the sake of peace I would gladly have given up my coal. Not only that but I was quite prepared to present the report in the *ghusul khanna* if it pleased her ladyship.

All this I poured out to the super. "Why is she picking on me? Can she dismiss me summarily? If she does, it might be too late to come to you then—so I thought you had better know it all beforehand."

He laughed. "Oh, you silly girl—I thought it was something quite different," and he looked relieved. "Run along now, and forget your troubles. She cannot dismiss you entirely on her own, I should have to be consulted." We talked for a while, then taking me to the door he repeated, "and I thought it was something much more serious; something quite different." It was only that night lying in bed going over all this wretched business I wondered what he meant. Then suddenly I saw light. Goodness gracious, did he think? Well If he thought what I think he thought—no wonder he sounded and looked so relieved!. . . . . . . No one believes I am a good girl, I thought miserably before falling asleep.

No one, except Uncle Jim Clark. I often took my troubles to him. I told him how difficult it all was. He was sympathetic, "'Phone me whenever you are free or feeling blue; remember you always have me," and he would pat my head. He was a lay-preacher, a missionary of sorts—a little more than middle-aged and fat. He ran socials for his flock and when able I went along to help entertain the soldiers: we played parlour games, and there were competitions. The other women and girls present were mostly non-club members.

Uncle Jim could not drive a car himself, so kept a Pathan driver. The car was always sent for me after I phoned and my favourite eats arranged. For tea lashings of mulberries and cream. This luscious green-purple and very sweet fruit grew in his garden. If I dined with him, there would be a spring chicken. One or two of the sisters were suspicious about this friendship: they just could not believe it was purely platonic. This made me mad, and I told Menelaus. "Why, he's old enough to be my father! How can they have such vulgar minds."

"*Let them say what they say*," she quoted.

"When I am alone with him he behaves in the same manner as when you or others are around," than I added. "It's such a comfortable feelings I can relax with him, not having to be always on one's guard is a relief." She nodded, and I continued. "When the car stops it *is* to admire the view, and for no other reason."

Well so it was—for a long time, and then little Irene had a rude awakening. One day the driver was told to stop; he usually wandered away a short distance to sit and smoke until called. Now Uncle Jim did a most unusual thing, he picked up my hand and began shyly to stroke it; I felt silly! Then after a long silence—in which I had time to conquer a mad impulse to get out of the car and run—he asked me to marry him! I thought: has he suddenly gone mad or am I having a nightmare? After a few moments of confusion I found my voice and thanking him for the honour he was doing me I emphasised the difference in our ages; then brought in Queen Charlotte's and the 'midder.' I prayed frantically for the right things to say as I did not want to hurt him. I ended with, "you have been kind to me, and I am grateful." He did not press the point, and we finished the drive. I saw him just a few times after that—but never alone. Then I heard he had suddenly left Peshawar and I was relieved.

CHAPTER 23

Frontier Finery

One of my nicest winter memories of Peshawar is the Fraser-Bolam wedding. I remember particularly the huge white flower-covered bell the bride and groom stood beneath to receive their guests, and when a few years later Doreen married, I made one for her and her husband.

Another pleasant memory I have is the dinner party given by Eric Wilkinson, one of the young masters from Islamia College. Only young unmarrieds were at this, and after dinner we went on to the club dance. I had wanted a new dress, but after the expense of the dress for the Fraser-Bolam wedding, I felt I could not afford it. So I decided to freshen my old white organdie evening dress.

Next morning in Family Block I hung back until the doctors had gone ahead, then getting the old *dai* to one side I whispered to her to get the bazaar *dirzee* there that afternoon. After lunch, returning to duty, I took my organdie in a pillowslip up with me. When the *dirzee* arrived the *dai* came for me. I did not want to be caught at this frivolity in the duty room by anyone in authority so picking up the pillowslip I hastened to 'Families.' There with the *dai* squatting by my side I showed the *dirzee* my sketch of alterations and explained what he had to do. "From this yard of muslin make a cape like this; then take this dress and remove the sleeves, make a petticoat top and add wide shoulder straps. *Samajtha* (Understand)?" He nodded. Encouraged, I continued. "Then sew the yellow and green ribbon round the hats in alternate rows."

As he was not a *pukka dirzee*, to help him I sketched as I went along: but I had reckoned without the patients. In a very short time every Pathan woman who could had left her bed and crowded round us, each one making her own suggestion; in the meantime breathing onion and garlic over us, this with the stink of iodoforms and sweat was a bit much in that heat, and I wondered if after all I had been wise in coming up here. Perhaps one of the *ghusul khannas* in Bolton— bolted against intruders—might have been better, but would the *dirzee* have objected? Anyway, at last getting the idea he packed his bundle and was glad to leave.

This is the sort of thing the Pathan and Indian women love, discussing clothes, cooking, homes and children. Here I had the advantage over the other sisters in being able to speak *Urdu*. So now through the *dais* the *Pushtu wallahs* heard all about the dance; and they were delighted when I clasped the fat old *dai* round the waist and waltzed her about to show them how it was done. "Do the men and women really hold each other like that?" I was asked. "*Thoba thoba, Bapre Bap*", expressed their shock. Though a little girl showed her approval, clapping her hands she shouted, "*Shebash!" Shebash!*" Next day, just before the lunch break I noticed the old *dai* hovering outside Bolton. When I got up to her, looking round carefully, she whispered, "The *dirzee* has arrived and your dress looks very pretty."

I had visions of the Pathan women pawing my dress, so grabbing up the bunch of little yellow silk rosebuds I had made to slip into the green velvet ribbon tying at the waist, I flew along with the old *dai*, waddling after me. After inspecting the work I asked the *dirzee* how much I owed him. The figure named was twice what it should have been, but with so many pairs of eyes fixed on me I did not argue! His "*Bahut, bahut, salaam*, Miss *Sahib*," confirmed my suspicions, and I knew full well the old *dai* would collect a rake-off later. After he left I slipped the posy in position and held the dress up for all to see. They begged me to get into it. "We'll make this old *buddis* sit outside in the pathway, and call out if she sees the Matron *Sahib,* coming." The old woman referred to shook her head in agreement, and said she would cough loudly three times if matron appeared.

I knew there was no need for this signal as matron was in the mess. It was not her I was thinking about, but I was remembering a similar scene years before when Doreen and I were children at a village tea-party when they laughed at our long old-fashioned white cotton bloomers. What would these Pathan matrons say to my short, pink, lace-trimmed panties? I dare not risk it so being a coward I said, "No, thank you."

The following evening I knew my dress was a success. I guessed this from the sour looks I got from the girls when I walked into the sitting-room where the guests had collected. Though it was the cheapest, probably the only *dirzee*-made there, it was pretty in an unusual way, and I was pleased that for once I had pipped these other girls with their fathers' fat cheque books, and lovely homes. At dinner I chatted gaily, collecting more black looks which added to my sparkle.

More than one man paid me a compliment and I remember that evening as a 'Proud moment', but I also remember that night being unable to sleep with my unhappy thoughts: the realisation that no matter how well I dressed or looked or was admired—colour prejudice would swamp the lot. Waking the next morning and having *chota*, I wondered if coming up here had after all been a wise move. My Peshawar adventure seemed to be turning sour on me. I was determined to leave the Frontier after completing my five year contract, get my 'midder', then nurse in some big city where petty envy did not exist. For some time now I knew that I would never be able to marry an Anglo-Indian; Frontier life with its close contact with the army and government services had spoilt me for my own community. I was unsettled and confused.

CHAPTER 24

Summer Madness

After Eric Wilkinson's party, in this disillusioned mood at a mess dinner the following summer I met Captain Paul Mitchell. He was slim, tall with brown eyes and hair going slightly grey at the temples. I had been kept late on duty that evening; getting bathed and changed had been a rush and I only managed to join the others as they got to the dining-room. I was sorry I had missed my sherry which we always had in the sitting-room before the guests arrived. This gave me a flow of conversation! There were about five or six men guests, most of whom I knew, but a subaltern who stood near the door through which I entered was new to me.

After we were introduced I saw Paul across the room with the dining-table between us. After our introduction our eyes held, and I had to force myself to look away. My 'enchanted evening' had come. At that moment I knew I had at last met the man I loved. As he was an older man he was placed near the top, whilst I was at the bottom flanked by two young men. I found this position irksome that night, as I wanted to be near him. I watched the wrinkles which appeared round his eyes when he laughed, which he did very often, yet gave the impression of sadness and tiredness. Our eyes met often during the meal.

We left the men in the dining-room and waited for Kareem Bux to bring coffee; I joined Menelaus on the sofa and in low tones asked if she could tell me anything about Paul. "He's nice, don't you think so, Menelaus?" She agreed with me, but could tell me nothing about him as she had met him only that evening for the first time.

"I see you have taken a 'header' Green. I watched you over dinner: be careful. Let's hope the others have not noticed or. . . ." But she got no further as we were called over to where Miss Creighton sat pouring coffee. Then the men joined us and the conversation was general until someone started card tricks which led to parlour games. In the middle of one of these I was suddenly swept off my feet. It was Paul who had done this, coming up silently behind me. My startled cries made the others laugh, taking advantage of this he whispered as he held me aloft,—"Where have you been hiding all these years?" That and a squeeze of my fingers told me enough to make me starry-eyed for the rest of the evening. Later there was dancing on the verandah, and before he left he kissed me behind a large palm and asked if he could, see me again. We arranged to meet the next evening.

After the guests had gone, it was our custom to collect in the sitting-room for a final nightcap and chat. That evening I wanted to miss that—but in order to avoid comment I joined the others. Then Menelaus managed to whisper the first minute we were alone together, "I want a word with you—it's about Mitchell." I was full of curiosity, but before she could say any more we were joined by Miss Snob, and even before she spoke I knew she was going to be catty—she had that gleam in her eyes.

"Had a good time, Green? Mitchell is a good dancer, don't you think so? You danced with him very often." Then she paused, savouring the moment, whilst I waited, hardly daring to breathe. "But I should be careful if I were you—he has a very jealous little blonde wife, I am told!"

The gasp, which I could not control as I sat down heavily, gave her all the satisfaction she wanted. I escaped to my room as soon as I could, and later Menelaus joined me. "I wanted to warn you before it was too late: we were together when she pumped one of the other men about Mitchell. I'm sorry for you, Greeny!"

"Oh, Miss Menelaus, why does he have to be married? Why did I meet him so late?" And in saying this I was reminded of his words, "Where have you been hiding all these years?" They had a new meaning now. Feeling very upset I continued, "do you know it's the first time I have felt this way: I have never really been in love before—it's just been light flirtations. Trust me to fall for a married man—just my luck!"

"Well, keep your head and try not to get hurt too badly," was her advice.

Paul came for me the next evening, we dined at the club and then went for a drive. He stopped the car in a secluded spot and then without any preamble told me he loved me, and in the same breath told me he was a married man. "Not only that, but I have twin girls, but that does not stop me from loving you, Now tell me I am an old fool."

"Well, if you are an old fool, you are the nicest one I have ever met—and I only wish I did not like you as much as I do!"

"You only like me? I was hoping for more than that, darling child." And that remained his name for me—except when we were with others—when he would call me 'Irene.' He refused to use any of the other silly names the subs had given me. So it was at that and subsequent meetings. The more I saw of him, the more I loved him. It was his gentle ways, his quiet manner, his tenderness and his silly little vanity that appealed to me. He was very short-sighted, but refused to wear glasses. One evening we were on a favourite subject—books. "I have a short list here that may interest you. I'll make a copy, darling child, you get the top three or four and I'll get the others; then we merely swop and that way we'll read the lot sooner." He started writing after screwing up his eyes and peering closely at the list he was given.

"You funny old thing, Paul, why don't you get glasses. You'll do your eyes a permanent injury of you are not careful."

"All right, nursey, I'll take your advice some day." he said with a laugh.

When I presented this list to the librarian at the club the following afternoon, it was soon handed back to me with the remark, "Sorry, Miss, I don't read Chinese."

"That happens to be Captain Mitchell's best English, now I'll have to find someone to write it out clearly."

I left the library and passing through the hall outside the main door on the pathway I saw a group of men, with them was the sub. who had been to our mess with Paul that first evening we met. Seeing me he detached himself from the group and moved forward. I smiled in recognition.

"Hello! You're the young 'un they call Jessie, 'Tuppence' and 'Baby Face.' Have you any more names or is that the lot?"

"As a matter of fact I've lately collected a new one, but as its rather special, I'm not telling you."

He laughed in a knowing sort of way and said, "I get it."

"Now will you help me please, Mr. Rogers, as you are in Paul's company you must be familiar with his handwriting. He has given me a list of books but the librarian cannot decipher it—he told me he could not read Chinese!" Handing him the list I added, "you see its only a short list, and I'll be very grateful if you can spare a moment to rewrite it." Then catching sight of a *kit* carrying some drinks I said, "If you do I'll stand you a drink."

"Of course I'll rewrite it but the drinks are on me. Come on, let's bag that table over there, quickly!" As he wrote Dick Rogers remarked, "the trouble is, the old boy is as blind as a bat, but will not admit it: he really is a good old stick otherwise, if he wasn't I should have knocked his block off the other night," and he looked up with a smile.

"Why, Mr. Rogers?"

"Look here, if you call me Mr. Rogers again you'll jolly well pay for the drinks—the name is Dick."

"Thank you, Dick, and now will you answer my question!"

"Well, I intended asking you to go to the pictures with me but Paul was doing his stuff, so I kept clear. Then the next night you dined here with him, a little bird told me—right?"

"Right! But there's always the winter when his wife returns from Kashmir: I shall be on the shelf, then you can take me to the pictures and mend my broken heart; yes?"

"O.K. Dicky will pick up the bite, but I warn you, keep clear of Stella or I won't be able to find the bite."

I had been brave in front of Dick Rogers, but I was upset and that night I told Menelaus about this meeting with him and his remark *re* Stella Mitchell. "Where will it end, Green? Don't you see you are going to be the one to get hurt—be careful!" I could see she meant to be kind.

"I'll never do anything foolish, Menelaus—I couldn't, but it's so lovely as it is."

It was lovely—just then, but the more we saw of each other the deeper grew the affection. I know I should have broken it off from the very beginning, but it was too strong for me. I kept hoping something—anything—a miracle would happen; and then Paul and I need never part. By now we had given up dining at the club or Deane's but would dine at his bungalow on a little table in the sitting-room by a window overlooking the garden. After dinner we would move out to the garden and sit in the semi-darkness with an electric fan to help keep the mosquitoes away. We sat with the scent of roses and other flowers mixed with the smell of citronella oil which Paul would rub on his face and hands. In spite of the citronella oil and the smoke from Paul's cigarette an occasional stubborn mosquito buzzed about our ears. We would sit out there holding hands and talking, and Paul would tell me how much he loved me. He would often sigh deeply but I refused to look beyond the present lovely moment and was happy. I would ask him to tell me about life in England, and was interested in all I heard.

Once he asked me about myself—my home and family. I then told him the old story which by now I had almost come to believe was true. I told this story reluctantly, the answer I wanted to give Paul and those others before him, including the sisters, was—"*Here I am, for what I am, and what I am, I IS!*" but I felt this might be thought evasive and prompt further questions. So I told Paul, "My people left England, Ripon, somewhere in Yorkshire I think it is, many years ago to go out to German East Africa, and from there they went out to India—where I was born." Why did I pick on Ripon? Because Grandpa Green and Grandma "Queen Victoria" did in fact go to India from there, I have forgotten now whether Grandpa was army or what, but he had something to do with the engineers. I can only just remember my father telling me this when I was a little girl. Why German East Africa? Because my mother's first husband did leave India to go to that country to join the railway, leaving Mama and the children to follow later, but before they were able to do this he died from black-water fever.

I felt safe in speaking about Africa, because Mama, through the letters she had received, had learnt much about that country, and often told us about the wild animals, and why the houses had to be built high on stilts; about the little black boys that were called '*totos*'. Then we had many curios from there. The horn of a rhinoceros; an ostrich egg; an *assegai*; and other things. I would tell this story only in self-defence, as it were: when questioned about my people and home, telling a story that was only half-true and always ending with, "We were too poor after my father's death to move further then from one house to another in Mhow; then when I was old enough I went to Bombay to train as a nurse, and now here I am." This last bit, thank goodness, was the whole truth and had, I felt, the right ring, though what Paul and the others believed or guessed I was never to know. Whenever I had to tell this story I felt humiliated but snobbery made it necessary.

If I had stated the plain truth would I have held my post? As long as I was able to get away with it the authorities turned a 'blind eye' and as the money coming in was useful—it made life a little easier for Mama, and brought my 'midder' closer—I had to go on with the act. So the weeks flew, then I noticed s restlessness about Paul and one evening he surprised me by talking about a divorce. "This situation cannot go on, it's not fair to you—I'm going to see a fellow in Lahore. . . . ." I would not let him go any further. Apart from the twins there was my mother. I told him she was a Roman Catholic and did not recognise divorce.

"I would never do anything to make her unhappy, Paul. She has had her fair share of that already."

"That may be, darling child, but what about us?"

"Oh, Paul, don't think farther than this lovely evening, let's be happy now, the summer will soon be over," and seeing I was near to tears he changed the subject and said something to make me laugh.

Occasionally after this—on other evenings—after a long silence he would suddenly get to his feet and pull me up saying, "Come on, I'm taking you home," and in spite of my protests that the evening was still young, I would be bundled into the car and driven back to the hospital in complete silence. Getting out of the car Paul would take my face between his hands, kiss me, and without saying a word would walk back to the car. I would stand where he had left me, just by the steps leading up to the mess verandah, and listen to his car being driven away down the drive, out of the gate and over the road past our bungalow on towards the fort. It was only when I could no longer hear it that I was able to move. In my bedroom I would fling myself on to the bed to lie fully dressed, with my miserable bewildered thoughts. One evening in a bitter mood, and I suspected he had had an extra drink he told me a little about Stella; usually he never mentioned her at all.

However what he told as was what I had already more or less heard from Dick Rogers. "I am not giving away any secrets when I tell you that Paul and Stella do not hit it off—it is common knowledge; it's only the twins that keep them together. She is a mean, selfish, cruel woman, Jessie, but she will never let him go. We are all sorry for Paul—but there it is!"

Now Paul told me about her various affairs. "I've known about them for a long time, but I've never tried to get proof: I've just ignored them and that hurts her. You see I have to think about the twins, they mean a lot to me, it is this she uses as a whip," as he said this his voice went quite hoarse.

"Oh, Paul stop, don't—don't say any more," I cried, trying to stop him, but he smacked my hand impatiently and continued.

"Then I've only my captain's pay. I've no training of any sort, the army's all I'm fit for—so you see what a nice old lame duck you have fallen for, darling child." By now I was sure he had been drinking— and I did not like him in this ugly mood so I was glad when he said, "Come on, I'll take you home."

I did not see him after that for three or four nights as he rang up to say he was very busy and would be taking some office work home. Then one afternoon off-duty at 2 p.m. I stepped on the verandah to hear our 'phone ring; with a sudden happiness I *knew* it was Paul, but Kareem Bux beat me to it, and I heard him say, "Yes, *Sahib*, Missy Green is here." Handing me the receiver he remarked unnecessarily, "For you Missy—Captain Mitchell *Sahib*."

Sometimes I felt our bearer was too smart. "Hello, Paul!"

"Hello, darling child, what about tonight? It is your free evening I know but has some little whipper-snapper fixed to take you out?"

"Even if he had he would now he dropped and you know it!"

I heard him chuckle. "Right then, be ready at the usual time, and wear your pretty frock." This is what he called the old white organdie that I had altered for Eric Wilkinson's party.

I spent my free hours after lunch damping my hair and coaxing in deeper waves, manicuring my nails and ironing my frock. I was too excited for sleep but got into bed and tried to rest. How the hours dragged. I was ready an hour before he was due, and the minute I heard the car on the gravel outside I rushed from my room. "Oh, Paul, how I have missed you," I said, as he got out of the car.

He looked towards the guardhouse before taking my two hands in his. "Confound that guard. I want to kiss you—but that will have to wait."

On the little table which was fixed for dinner in his sitting-room I noticed my favourite flowers, St. Josephs lilies—Paul had once told me he found them overpowering—I had to admit they were rather heavily scented, but as they always reminded me of the four happy years we had spent in Neemuch I loved them. Seeing them there I appreciated his kind thought. Then I noticed the extra glasses on the table, and on a low stool I saw the bucket of lead champagne, "What are we celebrating, Paul?"

"Your return darling child; I have missed you very much these last few days, but I wanted you away from me so that I could think clearly." Then seeing he was about to pour me out a sherry I stopped him.

"No sherry for me, Paul, not if I am to drink champagne: my head will not stand the mixture."

He laughed and sipped his own before continuing, "I have been doing some soul searching, but we will talk after dinner—Abdul has fixed all your favourite eats." At the sight of the iced asparagus tips I smiled at Abdul and said, "*Shabas Abdul.*"

"Now he is your slave for life," said. Paul approvingly. As he was gay I fell in with his mood and with a glass of champagne inside me—I sparkled. We laughed a good deal over that meal and were happy. But out in the garden sitting together on a sofa—(I with my feet up on a garden chair, as I was always frightened a snake would crawl up the folds of my long skirt), he was very quiet. At first I did not mind as I thought it was just the comfortable satisfied feeling following a good dinner, but when it, continued I guessed he was brooding and said, "Paul! What is it? I thought this was a celebration, why are you so quiet?"

"Little girl, do you really want to know?" I nodded dumbly, but felt a little frightened. He sighed deeply, then said, "darling child, I don't want to hurt you, but don't you see, this is intolerable, I cannot stand it much longer. I love you, don't you understand?"

"Paul!" I said, sitting upright. "What is it you are trying to say; don't tell me we have got to part, there's *weeks* of summer left yet!"

"No, darling, but we have either got to stop seeing each other or .. . . . ." and he leaned over and whispered the rest in my ear. "You have got to let me love you properly."

"NO! Paul, I am sorry. You know by now I am not that sort, and anyway love does not only mean *that*. . . . . " I got no further because he interrupted me with a harsh laugh.

"All right, never mind, Irene, I guessed what you would say, but I wanted to hear it. Though if you really loved me your answer would be a different one." Then he rose and walked to the tray left on the verandah to help himself to a whisky. Returning he sat silent, then after a while spoke again, "Well what are you thinking? That I am a dirty dog; that you wished you had never set eyes on me, and that you hate me."

"On the contrary I was thinking how much I loved you—to be here in this garden—even when we are not talking or holding hands,

I am happy and content; why cannot it be like that for you? Then perhaps in the future anything might happen."

"What might happen?" he demanded.

"Well—er—she may run off with a rich man and then everyone, including my mother, will understand our position and we could marry. You will have the twins whilst I will have you." The evening ended on a discordant note.

After this our lovely happy evenings were rare, and, we nearly always argued every time we met. Sometimes Paul was gay and his old self, saying he loved me and wanted no more—that he was content—other times he was restless and unhappy; and he would try to get me to change my mind, whilst freely admitting he was asking too much, and not being fair to me, but "*love is unreasonable,*" he would quote. Sometimes I felt myself slipping and in the privacy of my room would pray for strength, and for this situation, to work itself out, "Oh, *please* let a miracle happen." What I hoped for, even I did not know! In this unhappy confused state I had to go on 'nights', as a patient was admitted to Bolton and it was my turn for this duty. I was glad of this respite, so I rang Paul and told him I could not see him for a while—I suggested we take this opportunity to think things over and not meet at all until the patient left.

Then for the next two nights after settling my patient, I would sit with a consoling 'cuppa' to go over the whole wretched business. "If only I did not love this man so much; if only I could be like other girls, fall in and out of love easily; if only I did not feel everything so acutely; if only I had had my first love affair at fifteen instead of at twenty-five, and if only I had not stuck my head in a book learning about love second-hand instead of going out and meeting it in life. So my thoughts went round and round, I would pick up the sewing I was doing and tiring easily throw it aside, take up a book—only to find this boring. Then I would end by getting into a deckchair and with my hands behind my head I would sit and think about Paul. On the third night I was seated like this when the unexpected happened. At first I thought I had fallen asleep and was dreaming until he spoke, then I knew it was no dream.

"Paul!" I cried, springing to my feet. "What on earth are you doing here? Hell's Bells! You'll get me into a serious row if you are caught. It's two o'clock in the morning—you should be in bed!"

"Hush, nursey, don't got alarmed, no one has seen me except the friendly guard who let me in quickly when he recognised me." And Paul calmly proceeded to kiss me. I soon disengaged myself.

"Paul! You must be mad or drunk—are you drunk? What have you come for?"

"I just felt lonely and wanted to see you—no crime in that is there? And, Sister Green, for your benefit I am *not* drunk— so let's sit and talk," and he pulled up a chair to place near mine.

"Oh, NO, you don't," said I, taking this from him, "You must go at once."

"Now don't panic, darling child, I'll go as quietly as I came, no one will know, so let's talk."

"Paul, you have been drinking. . . . . ."

"Now, my dear little one, I may have had an extra drink or two, but no one can say I am drunk. Come on, aren't you going to kiss old Paul?"

"I will, but only if you promise to leave at once afterwards—I am terribly nervous with you here—really, Paul, you should never have come here drunk."

"Don't keep on harping so, I am NOT drunk! You little goose. . . . ." and with that he sat on the edge of the large writing-table. He picked up the open report book which I swiftly took out of his hand. He then spotted my sewing lying on one end of the table. "What have we got here? Ah, pink silk pyjamas! Whoopee!" And he stood up to hold them out in front of him. I grabbed them from him.

"Shut up Paul, for goodness sake, and go home." I then got him by his arms and pulled him out of the duty room, "Go on downstairs—go quietly now, don't fall or make any noise. I am nearly sick with fright." Then seeing I was really upset, he was suddenly serious.

"All right, I'll go—but those pyjamas!"

"Oh bother the pyjamas—GO!"

"First you kiss me goodnight, then I'll go quietly."

At the bottom of the stairs he looked up and called, "Those pyjamas . . . ." I did not wait to hear more. Back in the duty room to keep myself from collapsing I quickly brewed an extra strong 'cuppa'.

Waking me at 4 o'clock that afternoon with my tea-tray Kareem Bux gave me a letter, "Captain Mitchell's *syce* brought this for Missy"—he did not miss much, our bearer. Paul had written to apologise—it was a long humble screed, very touching, but what made me smile, right in the corner of the last page in very small letters were the words, "Pink silk pyjamas."

Going on duty that night, I was informed the patient was being discharged next day. After getting him tucked up for the night I made my tea and settled down to reading—then sewing—but the night seemed dull after last night. Though the visit was wrong—it had been fun. Or so I thought now, and in a forgiving mood I decided to write him a long letter. I could then tell him I should be free the next evening—Kareem Bux would see he had it before lunch.

So we met the following night. At dinner Paul said, "If we are quick we can go to the pictures—a good film being shown—*Congress Dances*—with Lilian Harvey— you like her. After the pictures, I'll take you straight back as you look very tired. . . . ."

Here I interrupted to say "You mean you've got a thick head after last night!"

"Now don't rake up the dirty past—be kind, darling child—I am truly ashamed."

We enjoyed the pictures—taking me home that night he was very quiet until we got to our 'parting' corner—this was where we left the main drive between the hospital gates and turned down the garden path that led to our mess. There was an old grave here; a *saiid* or Moslem holy men had been buried long before the hospital had been thought about—and to keep it undefiled by the passing *gora log* a wall had been built all round. Getting behind the wall gave a certain amount of privacy from the curious glances of our police guard. When he kissed me goodnight, he whispered, "I'd like to see you in those pink pyjamas one night." After this the pyjamas kept cropping up at regular intervals. I was very unhappy, I loved Paul and it seemed so mean to see him suffer. "No one need know," those four devilish little words kept popping into my head teasing me at odd moments; going round the wards with the doctors; helping in the theatre or nursing in Bolton.

Then towards the end of one evening, when Paul had been his old self, gay, kind and understanding I whispered, "I have decided to bring the pyjamas tomorrow night." The next day would have been difficult to get through in my state of mind, but a sensational bit of news was brought to us. In Mardan at the mission hospital a Pathan orderly had run amok—he had been in love with one of the Indian Christian nurses who had spurned her. As she was helping an English sister with a dressing this man attacked her with a knife, the sister went

194

to her rescue and was seriously wounded.

That evening changing to meet Paul I felt nervous and keyed up, but when we met he was so casual and at ease that I soon relaxed. We had our usual sherry in the garden, and then I told him about the Mardan affair. Then Abdul announced dinner. Going in I found my favourite flowers had been ordered, and saw the bottle of iced champagne. Paul was gay, and so was I—at first—then gradually in spite of the 'bubbly' I found it difficult to be gay, and the food did not go down easily—I ate slowly, toying with my chicken; even my favourite pudding—a half peach filled with cream—would not slide down. We had been a long time over the meal. Paul was patient, giving me time. Then abandoning pretence I fell silent, and looking up saw Paul watching me. He jumped up then and grabbed me by my hands, pulling me out on to the darkened verandah—here he found my evening bag—thrusting this into my hand he said, "Come on, darling child, I am taking you home right now." I could only stare at him.

"Don't you understand, you poor little frightened goose— HOME," and with that I was marched down the stairs and bundled into the car. Nothing was said until we got near the hospital gates, then very quietly Paul spoke, "You realise, I think Irene, that this is the end; one day you will know how much I loved you." As I was still dumb, he continued, "darling child, it is best that we should part this way." I was beyond saying anything, and could only stare straight ahead—swallowing hard all the time. At the 'parting' place he merely took both my hands in his, and squeezing them very tightly left without saying a word. I stood where I was until I could no longer hear the car. Next day I asked matron to let me go on leave at once; I allowed her to think there was trouble at home. She kindly arranged this.

On that last leave home from Peshawar I had to work hard not to let Mama guess I was unhappy. I went out more than I had done on my previous holidays. Accepting invitations from any of the fellows I met at the sergeant's dances, or the Railway Institute—but it was never a success. I kept making comparisons. I was now 'class conscious', the years spent in Peshawar had shown me the difference, I am not suggesting that there were no educated gentlemen amongst the Anglo-Indian community or the sergeants or even the 'other ranks'. There undoubtedly were—only I was unfortunate enough not to meet any—except perhaps one—he was a railway man, a friend of the family. He was well educated and had very good manners, a 'natural gentleman' my mother called him, but unfortunately he was coloured! We met very often, and one day when I had only a few days of my leave left, he asked me to marry him. As I had never given him the slightest encouragement this was more than a surprise, it was a shock! I politely refused, and had to refuse many times. In the end when he was determined to get my reason I told him as gently as I could, "I do not wish to have coffee-coloured children. I wanted to spare you this but you asked for it."

"What's wrong with coffee-coloured children, Irene?"

"Nothing, bless them—it's the attitude of the world towards them that's wrong. If I ever marry, it will have to be a white man, then the chance of my children being coloured is remote, possible but not probable. Oh, you must know what I mean," I said impatiently—then I had an idea. "Do you know the Bowmans? He used to be a guard in Neemuch when we were there—they did not have children for the same reason. It's not snobbery, please believe me; merely a wish not to produce children to be hurt."

"Then why haven't you married a white man in Peshawar?"

"For the same reason, the colour bar is in operation all round, don't you know? They won't risk marriage with a girl who is a quarter coloured."

He was persistent. "Then that means you will never marry?"

I laughed at this, "I'm not worrying, I'm trusting my mother's instinct which tells her there is a 'Mr. Right' waiting somewhere in this world for me, who will, I hope, be brave enough to marry me after being told I am not completely white."

On my return from leave I threw myself into the work. I am sure the ward orderly thought I had gone mad the way I turned out cupboards and washed and relabelled the already clean bottles. Off duty I took up tennis and golf, and so met the young men again; then the gay rounds started. Soon it was winter and with the return of the families we were busy in Bolton. The Saturday night club dances were resumed. Now I cannot remember who took me to one of these early in the season, but dancing round I saw Paul; we exchanged smiles, but he did not come near me. Then to my horror when we wanted supper my partner and I were ushered to a large table round which the Mitchells and Dick Rogers were already seated with some others. It would have created a scene had I tried to move away as the men were already on their feet, so with some misgivings I sank into the chair pulled out for me. To cover my nervousness I immediately started a conversation with the men on either side. Now and again I caught an encouraging smile from Paul.

When the conversation became general I was able to relax. There was much laughter at this table, then with a lull Stella Mitchell seized her opportunity and pounced! Smiling sweetly at me she said, "I hear you have been very good to my lonely husband, Miss Green, so kind of you, but I hope he has not taken up too much of your time: he is an awful old flirt, you know!" I felt crushed and could think of no reply, but Paul jumped to my rescue.

"Come now Stella, refrain—you know that last bit is untrue, though Miss Green has taken pity on me occasionally."

She laughed at this, rather loudly and meaningly—making more than a few uncomfortable. Dick Rogers then helped by saying, "Our Jessie is quite able to look after herself, I assure you, Mrs. Mitchell. she tells me she makes a habit of falling for the old boys." Then turning to Paul, he added, "You pipped me there, sir, I intended making her my summer time girl." The awkward moment passed with this remark, and when the conversation and laughter were resumed, Dick said, "Come on, Jessie, I can see you are not hungry and I want to dance: John will forgive me if I borrow you for this one." So he got me away from that awkward situation.

We waltzed for a while in silence, and when I was able to speak again I pressed his hand and thanked him for his help. "Dick, if you are on your own tonight, will you take me home now, right away, you can see John later and tell him I had a headache or something. You see, my dear, you are picking up the bits as I warned you in the summer you would be doing."

He smiled and nodded, "And I warned you about her claws, Jessie—anyway you go and get your coat whilst I bag a *tonga*, no, I don't see why we shouldn't take Paul's car—he won't mind," but I stopped him.

"Please, Dick, I'd rather go in a *tonga*."

He understood. "All right, Jessie, *tonga* it is, but don't look so glum, it will pass!"

It did pass—in time. Unfortunately Menelaus had left us to work as matron in an Indian State hospital, and I missed her comforting presence. Dick took me out several times—he was very kind and I could have turned to him for comfort, but he seemed every now and again to withdraw. This I put down to the colour business, but months later I learnt in confidence that he was supporting a crippled mother and would never be able to marry.

CHAPTER 25

Off With the Old

One afternoon in the spring of 1934 I had a 'phone call. It was from a young 'civvy' who asked if I had been dining at Deane's the night before with Dick—"and you were wearing a green and white frilly dress with a string of green beads, is that right?"

"Yes, that's right; but this is all very intriguing—will you explain?"

"Well, Jessie, there's a fellow here, a *box-wallah* on tour, who dined there with a couple from our crowd—these chaps said they thought the girl was the young sister from the L.R.H.—this chappy wants to meet you—he's crazy about you, are you free tonight?"

"He sounds like a wolf—are you trying to feed me off to him?"

"Now look here, if I did not think he was a suitable person to meet I would never have rung you—but why not judge for yourself—can we meet you tonight?"

"No, sorry, not tonight, nor tomorrow night, but the night after that we are having a dinner party here; unfortunately the table arrangements have been made, but you two can join us for coffee on the lawn."

"Thanks a lot, Jessie, you have saved my life: it's your fault for looking so charming."

"Now, now, Mr. Flatterer, no more nonsense. Goodbye—see you Wednesday."

Putting the receiver down I wondered who my new admirer was; I had noticed a very big man looking at me several times the night before—in the end I avoided looking in his direction, but all the same I had liked the look of him. He was the tallest men I had ever seen, well over six feet, and in his middle forties—'tall, dark and handsome.'

On Wednesday, just as Kareem Bux appeared with coffee, a car pulled up before our mess, and out stepped the young political with the stranger, and it *was* the big man. He had such a distinguished air as he walked from the car towards us that I was thrilled. He was introduced as Merrill Harvey, and when he spoke I was surprised to find he was American; the first I had met since leaving Bombay. We often had fellows from the American Express Company in St. George's and several of the student nurses had boyfriends amongst these, but here he seemed strange, the N.W.F.P. was so very British! When the others were deep in conversation, Mr. Harvey asked me to dine with him the following night at Deane's. "And the night after that we will go to the pictures. Then Saturday night we will dine at the club and dance later." Noticing my raised eyebrows, he added in haste, "you see, I have not many weeks left up here, and I want to see as much of you as I can: I've fallen for you in a big way, honey—you must have noticed how I stared and stared at you in the hotel."

"Yes, I did, and I found it most embarrassing—is that your usual approach?"

"Oh, I don't go around picking up dolls, but you have that something extra. . . . . ." and he snapped his fingers and thumb in the air, "I can't explain it, but when I saw you I knew at once we had to meet. . . . . do you follow?"

"Er. . . . . I think so, but you are rather a fast worker, and I find it difficult."

Now Mr. Harvey drew his deckchair nearer mine and whispered, "Don't try—just take my word for it, and now after hearing your cute little accent, I'm more than a little in love with you."

My cute accent! This made me smile, remembering the 'sing-song' of not so long ago. So taking his word for it I embarked on 'Fiasco No. 2' as I called it later. Though I admired him and was always proud to be seen with him as he was everything a young girl could wish for— he had travelled widely, and I heard many interesting stories about Japan, Java, Sumatra, Malaya and Singapore, "*Those faraway places, with strange sounding names. . . . .*" Then he had plenty of money and spent it freely. He knew how to entertain a girl and make her feel like a queen, but in spite of all this, I never really completely lost my heart to him.

The week after we met he gave a big moonlight picnic in the garden of an empty house standing on the Mall—two or three were asked from the mess and many others from cantonments. The refreshments and arrangements were lavish, the catering was done by a well-known Swiss firm in Lahore, and the decorated boar's head, chickens in aspic and ham made me gasp. Noticing my amazement Merrill came and taking me by the elbow he whispered, "This is all for you, honey."

After the meal—at which champagne flowed freely—we played games, 'murder' and 'sardines;' in the dark with unfamiliar furniture about this was fun! Two or three cocktail parties followed—given in his private sitting-rooms. After these Merrill reserved his charm and entertainment for me alone. How I was dined and wined at the club or Deane's every evening. Then on Sundays we lunched at the club. These Sunday 'Curry Tiffins' in the season were popular; in fact it was the fashionable thing to do—to collect there after parade service and show off one's smartest clothes. The band played on the lawn outside adding a gay note. I had a new two-piece made that spring, and I wore it for the first time to one of these Sunday *tiffins*. When Merrill saw me he said, "Now why didn't you tell me you were going to get all dolled up—I'd have worn my spats!"

As it was he was well dressed and when we entered the crowded *murghi khanna* I felt many pairs of eyes on us. Putting up my chin I forced myself to walk slowly across the lounge and thankfully sank into a chair that Abdar the Number 1 bearer had pulled out for me. When we were seated Merrill said, "You certainly can make an entry, little English girl, I felt mighty proud just then,"—the 'little English girl' part of this so nice speech made me want to giggle. When he gave an order for eats or drinks he was never quite satisfied until he was absolutely sure we were having the best that could be produced. This was not done in an ostentatious manner, but quietly yet firmly; he was used to the best and had every intention of getting it when and where he could. At hotels when I looked for the menu card on our table, I was often told, "We are having a special meal."

Sometimes champagne accompanied one of these meals—on the first occasion when we had one of these 'specials' I asked, "What are we celebrating, Merrill?"

"Your dress—when I saw you come down the stairs in that tonight I thought 'that calls for a special'—that frilly white thing suits you." After about ten days of this treatment I wondered when the 'pay-off' demands would start. Then one evening after dinner and a drive he suggested we go back to his sitting-room for a final nightcap and a chat, Ah! Ah! here it comes, thought I getting my defences ready, but after pouring out drinks he surprised me by placing me in a chair and pushing a small table between us he took a chair opposite. "I want a serious talk with you, honey,—you tell me you finish here in June—about then I should be back in Calcutta, my headquarters. I have a suite in the Great Eastern, and so have a charming English couple I know—I have many friends in Calcutta. Now will you come there as my guest? All on the level—this couple I have told you about will act as chaperone—I'll give you a whale of a good time if you come."

"Whew. . . . . !" I whistled slowly and smiled.

"What does that mean? Honey, why that smile?"

"I'm wondering what you are getting out of this, or hope to get. You see I am not the sort of girl who welcomes sleepwalkers to her room in big hotels—do you sleepwalk, Merrill?"

"No, and let me tell you, sister, if I thought you were that sort of girl I should not be bothering with you. I want more than a dirty affair with you—but I'll go into that later. What I want you to think about now is this holiday; work it into your plans. I'm really keen about it." After I promised to think about it, and we had finished our drinks I was taken home.

But every time we met after that I was asked if I had made up my mind, and each time the holiday was made to sound more and more exciting, not that this was needed, as Mama had often told us girls shout Calcutta and the gay life there. "Many of the senior commercial representatives who do not have permanent homes in the select Alipore area have luxurious sets of apartments in hotels such as the Great Eastern or the Grand. They have marvellous food and music and dancing every evening; then there is the famous Firpos restaurant with its Italian cuisine."

I had also heard about these places from some student nurses in St. George's, and I had longed to visit this gay city, and now here was Merrill Harvey, a rich American, actually asking me to go and live in the Great Eastern Hotel as his guest! The temptation was great. Pressed for an answer I said, "I have thought about it, but it's that business of sleepwalkers in big hotels that frightens me. Are you *sure* you do not sleepwalk, Merrill? Promise me *faithfully* you don't."

"You silly goose, of course I promise—you'll be quite safe with me, I'll tell you later just why."

"Why cannot you tell me now—you have made me very curious."

"No, honey, it must keep for a little longer," and Merrill gave a queer smile. There was something strange about him, strange and charming, and though I still loved Paul dearly, being petted and spoilt by him was having its effect.

"I must not be stupid, I must not lose my head, or fall for him—I don't suppose he thinks of me as anything but a plaything," I warned myself.

Merrill left Peshawar for a few days. On his return I noticed an air of excitement about him. "Oh, do tell me what it's all about—this mystery: what's happening?"

"I will be able to tell you any day now—you must be patient for just a little longer, I am expecting a cable that is going to clear up everything. Oh, honey, I am longing to give you my news, but I must be quite sure before I can speak."

Then, when there was only a day or two left at the end of his stay, before he was due to leave Peshawar for Hindustan, as he called it, he rang me and said, "It's come! That cable I was waiting for—can we meet early tonight, I want a long talk with you." That night for the first time I noticed he seemed indifferent to what he ate, he barely glanced at the menu, and for once made no rude remarks about English cooking. He offered me a sherry but drank only water himself. "Tonight I need none of that," he said with a smile. When we got to his sitting-room, he put his arm round me and led me to the open window.

"Don't move," he warned, then went across to the light switch and plunged the room in darkness. He held me closely then pointed to a star. "Do you see that little star away up there? Very far away." I nodded, realising this was a solemn moment; I was also a little frightened and kept very still, "I've been working for that—very hard, just lately," and then he stopped and whispered, "It's a baby, yours and mine, which some day we are going to have—we can be married, that cable was to say my divorce is going through—one day I shall be free. Oh, honey, say you are happy—say you will marry me."

For a few moments I could not speak, I was so surprised. "Do you mind if I sit down, this is the last thing I expected to hear, and may we have the light? I can think better that way." After switching on the light, he drew me down on the sofa beside him and put his arm around me. I could find nothing to say, but stared in front of me.

"You don't look very happy, baby, what's the matter?"

203

"You have given me a shock, Merrill, I had no idea you were married. You never spoke of your private life and when I tried to probe you always changed the subject. . . . . ."

He did not let me continue. "Perhaps I have sprung it on you rather harshly, now rest so and listen, darling." Pushing my head down on his shoulder he told me his story, and, listening I was more and more disturbed.

At the end of the First World War on his return to America he had discovered his wife had been more than gay in his absence—a divorce followed, he got custody of his child—the girl was now seventeen years old. He married again soon after; hoping for a happy married life, then he was offered a job abroad, with excellent prospects. His second wife accompanied him for a while, and though he gave her everything to make her comfortable and happy, she never settled and rows commenced. Finally she left him and returned to America. For some years now they had lived apart. At first, being young, he found compensation in the giddy whirl of big cities where his job took him, but as the years passed, getting older he wanted companionship and family life. Even before meeting me he had set the ball rolling towards a second divorce.

Whilst he was speaking I wondered if spotting me in Deane's that night he thought, "Ah, she looks a passive little thing—she'll do as wife number three," and the naughty thought, he's halfway to being another Henry VIII, how will I in turn be dismissed? Then remembering his romantic speech about the little star and baby I felt ashamed. For all his money, travel and gay parties, I now knew he had known very little happiness.

Then I heard Merrill saying, "After meeting you I decided definitely to get on with the divorce, and cabled my solicitors. You see, honey, I don't want you to slip out of my life, so I have to act fast— your talk of going to London scares me: that is why I want you to come to Calcutta to meet my friends—all 'box-wallahs' as you call them. There you will get to know me better, away from these British Army boys: you will get a glimpse of a different sort of life altogether. The women play bridge and shop and— well, you will learn all that from Doris Walters. And later, we will move on to another of those 'far away places.' Will you like that, honey?"

Living in expensive hotels, having lovely clothes and food all the time, being waited upon, seemed like a bit of Heaven to me, a girl from a railway colony. But—two divorces and a seventeen year old daughter were also going to be part of that life. I could never pretend they had never been—why every time he kissed me I should be thinking of the two exs, and wondering how I compared with them! However, I could not bring myself to tell him all this just then—I felt too shy—the fifteen years between us was another stumbling block. He often made me feel very young; I remembered how once when I wanted to dance again soon after we sat down he had said, "Think of my old bones, darling." Then it meant nothing to me and I laughed, but now it was a sobering thought. I remained silent until Merrill shook me. "Wake up, honey, I am waiting for an answer."

"Hell's Bells! Merrill, you don't expect me to say 'yes' and 'no' just like that right now, do you? This is serious and wants thinking about. Besides you know very little about me—I shall have to tell you something which may make you change your mind. I have been hurt just lately and I must be very careful."

"Oh, I know all about that, honey," said Merrill, interrupting me. "It does not matter one little bit to me—we will be very happy."

But I was not so sure. So getting to my feet I said, "Please, Merrill, I'd like to go back to the mess now—I've had a shock. This is just the sort of thing that would happen to me—a tall, dark, handsome man enters my life—he has money and wants to marry me—the answer to a maiden's prayer—but for the divorce. . . . . ."

"Well, what's wrong with that?" said Merrill fiercely, "I was the innocent party to both occasions—as a nurse you should be more broadminded." He looked puzzled, but at that moment I did not feel like going through any more: I did not feel up to explaining what the stigma of divorce meant to me with my mother's strict upbringing. That he was thinking of me as Mrs. Harvey III when Mrs. Harvey II was not even quite out shook me! Just then all I wanted was the privacy of my room.

In my room I lay awake and thought things over—If I tell him I am coloured, that will be the end—goodbye posh hotel holiday! But need I tell him that? By now I was very reluctant to part with this secret of mine, besides it was none of his business—all I had to do was to tell him that I could never marry a divorced person—innocent or otherwise, and deciding on this plan I fell asleep.

Next evening I did the talking. I first asked him what he knew about me, and from his reply I realised he hadn't a clue that I was partly coloured. I then told him about Paul Mitchell who had once suggested a divorce would free him to marry me: that I had discouraged him was not due only to the fact that my mother was Roman Catholic and would never give me her blessing. In my own heart I firmly believed that a marriage should last in spite of everything—as my mother put it. "All the faults and sins of one's partner must be forgiven again and again and love and kindness shown to the erring one—then with time, peace and perhaps even love may return—but if people get divorced there's no chance of this happening." So how could I come between a man and his wife?

"But you have not come between us—we had already parted before I met you," Merrill protested.

"Yes, I know, but the thought, 'If I hadn't married him, he may have gone back to his wife' will haunt me," I answered, Merrill listened but was not impressed—my views were totally alien to him. He talked and argued and made me promise to meet him in Calcutta.

"We will have that holiday together anyway, and perhaps Doris Walters will get you to change your mind."

CHAPTER 26

Indolent Interlude

So he left Peshawar, and his letters were very sweet. I was glad I had met him and had this holiday planned, or the thought of leaving Peshawar and returning to that 'other life' would have been very depressing. Sometime in June I was back in Mhow, and found my mother's love for me was very comforting—nothing else mattered just then: all men married or single, coloured or white, were pushed to the background. I was able to relax, and could hardly bear her out of my sight. "Get all your work done quickly, Mama, and we'll sit on the verandah and have a good long chat." Most evenings she and I would share a bottle of beer. Her favourite meal was a kipper with a cold boiled potato, whilst I revelled in the curries which she ordered for me very evening. This kind of spoiling, this 'mother love' which asks no return, was only now fully appreciated by me. As I was getting full pay for the next six months, the 'money bogey' was absent and we were happy in a quiet way.

I missed Doreen, who was now nursing also at Dohad, but was glad to have Mama all to myself for most of the time: Vi only returned from the stores late in the evening and then after dinner most nights played bridge. Now Mama and I would get into our beds and have long chats. I never told her of my miserable muddled love affairs, but I think she guessed I had met difficulties, and still had problems to face. Once after a long silence, when she heard me sigh, she put her hand out and covered mine. "It will all come right," she said, "God will look after and help my girls— you see, Irene, I asked this help—He knows I want you girls to marry. I do not want you to work—that does not seem natural, I want good steady men, not necessarily rich or handsome ones, and your Mr. Right will come along some day."

207

Wishing to change the subject I told her of the advertisement I had seen for a nursing sister who was wanted for the Civil Hospital in Quetta. The salary was good and being a Frontier city it had an appeal, but Mama was against it. "You have had enough of those wild barbaric places, why not take a job somewhere close round here, so that I can see something of you for a while before you go to London. Anyway, you must have at least two or three months holiday first."

So it was that I never answered that advertisement, and when Quetta suffered that severe earthquake in the following year, Mama assured me that *Kismet* had prevented me from being there—she had had nothing to do with it! After I had been home a month I heard from Merrill, he had gone back to Calcutta and was all set for the holiday. So packing a suitcase I told Mama I was going to friends.

I was met by Merrill at Howrah station, driven across the famous pontoon bridge which was in use over the Hooghly until 1941, along Clive Street—the main business thoroughfare now renamed Subhas Chandra Bose Street, and so to the Great Eastern Hotel. In the foyer Jim and Doris Walters were waiting for me. I loved Mrs. Walter from the moment she tucked her arm into mine and marched me up to the reception desk, she stood by me whilst I signed the register, letting me and anyone else who cared to hear know that I had a room next to hers. That I was well chaperoned she made abundantly clear! Going with me up to my room, she said, "Knock on the wall if you want anything, please. Jim and I are dining out tonight but we will meet sometime tomorrow."

In the days that followed Mrs. Walters took her responsibility very seriously and every now and again popped into my room, and walking down the corridor with me she made sure everyone saw us together. And she and Jim often joined us for drinks. Occasionally we four had a meal together. However, in spite of all this I felt a sense of guilt, and was not too happy in my position. "Mama would not have approved" this thought weighed me down. "But I am not doing anything wrong, and if they think otherwise, that's their business." Telling myself this I would force my chin up and join Merrill in the crowded lounge ignoring the glances of the women.

When I told him how I felt he dismissed it lightly. "Take no notice of the sour pusses," he said with a laugh. In fact he treated all my fears as a joke, making me gasp the first day, when in front of the Walters he pointed to his room, which was at the end of the corridor, and said,

"Look, honey, if I walked in my sleep my bare feet on the cold marble floor would soon awaken me," then turning to Jim he said, "She is frightened of sleepwalkers: are you safe?" I could have killed him but I realised then that I had nothing to fear and felt rather foolish.

After I had been there a day or two Merrill said, "I want you to go shopping with Doris—get yourself some real dresses, honey." I was hurt and asked what was wrong with the ones I had. "Oh, your dresses are very pretty—suitable for private clubs, but you will find the women here are very posh, and you don't want to feel odd: besides which I want to feel proud of you."

"Those *dirzees*-mades are all I can afford, Merrill."

"I've thought of that and it has all been fixed with Doris, she will have the cheques sent to her, and I'll settle with her later."

So it was that Doris and I had a lovely morning shopping, which I enjoyed all the more after our break for coffee, when she remarked, "If Lord Merrill, does not approve of your dresses and wants you to posh up—well! It's only fair that he should pay." We bought two evening dresses—a black chiffon velvet and a green taffeta—and an evening fur. This might sound a queer buy in that climate but as the dining-room-cum-dance-hall was air-conditioned at the Great Eastern Hotel it was necessary to have some sort of wrap for one's shoulders. Leaving these rooms to face the hot blast outside, one was struck by the con-trast' I wore the green taffeta the night Firpos put on a 'gala' do. The dining-room walls were festooned with garlands of huge pink roses and 'maiden-hair' fern. Orchids were placed on each table. And every woman guest was presented, with a large French doll. Everyone was drinking champagne. The menu was it least eighteen inches long and beautifully decorated. It was years since I had been to anything like this and I was very excited.

When the cabaret started I jumped on to a chair to see better—a girl in black lace tights pirouetted on the toes of one foot only, it was very clever; after it was over Merrill put a hand out to help me down whilst a young man standing near took my other hand. Smiling, I thanked him, then turning saw Merrill flush with anger, I hoped the young man had not noticed and felt ashamed for Merrill.

We dined and danced at all the posh places. At one of these I saw for the first time a European waiter pushing a trolley round with a chafing dish on it. I asked Merrill what he was doing with it, and he immediately called him over and ordered a crepe suzette. Then the fuss and palaver was almost more than I could bear, the man standing over me whilst I ate the first bit, waiting anxiously to ask, "Does Madam like it?" And Merrill looking at me as if he wanted to eat me—neither of them knew that I swallowed the first bit without tasting it! When he could get away from the office Merrill took me out showing me the attractions of Calcutta.

I cannot now remember the many places I visited, but the Victoria Memorial on the *Maidan* and the Botanical Gardens I do recall. There is a famous banyan tree in the gardens which has, over the years, thrown down roots all the way round from its branches, and now covers a very large area of ground. It is one of the main tourist attractions. In the days that followed my host set out to be charming—he was kind, gay and understanding, and it was very hard not to fall completely in love with him, but always at the back of my mind I knew nothing could or would ever come of this—there was an invisible obstruction between us.

One evening when we were driving back from some place or other he asked, "Well, honey, are you enjoying the holiday?"

"Of course I am! I would be very unnatural if I were not: you are most kind and I am very grateful."

"It's not your gratitude I want—you know that, don't you?"

"Yes, I do—Oh! why should this have to happen to me twice—it's most unfair!"

"What are you talking about, Irene, what do you mean?"

"Why should you both have to be married men—do you know I think there should be a law—married men should be compelled to wear a badge so that unsuspecting girls would not fall into any traps: seeing that badge a girl would veer away, as it is, a poor girl like myself meets a tall, dark and handsome man and falls in love only to discover—when he chooses to tell her, that is—that he is already married!" I saw Merrill smile, but he did not say anything—"well, don't you think I am right?"

"Humph," he murmured, "I suppose you are right—I have never thought about it. . . ."

"Well you ought to think fast," I said interrupting, "You have a nearly grownup daughter, haven't you?" He did not answer but turned and putting out a hand gently squeezed mine. In the long silence that followed I wish I had not added the last bit.

It was whilst I was at one of the restaurants that I heard for the first time that lovely song, "I'll see you again," from "Bitter Sweet". As we danced, the lights were dimmed and a girl joined the band to sing this: to my surprise and delight Merrill hummed and sang it very softly. When we sat down I asked him what it was called, and told him I loved it. I think it was that night whilst we were dining that I remarked how strange it seemed to me to be in a room where, apart from Merrill, I did not know anyone. At the dances in Neemuch, Mhow and in Peshawar I knew nearly everybody, some well, some not so well, but I knew bits and pieces about them all—that's how it was in garrison stations. "It's not so easy to make friends in a large city, is it Merrill? Though you seem to know quite a number." Now he started telling me about the people all round us—he knew most of them, or 'bits and pieces' about most of them.

"Do you see that chap sitting by that palm? He has been drinking heavily—had D.T.s not so long ago—they were thinking of shipping him home. Then that fellow with the beard behind you, don't look round now, he keeps an Indian woman in the bazaar, that's his wife with him and she doesn't know a thing! Those two young fellows away there with the girls dressed alike—they are twins, I think—those boys are heavily in debt. Oh, yes, honey, do you see that woman all covered in jewels, that red hair is a wig, it's a new one. She lost her old one in a storm on the Maidan, not so long ago. Then the fellow across there with the two girls, one is his wife, the other is her sister just come out with the fishing fleet—his mother is as black as your dress, you wouldn't think so, would you? That chap there......" but I did not hear any more, ".... his mother is as black as your dress." Those words went echoing round and round, whilst I stared at him, and a little voice inside me whispered, "Go on, Irene, here is your chance, tell him and test him—and end your lovely holiday," but I remained dumb.

One afternoon we went out to one of those country club places for tea. Later we were joined by three or four men and their girl-friends, Merrill only knew one or two of the men, the others were friends of these. I found to my delight that one of the girls was a nurse who had just finished her training in the Presidency General, so she and I had much in common. We sat on and on chatting and drinking until it was quite late. Then Merrill asked the whole lot back to the hotel as his guests. When we got there he ordered dinner to be served on the side verandah, and whilst the preparations went ahead—the small tables were joined up to make one long one—we sat and listened to the hotel band, and to my delight they played, "I'll see you again." Merrill now approached me and suggested I take the girls up to my room; as there was a perfectly good 'powder room' on this floor I thought this unnecessary and told him so. Unfortunately one of the girls had overheard us and asked me in surprise, "Do you live here?"

"For the moment I do."

At this her eyebrows were raised and with a haughty "Oh!" she walked away. I turned to Merrill and said, "That was your fault!"

That was not all.

When dinner was announced Merrill wanted me to seat everyone—play hostess, in fact. He came to me and said "Go on, honey, do your stuff—this is *your* party." I was really cross now, I wanted to say, "My party? Since when? *You* asked them." But as this would have been ill-mannered I remained silent. The guests now stood about awkwardly, chatting, and no one made a move to sit down. I could feel Merrill looking at me, so in desperation I said, "Go on, everybody, sit down anywhere." I guessed Merrill wanted me to sit at the bottom and as he had moved to the head; hoping to score a point, I moved round to the side and sat somewhere near the middle between two very young men. We laughed and joked right through the meal and I avoided looking at Merrill, When they had gone we had our first quarrel! "Why did you try to push me in the limelight, you know I don't like that sort of thing," I told him in answer to his question, "Did you enjoy *your* party honey?" "I was not hostess, and you know it. I did not want to give these girls the wrong impression."

"Well! For Pete's sake! Do you care what they think?"

"Yes, I do—I am not your—your. . . ." (I could not bring myself to say the word). "So why should they be allowed to think it?"

"Well they probably think it whether you play hostess or not, but I shouldn't worry. . . . . ."

"No, you wouldn't," I said, "But I do, anyway, it's my fault: I should never have come here." And nearly in tears I fled to my room. That evening had ended on a discordant note, but the next evening even worse was to follow. We were dining at one of the posh restaurants when suddenly the respectable quiet of the place was rudely shattered by a sudden brawl at the entrance, I could not see what was happening, but the European waiters rushed to the door telling, each other, "Keep her out—keep her out?" I heard a bearer tell another "*Phul wali a-gaya.*" Then the familiar Cockney voice was heard singing in a drunken way, "won't you buy my pretty flowers?" The bearers were right—the flower seller had come! "Oh! It's darling old Fighting Flora," I cried, jumping up and rushing towards the door—however I did not get far as Merrill grabbed me by the shoulders and stopped me.

"For Pete's sake, honey, you don't want to have anything to do with that old drunken bitch."

I tried to free myself, saying, "Merrill, I know her—I want a word with her—let me go!"

"Come on sit down, they are all staring at us, don't tell me that old dame is a friend of yours," and he pushed me back into my chair, I looked towards the door but they had got Fighting Flora out and all was quiet again.

Turning to face Merrill I said fiercely, "Yes, she is a friend of mine—are you shocked? She is a friend to every nurse, and is not a drunken old bitch, at least not all the time, and she is a darling at heart and she wouldn't hurt anyone."

So started a second row—later in his sitting-room he tried to pacify me and said, "I'll give you a cheque tomorrow, you can send it to her."

"No, thank you, I don't want your money for her, she would be very hurt if she knew I had been there tonight and did not speak to her—money isn't everything, you know."

"But respectability is, my prim and proper little miss, you went stiff with it last night—yet tonight you want to go and hobnob with that old has been streetwalker. I just don't understand you, honey."

"No, you wouldn't—you are too much of a snob!" I answered, swallowing hard.

Next day after a long morning in the New Market I was sitting with Doris Walters in their sitting-room, enjoying a long, cool orangeade, when in sauntered Merrill, We were surprised as he usually lunched in his office. Our greeting was rather stilted, and I left the conversation to Doris and Merrill until Jim came along, he always returned to the hotel for lunch, and always had a naughty story or two to tell. He soon had us all laughing, "Have you heard this one—today one of my clerks who has not to my sure knowledge missed a day away from the office for over a year asked for leave. 'I want to go home to my district, sir, my wife has just given birth to a son.' 'But *Babujee* how can that be, you have not been home for ages!' I asked puzzled. with a wave of his hand he blandly replied, 'that's nothing, Sir, by the

213

grace of God and my brother it has been accomplished.'"

I joined in the laughter, but Merrill could not resist a little dig at me. "Be careful, Jim, you will be shocking our little prude here," and he touched my knee.

"You are being silly," I said crossly.

Doris said, "I feel you two have been quarrelling, that is a good sign," and she smiled at me. How wrong you are, I thought. That afternoon I was depressed; lying on my bed trying to rest, I thought of home. Then with my afternoon cup of tea the bearer handed me a letter. This was from Vi; she had written, " . . . . Mama is not well, and if you are not doing anything very important, will you come home, as she will not stay in bed as the doctor has ordered." As Mama was very dear to me I decided to go home as soon as I could—the next day if possible. Merrill made a fuss when I told him I wanted to leave the next day.

"Are you sure it's not because we seem to be edgy with each other just lately, honey?"

"No, Merrill—I am not edgy, but if my mother needs me I must go, and, at once."

Then after making me promise I would meet him in Delhi that winter, he set about arranging for my journey back. Next day, as my luggage was being carried out of the hotel and placed in the waiting car, I saw the young man who had helped me down from the chair at Firpos on the Gala Night, and we exchanged smiles. We had seen him in the Great Eastern Hotel dining-room occasionally, and at other places—he did not appear to have a girlfriend and seemed lonely. He was now going into the hotel, but waited until the car moved away, then blew me a kiss which I returned. Merrill, not missing a thing said, "I knew he was going to do that," and sounded cross, but in the train saying "Goodbye" he was sweet, and I felt sad especially when he produced the record, 'I'll see you again,' and said, "whenever you play it, remember I am singing it to you."

CHAPTER 26

Nostalgic Moments

Back in Mhow I found Mama was already better. "She improved the moment she heard you were returning," I was told.

When she was quite well again our family doctor, who was a hard-working Indian Christian, asked me if I would like some work. "Yes, please, I would like to nurse round here for a while as my mother does not want me to go far away just yet."

So started my private nursing career. The first case was from the convent. One night just as we had finished dinner a note came from the doctor asking me to go across and help a nun who was sick. Next morning the convent *chaprassi* brought me a note asking for my bill, I replied that I had been pleased to help and as it was such a small job—there was no charge. I felt privileged at being able to help a nun and hoped this was going to prove a good augury. My next case was a Parsee, a member of the Illava family. They were respectable well-known business people who lived in a big house with a beautiful garden on Station Road. It was Granny Illava who was ill and I had about ten happy days nursing her. Parsees are known to be generous: they are very charitable, and never fail to subscribe to a deserving cause. It is said there are no Parsee beggars; the community sees to that. So when I presented my bill I was not surprised to find a fat tip had been added. In those days the fees were for day duty Rs20/- per day/£1/10/-. Night duty was Rs25/- or £1/17/6d per night.

A Sikh doctor then asked me to nurse a rich Hindu. On the final day I presented my bill; the exact amount only was given, though as I left some one kindly put an enormous garland of marigolds round my neck, and a posy of flowers was pushed into my hand. Then a jewel-laden *bebe*, presented me with a *pan*. Decorated in this fashion I felt extremely foolish climbing into the *tonga* which was surrounded by Indian children, and would gladly have given the little girls the flowers and *pan* but for the watching *bebe*. Out of sight of the house I presented the *tonga wallah* with the lot, after pocketing the cheque.

"Well! You know what to do in the future if you have to choose between a Parsee and a Hindu patient," said Doreen, who had now returned to Mhow..

I spent the next day or two calling on all the doctors. I also called on the matron of the British Military Hospital, and left copies of my references with them. Before leaving Peshawar I had armed myself with these. It is interesting to note now that Colonel C. Brierley, the Inspector General Civil Hospitals N.W.F. mentions amongst other things, "..... she is leaving entirely owing to the fact that her five year contract is up, and it has been decided to cut down the European nursing staff in order to increase the Indian staff." So from those early days the Europeans were gradually being pushed out—yet the majority of Anglo-Indians seemed blissfully unaware of what was happening until the rude awakening of 1947! I had chits from our surgeon superintendent and medical officer, also from the senior Asian doctors and the matron. When I called at the Zenana Mission Hospital to say "Goodbye" to Doctor and Mrs. Cox and the staff, Doctor Cox asked me my plans. I told him about the 'midder' I was hoping to take one day in Queen Charlotte's, "Let me know if there is anything I can do to help you—perhaps a reference or something," suggested this kind missionary.

"That's an idea, Doctor Cox, please write one now, not about nursing—I have enough of those already from the L.R.H.—but one about me personally; it might be useful to have a *chitty* from someone outside the hospital. I will be very grateful."

He left us for his study returning in a short while and said, "I have put it in an envelope to keep it clean—you can read it when you get back."

Amongst other nice things he had written, "......a girl of exemplary character." This coming from such a well-known missionary as Doctor R.J.H. Cox of the Afghan Mission Hospital as it was also called, was praise indeed! And I was very touched. Now the work was coming in steadily. Mama felt very proud when a car was sent for me, which was done more often than not. She would call out quite unnecessarily, "Your car has come, Irene!" This was to 'show off' to her women friends. Darling old Mama, I loved her for this little vanity. I was called upon twice to nurse an army officer's wife who did not fancy going into hospital—she was not very ill and had plenty of visitors. I had little to do besides taking an occasional temperature, pouring out her medicine and giving a daily bed-bath. There were plenty of books lying about and I was soon deep in one or two. Amongst her visitors were several young subs; and I was given the 'come hither' once or twice; these I chose to ignore, as in Mhow I was an 'outsider'. I could not join the club here—for the same reason as Celia could not in Peshawar—the family was in evidence.

But it was sad to hear the music from the club and to know they were dancing in there and I was shut out! Then one Saturday evening a crowd of young people came over from the club to see my patient. The women in pretty evening clothes, and the men in mess kit—I was filled with nostalgia. The uproar in my patient's room was terrific! The bearer was kept busy carrying in drinks, then someone thought of sister, who was sitting on the verandah reading, and a sherry was brought out by the bearer. I felt a real little Cinderella.

However, to cheer me up I had letters from Merrill, who kept reminding me that in the winter he would be in Delhi, and promised me a marvellous time when I got there—racing—the horse show, and all the other attractions of the Delhi winter season. Now more than ever I wished the man had not already had two wives. I wrote back promising to join him some time, but I was not too happy about the whole thing: the old conscience was at work again. Especially was I made uncomfortable when Mama in her naive way told friends—often in our hearing—what confidence she had in her daughters. I never went to any of the dances at the railway or the sergeants' mess—they had now lost all attraction for me. For recreation I went for an occasional game of tennis to the Institute, or S.& T. Club.

So with an occasional 'case' which helped to swell the savings in the post office, bringing my 'midder' nearer, the months flew past, and winter came to Mhow—this was lovely there and could be compared to a good English summer, plenty of sunshine and cool evenings, when a light coat was needed and occasionally a fire. Merrill wrote often now, asking about the Delhi holiday—he wanted me to spend Christmas with him; this I told him, was out of the question, as I had been away from home for so many years at Christmas that this year Mama was looking forward to my being with them.

"We'll have a goose, my girl—I'll buy one a fortnight before and I'll have it fattened up."

"You and the girls can have the goose with the Walkers, I'll have my curry, as usual: do you know, Mama, I never get a decent curry away from home, no one can make them as well as you can." This was the truth—I had often asked for a curry in the big hotels in Bombay and Calcutta, and had been very disappointed, with the dish presented. They gave fancy names for the same tasteless, yellowish-brown mixture: 'Madras Curry,' 'Casanova Kofta,' 'Fire Eaters Special,' and whether they were made of fish, fowl or the stringy goat, I was never able to discover.

Susie Pinto was in Mhow for Christmas, and one day in a burst of confidence I told her all about Merrill and the Delhi holiday—"To go or not to go—is the problem, Susie. It has been nice having Christmas at home, but otherwise I have found it dull—I miss my 'Posh' life." Susie knew to what I was referring as I had told her how I had spent the last five years, and she understood.

"Well, why don't you go, Irene—he sounds all right to me—a man with a seventeen-year-old daughter is surely not a wolf, and anyhow, goose, you can always bolt your bedroom door."

So I told Merrill in my next letter that I would definitely be in Delhi in January. He answered at once, saying that was a date and was glad I had at last—after all the 'shilly-shallying'—made up my mind! He softened this last bit by asking me what I wanted for Christmas. I asked for a good book. He did not give me just a book or two books—but a year's subscription to the London Book society.

Whenever they were very busy in 'Families' in the military hospital I was asked to go and help out—usually to 'special' on night duty. Then at Christmas that year I was asked to relieve the sister-on-duty the evening they had fixed for their mess dinner. That night alone in the strange duty room, my thoughts wandered back to the last five Christmases I had spent in Peshawar, and I was a little sad.

CHAPTER 28

Things That Go Bump in the Night

So January 1 1935, dawned and I was wondering how to tell Mama about the trip to Delhi, when one afternoon something happened that put this right out of my mind. I was fast asleep after a heavy curry lunch, when Mama's old *ayah* came into my room and shook me awake. "There is a big doctor *sahib* on the verandah asking for you, Missy *Baba*." In a semi-somnolent condition I walked on to the verandah and found the M.O. from the cantonment hospital waiting for me. He told me that three or four English children—their father an ex-'Tommy' who had settled in Mhow on leaving the army—had contracted smallpox.

"The situation is perplexing as we have no isolation hospital in Mhow—the only way we can segregate them and so hope to avert an epidemic is by taking a vacant house on the outskirts of Mhow and getting them there with you in charge. You will have all the help you require and anything you ask for. Do say you will do it, sister, as you know apart from the Queen Alexandras, and we can't ask them, they have their own duties, you are the only nurse in Mhow. We are all in your hands. So?"

Though I felt the responsibility was squarely being pushed on to me, there was only one answer a nurse could give. "My mother won't like this—she will not like the idea of my living out there alone with only the children and Asian staff—still I'll get round her somehow," I promised.

"Well, I'll leave you now to get ready, I have to see Colonel Mc-Coombe, but I'll be back."

I woke Mama and was giving her the news when a car drove up; this time a British officer whom I had not seen before stepped on to

219

the verandah: he was the Health Officer for Mhow, Lieut.Colonel McCoombe, R.A.M.C., who had come along to add weight to the M.O.'s plea for help. Again I was promised all help, and the need to keep the parents and children apart was stressed. "You must be firm, we do not want this thing to spread—so we are relying on you. The parents will take the patient's food over daily, as we do not want to burden you with that responsibility. Your own meals will have to be sent from here. A *chaprassi*, a *dai* or two, and some 'boys' will be your staff. Please get there as soon as you can and get things sorted out. We have sent over a truck-load of furniture, and the patients will follow as soon as you are ready for them." Then thanking me profusely both men departed, greatly relieved, I looked upon this as a challenge, and determined to show them what I could do; actually I felt I was going to enjoy it all, but Mama was a little doubtful.

"You will be alone in the jungle—miles away from anyone. It's a large rambling old house called Porters Folly, built by an eccentric old Englishman who retired there years ago—since he died no one has lived there—and the place must be full of bats and snakes—I don't like it at all, Irene."

"Oh, don't be silly, Mama!" said Doreen. "After her dear Pathans and sofa-cobras of the Frontier, she will feel at home with a few snakes and bats."

I had no time, unfortunately, to answer this one, as I was too busy getting my uniform packed and making lists of the medical supplies I needed. A *chaprassi* waited on the verandah to take these from me. Seeing him and the car that had been put at my disposal made Mama very proud. "She even had a colonel come—for her—there were two of them asking my girl to take the case," Mama was heard telling Aunt Alice this, who after years was visiting her.

"Oh, Irene, you should have heard Mama—how she was 'showing off,'" Doreen told me when next we met, and we both had a good laugh! I had so much to do in the few remaining hours of daylight— that it was one mad rush. Getting to the building—no one could call it a hospital yet—I found my 'staff' contentedly squatting on the verandah. The two 'boys' sharing a *hookah* whilst the *mather* sat apart with his *biri* well alight; his wife sat near him busy with a 'Madras Hunt' whilst she feverishly examined her daughter's head—the little girl cradled her fat, naked baby brother. The two *dais* were busy with their *pan dan*.

My arrival put an end to their party. They were now all armed with brooms and pails, and were soon being worked off their feet. "*Jaldi! Jaldi!*" We concentrated on the largest room which must have been the sitting room—this I decided would be the main ward. I had the walls brushed free of cobwebs and got the *bhisty*, who had now joined us with his *mussack*, to throw down gallons of water which the *jamadar's* family swept round mixed with phenyl. The beds now arrived, with a truck load of bedding and other necessities. The two *dais*, and I set about making up the beds. I was determined my hospital was going to look right, so taught the *dais* how to make up the beds in the correct hospital fashion—corners 'square,' and pillowcase openings facing away from the entrance.

Slowly but surely order emerged from chaos in this room. With the oil lamps burning brightly and the beds all in a row (I wondered at this stage why twelve were sent when I only expected three or four patients—I was to find out later!) with their red blankets folded down neatly—the 'ward' looked quite respectable—how I wished now I had thought of bringing a big bunch of the champak flowers from our compound. I made a mental note to ask the *chaprasssi* to bring some the next day. Great bowls of these creamy-white sweetly scented flowers did much—not only to brighten the place, but helped with the disinfectants to hide the smell peculiar to smallpox.

Late that night the children arrived; the M.O. accompanied them, bringing their mother, a big good-natured Scotswoman. Mrs. Ferguson was to be a great comfort to me in the next few weeks. As this was such a big house even by Indian or Colonial standards the authorities had decided she could stay in one of the rooms, getting the patients' diets ready, which the 'boy' would take from her to the children. Later I allowed her to talk to her children from the verandah—hoping the strong breeze that blew out there would keep her immune; anyway, one could hardly do less. Her husband, who visited every evening, was not allowed through the gates. She had to go out there and give him daily reports.

After I had got the children into bed and left a *dai* on guard at the door, I marshalled my staff, and with Mrs. Ferguson went into a room, which later I turned into a duty room and surgery, to be vaccinated. After this was done, and before our arms got too painful, I rounded up the servants again, some carrying lanterns now, and we went from room to room cleaning, sweeping, dusting and killing the centipedes, scorpions and huge spiders that had made 'Porters Folly' their home. I was thankful not to see a snake about, the old *bhisty* assured me that the noise we had been making must have frightened them all away; I sincerely hoped he was right! I did not dare look up at the ceiling in any of the rooms or think about them too much.

In those old houses, with crude tiles on a thatch roof, the ceiling in the rooms consisted of a locally woven material whitewashed to give it added strength, and fastened to the rafters between the walls. This space between the roof and *chhut*, as it was called, became the favourite breeding place for civet cats, mongooses, rats and other nocturnal creatures that used the place as a home. One felt lost in a respectable house with nothing moving around at night. The ceiling materiel naturally only had a limited life, and if neglected, as in this old residence, the occupants frequently fell through, no doubt to their own and the consternation of those below. Even a snake has been known to drop from above, luckily on to the mosquito net of an unsuspecting sleeper. When the staff and I were nearly on our knees with exhaustion I had to say *khutum*—finished!

When I got to my room I found my *chaprassi* sitting over a brazier, he was keeping the meal warm that Mama had sent over; I was really too tired to eat but the old man insisted I should try. I fell asleep almost immediately only to dream of beasties and things that go bump in the night playing hide-and-seek on my bed. I woke with a start, and sitting up in bed thought of Merrill and the Delhi holiday for the first time! With a shock I realised that I had thrown this away ". . . . . . .for centipedes, scorpions and spiders."

"I do not agree with you, Irene, you threw the holiday and Merrill over for your duty as a nurse to the sick children who needed you more. You had no choice in that situation—did he not realise that?" Apparently he did not! Susie, who was back in Mhow after months had asked me how the Delhi holiday had gone.

"It never got started," I told her, than explained all that had happened. "I sent Merrill a telegram the next day saying, 'Unable to keep date as arranged—letter follows.' This was followed by a long letter explaining the position and apologising. I left it to him to suggest another date. He did not answer for ages, in which time I guessed everything was over between us. When he did write, he ended with the words, '. . . . . . .remember it is you who are making the break and not I'. So that's how Fiasco No. 2 ended, my dear."

"From all you have told me, Irene, that man should have been a *sultan* or *nawab*—women to him are mere chattels—you are really well out of it"

She may have been right but after that letter I was left with on empty lost feeling for a long time. Work again was to be an anodyne, and I had plenty of that! A few cases of mumps followed the smallpox, these in turn were followed by a case of puerperal fever; this little Hindu mother I nursed entirely myself, allowing none of the staff near her. I taught the *dais* to give bed-baths and do the simpler nursing jobs, whilst I did the smearing of the smallpox cases with some ointment or oil. I have forgotten what we used in those days to diminish the chances of 'pitting.' This was something I did very carefully, especially the little girls' faces and arms, and when the scabs fell—which had to be collected up and burnt—leaving a clean surface, no one was happier than I. Then with the temperatures to take, medicines to give, reports to write and stocks to be checked, I was busy enough.

After a few days a fresh outbreak was discovered, and two or three more cases were admitted, again European children, friends of those already in hospital. Now all the contacts were rounded up and brought in. Soon all the rooms were occupied. It was hectic now for all of us. special watch had to be kept on the Indian patients' relatives who meant well when they wanted to trip from room to room visiting all the patients, even wanting to take flowers to the smallpox children! In their opinion they were being sociable whilst I was being tiresomely officious. In the evenings, after a bath with a strong disinfectant poured in, I would leave all my clothes, including shoes, in the bathroom, changing into mufti to walk about in the huge compound. All traces of the once beautiful garden had long since disappeared, throttled by the weeds and jungle, which was infested with snake and rat holes—and I walked carefully.

Doreen occasionally visited me with her current boyfriend, though they took good care to keep a safe distance, and we conversed by shouting at each other. Mama knew she could not come close to me, so wisely kept away. "I'll serve her better by sending her good nourishing meals," she had remarked, and in that bitter cold—we were now having an unusually severe cold spell—her delicious ox-tail stews and cow-heel curries were much appreciated. Merrill had not robbed me, I thought, thankfully sitting down to one of these meals, of the healthy appetite and respect for food which I had always enjoyed. So day followed day, and gradually all the cases improved. After the quarantine period had been observed they were discharged. I returned to my family and 'Porters Folly' was embraced again by the jungle.

CHAPTER 29

Indore

Forgetting those things which are behind, and
reaching forth unto those things which are before.
(Philipi 13,14.)

In February that year I was sent two references and as both were dated 14th February, 1935, I spoke of them as the strangest Valentines I had received. One was from the Executive Officer, Mhow—Major A.L. Molyneux. This one had the stamp of the office of the cantonment authority. The other was from Lieut.-Colonel McCoombe, R.AM.C. Health Officer, Mhow. They were kind enough to say nice things about my work. I think it must have been these references which secured for me the post of Acting Matron at the King Edward Hospital in Indore, in the state of Holkar, thirteen miles from Mhow. I had written to Colonel M.A. Nicholson, I.M.S. the superintendent, after being told by Doctor Pinto that private nursing in Indore amongst the wealthy Hindus and *rajahs* should be lucrative.

I told Colonel Nicholson that I was to be in Mhow for about a year (Doreen was now engaged to Henry Busby, and I wanted to be in India for their wedding, so my going to England had to be postponed) and wanted some cases: I asked for his help. He replied asking me to Indore, I was to see him at the hospital; he gave me no idea why he wanted this interview. Imagine my surprise when the *tonga* stopped under the porch and I saw Josephine Manuel, one of the few coloured student nurses who had been my junior on a spell of night duty in St. George's, standing on the verandah waiting to greet me. "Hello! Green," she said, all smiles.

"Manuel! What a lovely surprise! What are you doing here?"

"I am the matron," she replied with a chuckle.

"Hell's Bells! As we used to say in St. George's some people have all the luck!"

She then took me into her office and we settled down to a comfortable chat and a 'cuppa,' after she had posted a little Hindu nurse to keep watch for the Colonel *Sahib* and to warn us in time if he approached. "I'm not supposed to tell you, Green, but he wants to see if you will take over from me for a year whilst I go to England to take an administrative course: I have won a scholarship for this."

"Congratulations, Josephine, how nice for you."

We sat talking about old times until the superintendent was seen going into his office.

"Now when he mentions the job, don't forget to look surprised," warned Josephine.

The *chaprassi* then came to say, "Colonel *Sahib* sends *salaams*," and once I was in his office Colonel Nicholson lost no time in coming to the point. He offered me the post of acting matron for the year Josephine was to be away on a Florence Nightingale Scholarship. A furnished house was provided, also a *tonga* for the journey between the house and hospital. I was given a typed sheet with full details, and asked after studying it to let him know what I had decided. On the train returning to Mhow I read over this, and by the time the *tonga* stopped at Champak bungalow I had decided to accept.

It was the experience I wanted. This was a training school for Indian nurses and medical students. Altogether there were between sixty and seventy nurses. The knowledge I gained there, plus my nebulous 'midder' from Queen Charlotte's should, *Inshallah*, be helpful in getting me a permanent job as matron somewhere in Central India. Mama was waiting impatiently on the verandah to hear my news. She was happy to learn I was going to be near her for another year. "I'll spend my time between you and the girls here: I shall probably spend a week or ten days with you, then return to them."

This is exactly what she did for the next twelve months; shuttling between us. After she had been with me for a week—in which time she would upset my cook by taking over the cooking, and what was much more to his disgust and alarm, the bazaar accounts were checked!—She would start worrying, about the girls at home. "I'd better get back, Irene, I don't know how those girls are managing." This, after having given repeated detailed instructions to the servants to ensure the smooth working of the house. When I told Vi and

Doreen how she worried about them when she was with me, they laughed and said it was the same thing in reverse when she was in Mhow. "My poor Irene, I wonder how she is faring: I don't believe that cook-boy gives her enough to eat, I think I'll go up for a few days, girls."

But all this came after I had talked over the offer I had received with Mama and the girls, and they agreed with my decision. I went into Indore to tell Colonel Nicholson I would like to accept the post, and met Josephine Manuel again. She was asked by the colonel to show me round the hospital, after which she took me to her bungalow and I was shown over that. Apart from the large sitting-room and dining-room there were two bedrooms with a bathroom each, a store room and the usual front and back verandah. Back in her office we sat to discuss a few more details, then Josephine said a strange thing. "You won't be making many changes, will you Green? As you are only here for a year I should carry on as things are, if I were you."

"Yes, I suppose that is what I will do—off-hand I cannot think of any changes I want to make." And I was not speaking with my tongue in my cheek.

Just before she had to leave for Bombay she vacated the house, and went to live with her family—who were Indian Christians. Then accompanied by Mama and one or two *chokras* to help us clean, dust and unpack, I settled down to my new home. After a day or two Mama engaged a cook-bearer and a *matherani* for me; then the *chokras* were sent back to Mhow.

At the hospital I found we had two Roman Catholic nuns who worked there, with no reward save that of knowing they were doing good. Mother Mary Claire had taken over the small ward for children. Mother Mary Theopen relieved in any ward or did any odd job given to her—both were a great comfort and help to me. For the first month I was content to 'pick up the threads', then the old bug, my enthusiasm, got going and the ideas kept flooding in—why should not these lovely Indian girls have a proper uniform? I talked it over with Chandra Bai, the head-nurse, who came in every afternoon with the ward reports. She was very impressed and really got excited when I made a rough sketch of what I had in mind, painting in the different coloured belts for the first, second and third year nurses—which would be worn over aprons.

She realised as I did, that even the most illiterate of villagers would soon learn that it was a waste of time asking a 'green-belt' for his sedative. He would also learn that it was not done to ask a 'red-belt' to give him a bed-pan, she being a third-year nurse: the 'yellow-belt', the middle one who took the temperatures, would give him this if he was an operation case, whilst the 'red-belt' would give him his pain-killing sedative, (in most cases a harmless mixture of soda bicarb. or mist expect., but it worked!) and the 'green-belt' who rubbed his back would give him his diet. I deliberately chose the colours green, yellow and red remembering that all Indian girls love their chilly, green when it is young and unripe—yellow when a little riper—and red when mature. So even the villager from the remotest jungle should get the idea. Chandra Bai was quite excited by now, then suddenly her face fell and she said, "Where is the money to come from, Matron Sahib? Already we are providing our own *dhoties* and *saris* and ward shoes, these aprons will cost a lot of money, I doubt if the girls can afford them."

"You talk it over with the girls and tell me how they feel about it, if they want the change, I'll see the Colonel *Sahib* and ask his help."

The nurses wore white *dhoties* or *saris* with white blouses and tennis shoes on duty. There were no belts or badges to distinguish between the ranks. Most of the girls were Gujaratis: Hindus from good homes in the Western districts of India, north of Bombay. A few were Moslems, and three or four were Christians—*protégées* of the Roman Catholic Church in Indore. All of these had a certain amount of education; in their own language. It was the Gujarati girls who wore the *dhoty* which was both ugly and vulgar, not only seen through Western eyes, as I have heard the *sari*-clad women and the peasant class women who wear the *sari* or *jugra*, as these very full ankle-length skirts are also called, criticise this mode of dress. The *dhoty* wrapped round somewhat like a *sarong*, with most of its fullness at the back, was caught up and drawn very tightly between the buttocks, accentuating these and exposing the leg up to the knee behind, and midway between the ankle and knee in front. It was neither pretty nor graceful. Full aprons to hide these would be a kindness, I thought, but I left the decision to them.

The very next day Chandra Bai told me the nurses were all in favour of the change. "Now we will feel like proper nurses," she said. Colonel Nick—I soon shortened his name to this—was most kind; he received the suggestion with sympathy and promised to help. After a few days I was told to go ahead with the scheme. As a tailor was permanently employed here we soon had the aprons ready, and as the hospital *dhoby* had to do the laundering the nurses had no additional expenses to meet. Very soon they came to realise that these aprons protected their *dhoties* or *saris*, but what pleased them most were those belts!

A few of the doctors and students told me it made things easier for them; getting hold of a 'red-belt' meant they had got the right nurse to do a round with them in the wards. For the first three months I did not allow the probationer to wear a belt at all; at the end of the three months, if she proved satisfactory, she was given a green belt and told if later she passed her first examination she would be given a yellow belt and called a Junior. Now they felt they had something to work for!

Then I remembered that in matron's office in St. George's Hospital, set into the wall, was a very big blackboard; this was chalked up daily by matron, and under the ward names one could see where each nurse was working. There was a sick column, a leave column, and one for night duty. This was useful when a nurse was required in a hurry. In no time I had one put in my office, and soon had many visitors in to inspect this; doctors, students and clerks. Then the nurses sent word that they would like to see it also, and it was arranged for them to come in small groups daily in the *tiffin* hour; then I would stand and explain the idea showing each her place in the scheme of things. All this they felt made them a little more important and they were happy, I found lecturing to the girls in my fluent though 'kitchen' brand of Urdu a problem as the students all spoke the high class variety. Still they were kind enough not to laugh at my efforts, at least, not in my office!

One of my daily chores was inspecting the nurses' quarters after 'Mrs. Mopps' had been around. These were long lines of single rooms opening on to a narrow verandah. The rooms were very dismal: a single small window in the outside wall had iron bars to it! Then the verandah was enclosed by expanded metal, and was grim reminder of the Mental Ward at St. George's. Getting the inspection over I was always glad to get out through the only door there was—this door was locked nightly at ten o'clock by the theatre orderly. To brighten their rooms most of the nurses had embroidered their white bed-spreads with strange-looking birds and flowers in bright colours and "Goodnight" and "Sweet Dreams" was usually added on the pillowcase. The only table in the room was shared by the two occupants; a cloth draped over this had "Welcome" added for good measure.

This table and the two *charpoys* were all the furniture they had—a tin trunk stood under each *charpoy*. One morning Chandra Bai joined us on this inspection, and leaving the place I asked her if it was necessary for these girls to be locked in at night. She assured me it was and added that in spite of this precaution there was much *golmal*—trouble. "Some nurses," she said, "are *matwala piyar*"—drunk with love! Very often I had reports from her or one or other of the staff nurses who in this hospital took the place of the sisters in the European hospitals, I was told that Lalita Bai, Sushila Bai or Sunder Bai— (the *'Bai'* bit is a courtesy title)—was seen in some *kala jugga* in the hospital corridors laughing and talking with a student, or actually seen on the street with a student. "Now we will all get a bad name!" was wailed in my ear.

To comfort her I said, "All nurses have a bad name—deserved or otherwise." All the same it was difficult to believe that these demure little creatures with their downcast eyes and 'butter-wouldn't-melt-in-my-mouth' expression could be naughty. I never tried to sort out any of these complaints myself, as intrigue, laced with spite and envy was really at work all the time: so I fell back on Chandra Bai for help and was usually guided by her. She was a high-caste Hindu, already a grandmother at thirty-two! Then often the staff nurse who worked in the 'Theatre' was reported: they told me she was much too familiar with one of the surgeons; though as she was one of the very few Moslems and these reports were brought by the Hindus I took no action. The nurses' food was another problem that brought me headaches—and not being able to solve it was a sore point. Two women were employed as cooks and it was my job to inspect the kitchen and food daily—yet as a non-Hindu I was expected to keep a safe distance—not to defile!

This was ridiculous, and I asked Mother Mary Claire one morning as we met near my office, "Why isn't the kitchen inspection done by a Hindu? Mother—I am really not doing the job at all well; the whole thing is unsatisfactory."

"Because no one will take it on—there has always been trouble. 'The cooks are good, the cooks are bad; not enough vegetables, too much vegetables; we want a change of diet, why can't we have our favourites more often.' They cannot all be satisfied," she said.

"Then what can I do? Can you suggest something, Mother."

"Yes, Matron, leave well alone."

I was sorry later I did not take this advice, I dismissed the cooks when three or four nurses complained almost daily about them. The new cooks had hardly settled down when three or four other nurses took up the daily moan—now I saw the wisdom of the nun's advice. I was too busy and interested in my new job to go into Mhow at first, and my family came to see me—often the Pintos came as well—I was always glad to see them as I could get news of Susie. She, like me, hated letter writing, so this was the only way we kept in touch. One evening we were all sitting outside in a huge circle when a Eurasian family came down the road—I had got to know them as the little boy could not pass my gate without swinging on it. The Beauchamps were going to the *dak* bungalow for their usual 'sundowner.' I waved and smiled and Doctor Pinto turned around to see to whom I was waving; then he shot out of his chair. "Anthone!" he yelled, and was halfway up the path.

"That's Mr. Beauchamp," I said after him. He stopped dead and looked round. "Beauchamp? That's Anthone, the waiter. . . . . ," and he was down the road before the poor fellow could escape. As they stood talking on the road I thought it would look well if I asked them in—then I proceeded to introduce Mrs. Beauchamp to Mrs. Pinto and my mother.

"Beauchamp? Beauchamp?" persisted Dr. Pinto, "I say, man, where did you pick up such a posh name? I bet you got it out of the hotel register."

We could see Mrs. Beauchamp was feeling this acutely, and after they left Mrs. Pinto rounded on her husband. "But, my dear," protested Pinto, "I've known that fellow since he was that high. His father was Francis, the Indian Christian head cook of the Majestic Hotel in Agra, who before he was converted was Ganesh, a low caste Hindu and only a dish-washing *misalchi*. Anthone was a waiter there." Now Mr. Pinto went deeper into the mire by adding, "since when has he been a Eurasian? And where did he get his pretty fair wife?"

"She probably married him from the Agra Convent, a lot of those girls were glad to marry just anyone to get away from the petty restrictions. I know because I was one of them," replied Mrs. Pinto, now covering her husband with confusion. She was paying him back for his rudeness to 'Anthone' or 'Mr. Beauchamp,' as that gentleman no doubt wished to be called.

Later when Mama and I discussed this in private, she said scornfully, "Talk about the pot calling the kettle black!"

Soon after this Susie came to see me—she was on leave again—and the Beauchamps passed down the road as we walked about in the compound. As I waved to them I remarked, "I am glad your father is not here, he caused quite an embarrassing scene not so long ago," and I proceeded to tell her what had happened, ending with "...... it was rather cruel."

"You should not be surprised, Irene, don't you realise that we are very cruel to each other?" By the 'we' I knew she meant the Anglo-Indian community. "Haven't you noticed when a new baby is born how they all flock around, not out of friendship, but merely to see which shade of brown has been produced. I am determined not to give them that satisfaction. . . . ."

"Ah! That reminds me," I said, breaking in. "What is this I hear about you and some sergeant? Has the great Miss Pinto fallen at last? I am told you only dance with him at the S. & T. Come on, tell me all about it—I am longing to know."

"Well! I am only human, he picked me out from all those girls at the S. & T.—ME! A little DARKIE! I was flattered at first, then this turned to love."

As we paced about I squeezed her arm and asked, "Are you going to marry him? Has he asked you? 'Are his intentions honourable?' as my Mama would say. I heard he is madly in love with you—of course I shall be your bridesmaid and. . . . ."

"Stop! Stop! Irene, you go too fast; he has asked me to marry him, and it has not been too easy saying 'no', but you know how I feel about these mixed marriages; Papa says I'm a fool. Mary is quite happy in England and he thinks I can be too. Do you know what advice he gave her before she sailed? 'Don't tell any of them you are a half-caste, say you are from the middle East—Persia will do nicely—as you know something about the Parsees and their religion'. With her olive complexion Mary will get away with it—but will I? Anyway that's not the question—it's the children I am thinking about—they are never accepted—not really. Some Europeans pretend to like them—but it's pity—not love!"

By now I was very curious. "Did you really tell him all this? Did you tell him you did not want coloured children? And what did he say? Oh, go on, Susie, do tell me, I am very anxious to know."

"Yes, I did, Irene, and his argument was that they might be white or near-white. I conceded it was a possibility, not a probability, but, anyway I was not brave enough to take this risk."

Then anxious to help I told her about the Bowmans in Neemuch, and how they had been married happily for years but had no children, as Mrs. Bowman held similar views to her own.

"But are you sure Mrs. Bowman is happy, Irene? Max. may well say, 'All right then, we won't have any children,' and he may be happy for a time; but later? No, my dear, it's not fair. And anyway, you must remember I am a Roman Catholic. Now don't you think I have done the right thing, or do you think I am a little mad?"

"Well, I often think we are all a little mad and for different reasons—think of Anthone and his silly vanity—selecting such a posh name as Beauchamp—and poor Mrs. Boodrie?" And thinking of that hard-working person I had to laugh. "It has its humorous side, don't you think?"

"No, I only see the tragedy," she answered.

"You are too intense—too bitter, and I'm damned if I am going to let you make me bitter, so some along, let's go to the '*Dak*' and drown our sorrows in beer—glorious beer. If I know anything of British sergeants, at least he will have taught you to drink."

We were enjoying the beer and chips when to my disgust Susie tried to bring this subject up again. "I can't understand you, Irene, you have not had too rosy a time yourself—there was a Miss Snob, you mentioned her claws; and the sly digs or hints from some young fellow in Peshawar. Then what was that remark about a 'black dress' from your last boyfriend, the rich American you. . . . .'"

"Oh, stop Susie, all that's past! Completely finished. I am now embarking on a new chapter and I have a feeling things are going to be different. Anyway I believe my mother when she says, 'It will all come right.'" Looking at her glum face I said, "Come on, let's share another beer, and I'll give you a toast—Here's to the future for you and for me, may it be happier—with lots of fun!"

CHAPTER 30

Mendicants and Wedding Bells

One morning Chandra Bai came to report that a nurse was ill. "Where have you sent her? Order my *tonga*, I'll go and see her, Chandra Bai," I said.

"Matron *Sahib*, she is in Beaumont—female—where did you think she had gone?" she asked, looking puzzled.

"Well! I know you haven't a special sick room for the nurses here, but I thought you must have some arrangement with another hospital or nursing home to take our sick nurses."

"Oh, no! We have to put them into any vacant bed we can find in the female wards." And Chandra Bai opened the report-book preparing to read, but I had not finished.

"This surprises me, *Baijee*, it is all wrong. Nurses work very hard and are entitled to a little extra comfort when they are sick. Why have you no special room set apart for them? I notice the students have a sick room."

Chandra Bai hesitated and then replied.

"I suppose because no one has thought about it: but it would be nice for us to have our own sick bay," she ended wistfully.

That set me thinking, perhaps I could do something to help these girls. A nurses' ward, just a three-bed small room would do. I thought and thought about this. On my rounds I had noticed a room that was not used much. The Indian lady doctor saw the ante-natal cases here, but if she could be persuaded to give this up and see these patients on that portion of the verandah which was near the maternity ward—this could be screened off and fitted up quite nicely for her. . . . . . These thoughts persisted. But where was the money to come from to furnish this room? I dare not ask the committee for any more. Then one night, unable to sleep, the idea suddenly came—beg for it!

Next day I asked Chandra Bai and Jai Bai, who was assistant head nurse, to come to my office. I then told them my idea. They agreed with me that a nurses' ward was necessary, but could not see where I was going to get so much money. "If I go out collecting from house to house, from rich and poor, will one of you accompany me?" Jai Bai volunteered, as Chandra Bai was needed at the hospital 'on call' for the maternity cases which came in at any time, day or night.

After getting permission from Colonel Nicholson, we got James, the typist, to make us several lists and then set out day after day in a *tonga* after duty hours. When any sum was contributed it was put down in a column, and the contributor was asked to sign alongside, after which either Jai Bai or I added our signature. When the householder or housewife was unable to sign, a thumb impression was taken. We first approached the two palaces: Lal Bagh and Manik Bagh. We were lucky in having; two *maharajahs* resident in Indore at the time; the ex-*maharajah* who some years previously abdicated in favour of his son lived at Lal Bagh, or the 'old palace' as it was sometimes called, We collected from both palaces, then went on to the millionaire mill-owner Sir Hukam Chand; after him we did the rounds of all the other wealthy Hindus in Indore before turning our attention to the less affluent.

It was tiring work—and the slowly trotting pony with his jingling bells seemed to mock us when we wished he would go a little faster, but we dare not even voice our thoughts, as those *tonga-wallahs* loved nothing better than to get hold of the whip and lash those poor half-starved beasts. We were able to do our begging in Mhow only at the weekends, when Mama would supply our meals and put up a camp cot in my old room for Jai Bai. In Mhow we had great success with the Parsee community; they gave generously. We went to as many European houses as we could, in fact we scrounged wherever possible. Some days we did better than others: the disappointing days made me wish I had never started this venture, but having started I had to go on.

It was some months before I could go to Colonel Nick and say, "Here's a good sum—now do we get started?" In the meantime the daily hospital work continued—for Jai Bai and for me. Lectures, inspections, rounds. I had got used to seeing some horrible sights on the Frontier, but here the leper ward never failed to make me shudder, and one day whilst in there a sudden gust of wind sent something into my eye. I bathed it at once, even so I was not happy about it for a long time.

Talking about my work I mentioned this ward to Doreen, she asked, "Why is it you nurses are not frightened, and how is it you don't seem to catch these horrible diseases?"

Then, I could think of no better answer than, "Because we are too wicked to catch anything." But now I would answer, "Because nurses, like children, have a special protection."

Mama had worried a great deal about my living alone, she wanted me to get someone to share the house. "If no one else, why don't you get one of your nurses: you can easily spare the dressing room off the second bedroom," she suggested.

So, when a private nurse called for the first time to register for work, and told me she was unhappy where she was living, I immediately took the opportunity to suggest her living with me. I made it clear that I was only doing this for company. As she was an educated Moslem girl from a good home I was pleased to have contacted her. She was of the Ismalia tribe of whom the Aga Khan is Spiritual Head; they are also called Kohjas. Gulabi Bai, or Rosey, then told me she had a maid servant and wanted to bring her along. I warned her that I could only spare the dressing room and wondered where the servant would sleep. "Oh, the verandah will do very nicely for her," she replied disdainfully. I was happy to have the comfort the presence of these two women brought. But after a while, when Gulabi Bai started nagging Geesie Bai, the maid, who never answered back but crept around like a mouse, eyes always cast down, I was upset.

Geesie Bai seemed to try hard, cleaning her mistress' room, shopping, cooking and washing her clothes; yet she failed to please and the nagging continued. In time I wondered if Gulabi Bai had this girl in her power for some reason:, why did she not rebel? 'Goosie' Bai, I thought, if only you would answer back, just once! You know, my dear, we have met before, only they called you 'mouse' then. . . . One Sunday—when the nagging went on practically non-stop all day—I was in my sitting-room working on the nurses' ward accounts, as I had been unable to go out begging that day, Jai Bai not being well—when a timid whisper "Matron *Sahib*" made me look up, and standing trembling by the door I saw Geesie Bai. She was trying to tell me something between her sobs, and not being able to understand I called out to Gulabi Bai to come and explain.

One look at her face told me she was in a rage! "*She* wants to be a nurse! *She* wants to be a nurse!" The emphasis on the 'she' needed no explanation, but her next words made it crystal clear. "This *pagali*"—mad woman—"Matron *Sahib*, tell her she cannot nurse, that you will not have her. I have been telling her that from morning and now she has sneaked in to ask you herself."

I was in an awkward position and had to think quickly. "Gulabi Bai," I replied, "You know it is a rule of the hospital that I must not conduct any of its affairs from my house—so I cannot answer here. If Geesie Bai wants to be a nurse, whether she can or cannot I can only say after considering her application, which has to be presented at my office," and with that I ended a painful scene.

However, Geesie Bai took the hint. She was not as dumb as she made out. The next time Gulabi Bai had to leave Indore and go on a case to one of the small states, Geesie Bai came to see me at the hospital. I found that she had about as much education as most of them and decided to give her a trial. She went away happy, then packing her poor possessions in a battered old tin trunk which she carried on her head, she returned to the office with the key to Gulabl Bai's room—this she handed over to me before proceeding to the nurses' quarters—the key I sent by Chandra Bai to one of the clerks to have locked up in the hospital safe. After a day or two I met her in the wards and stopped to have a word with her.

"Are you happy with us?"

"Oh, Matron *Sahib*, I am very happy: now I sleep on a *charpoy* again!"

I had noticed on my rounds in the nurses' quarters the pathetic attempts to brighten her share of the room—paper flowers were stuck in gaudy coloured vases, and cheap prints of some Hindu gods adorned the walls. In time I guessed the embroidered bedspread would appear. The early reports about her work were promising, the 'Staff' said she was conscientious and hard-working, though she had great difficulty in getting her to abandon, her habit of throwing herself at her feet when rebuked for any little fault. This humble gesture of prostration, the placing of hands and forehead on the feet of the authority in charge, is still popular amongst the poorer rural classes. When after a month her ward report stated, "She is kind, gentle and hard-working, and will make a good nurse," I was satisfied.

Though I was not looking forward to the return of Gulabi Bai, who had been away for six weeks on a typhoid case and was expected back any day now. What were her reactions going to be? I wondered.

I did not have long to wait to find out as the report about the case in Dhar, which should have been given in person was sent to the office. With this she sent a curt note asking for the key to her room, as she wanted to collect her possessions: she was leaving Indore for good, she informed me. I was thankful to have been spared an interview, which I knew would have been unpleasant.

After we had collected a respectable sum towards the nurses' ward Colonel Nick took me to Rasalpura to the Mission Training School for Indian Christian boys. There they were taught arts and crafts and light industries. They had a workshop, and Colonel Nicholson placed an order for three beds to be made entirely of metal. This was a precaution against the bugs which infested the wooden *charpoys*. After the order for the beds had been placed, Jai Bai and I started on the other requirements. We bought bed linen; also a few *saris* and nightdresses. The linen cupboard and the three bedside lockers were painted white. Our colour scheme was white, blue and silver. A blue and white checked lino was ordered for the floor. A corner of the back verandah adjacent to this ward was partitioned off by a joiner, and a little pantry and bathroom was built in this space.

I really let myself go over that pantry. A primus stove was bought and a few pots and pans, a pretty blue and white tea set was displayed on the white shelves, with copper and brass vessels which the Indians fancy placed alongside. I added some cutlery and finished off with jars labelled for tea, sugar and coffee. A mistake I made was ordering an English bath from Bombay. I wanted these girls to have all the comforts, but forgot in my keenness that the Indians consider this an unhygienic way of bathing, they prefer the showers, I suppose they used that bath the way all Indians use an English bath, they stand in it, and after soaping themselves, they pick up a pail with hot and cold water mixed and empty this over their heads. When all was ready the nuns from the Nursing Home came over to see the ward, which looked very pretty.

One of these nuns was overheard by me saying, "It's so good, it should be used by European patients." She jumped when from behind her an angry voice said, "This ward will NOT be used by any but the sick nurses." Colonel Nicholson now suggested we should have an opening ceremony, and that the ward should be named after me. The wife of a senior British officer in the civil service did this by cutting a white ribbon with a pair of silver scissors specially made and presented to her after the ceremony.

Doreen's wedding to Henry Busby, the eldest son of Captain Busby, our very good friend, took place on the 24th February, 1936. This event was the *finale* of my nursing days in Central India before leaving for London and the 'midder' course. Each member of the family was given a special job. I was asked to decorate the hall and with the help of two volunteers from amongst my nurses made a huge white crepe paper bell of flowers for the couple to stand beneath when receiving the good wishes of the guests. (This idea I had copied from the Fraser-Bolam wedding in Peshawar.) We made this in my spare bedroom at Indore, seated on the floor surrounded by pots of glue, wire, and the white, yellow and green paper which I had bought in Mhow.

The bamboo framework was made by the *chikwallah,* who haunted Champak bungalow for orders, selling cane baskets, tables, chairs and the useful *chik-mats.* The nurses and I had lots of fun making this bell. Word had gone round the hospital about the wedding, and all the nurses were agog; whenever they were free they strolled down to my house to see how the bell was progressing. I was asked many questions about Christian weddings, our customs and so forth. The interest they showed made it inevitable that I ask them all to the wedding. This shook the family, as the list of guests was already a formidable one; this was inevitable, as Henry and Doreen had lived nearly all their lives in Mhow. All the railway had to be asked, then they had many friends amongst the army and telegraph department: and Mama had quite a number of her own friends. "My old cronies and lame ducks must not be left out—or they will be very hurt," she had insisted.

After the bell was ready we realised it was too wide to pass through the railway carriage door, so had to take it into Mhow by *tonga.* A nurse and I sat holding the bell on our laps all those miles. Near the Octrol or Customs post on the border of the State of Indore and Mhow British territory, our *tonga wallah* was ordered to a halt, and to my astonishment I was asked to pay for the bell. I told the officials that the paper and other material used, also the framework, had all been bought in Mhow, but those *babus* were unrelenting and made me pay. They had never seen anything like this before and doubtless thought it had cost a lot of money.

The day of the wedding saw us all up at crack of dawn, then armed with broom and dusters Vi and I set off in a *tonga* for the institute. We found the servants we had engaged for the day waiting there with a large number of those ever useful *chokras.* We found jobs for all, and started them on cleaning and dusting. After the dusting and final sweeping of the hall we had all the little tables brought in and placed close together. As I knew the nurses would not be able to eat the refreshments supplied by our caterers—owing to the caste rules—I had arranged for Jai Bai to do the catering for them. To avoid confusion, we 'fenced' off a corner of the hall with white ribbon, and in this enclosure we put the tables and chairs for the nurses. As a further precaution I warned Jai Bai to get her party seated here as soon as she could after they returned from church.

Jai Bai and two assistants were at the institute early, arranging their refreshments. Indian sweet-meats *buggias* and *puries*. They portioned all these on to four plates which they placed on each table, with a glass of differently coloured sherbet by each plate. This looked very gay but was slightly unusual for the institute! To off-set this I arranged masses of pink and white phlox in vases and had the flower bell hung from the ceiling. This was to be the centre for the bride and groom to receive their guests. Time was passing and Vi got anxious. In the end she came and dragged me away from my flowers. "We will barely have time to get bathed and dressed," "he said. "I do hope Doreen is nearly ready." To our amazement, when we got home, we found har wrapped in an old *kimono* seated cross-legged on a bed calmly and amiably talking to Mama.

"Doreen!" said Vi, "You ought to be nearly dressed!"

And I added, "Do you realise that you are getting married in a couple of hours time?"

"Yes, that is why I am listening to Mama's last minute instructions on the facts-of-life," she replied, with a wink.

I can still remember what pleasure I had helping my lovely little sister to dress. Doreen, with her olive complexion, black hair and soft brown eyes, made a lovely bride. With a last warning, "Remember to walk slowly up the aisle," I left her to get into one of the many cars my helpful staff had arranged for us. At the reception in the Institute I looked in vain for my nurses, as I saw some Europeans and Anglo-Indians making for their reserved corner: however, on seeing the Indian refreshments they had the sense to move along to the other tables. Susie Pinto was standing at my side when I saw that dear lady Mrs. Boodrie, accompanied by Mrs. Bowman, making for these tables: the ribbon 'fences' must have been pulled down by the crowd. I was about to step up to them to move them along when Susie, with a naughty twinkle in her eye, stopped me. "Wait! Listen!" Mrs. Boodrie, seating herself, was now heard to say in her high-pitched 'chee-chee', "My!

Why they are giving such kind of food! Men, do they think we are natives?" Mrs. Bowman, that poor frustrated female from Neemuch, who was not allowed to have the babies she wanted, merely looked down at her plate bewildered! Susie was very naughty, she pinched my arm and whispered, "Another case of the pot calling the kettle black!"

When I could control my voice I walked up to them and said, "Will you please move along to these other tables which are for Europeans. These are for my Indian staff." That soon shifted them! Then I went to look for my nurses; they were standing outside feeling too shy to enter. Taking an arm of the two seniors, I led them inside saying, "*Challo, juldi, bahut chil hai,*" hearing there were plenty of 'hawks' around the others soon followed. We had yet another laugh, this time one in which all the family were able to join. We had decided a white wine should be served for economic reasons, there was no thought of trying to deceive anyone; so when a whisper ran round and Doreen and I heard it for the first time together, we nearly choked ever our own drinks. "Isn't it all grand! Champagne! Men, lovely champagne!" A little later we were joined by Henry who was chuckling. "They imagine they are drinking champagne! With the stuff flowing so freely they must think we are ruddy *rajahs!*"

"I suppose we really ought to do something about it," I said.

"Not at all," replied Doreen, "Why spoil their pleasure!"

CHAPTER 31

Charlotte's—Here I Come!

The nurses of the King Edward VII Hospital, Indore, were kind enough to give me a "Farewell" before I left. Colonel Nicholson, Josephine Manuel, the lady doctor and one or two others were present, besides as many nurses as could get away from the wards. This was held on the front verandah, and we had the usual tea-party, with garlands and a bouquet. Little Irene sat feeling very foolish whilst Chandra Bai, as head nurse, stood up to read an address in which all the usual pretty things were said. Though when she went on to tabulate the various changes made, the nurses' ward and uniforms, and ended by saying. . .". . . . . we cannot forget the happy days when you took charge of this place and taught, worked and improved in every department."

I could not help stealing a glance at Josephine. Catching her eye I winked, and her answering smile made me feel better. After all, were we not both the products of St. George's training? Colonel Nicholson followed this up by sending me a letter on behalf of the hospital committee thanking me "for raising contributions for providing a Nurses' Ward in the hospital." In the reference he was kind enough to give me he mentioned that I had collected nearly *Rsl*.500—about £112/10s. In those days this was a large sum, and we were able to do much with it.

After I left Indore I wrote to Miss McFarlane and asked if she could help me to get to England for my 'midder'. I told her I wanted to 'work my passage.' To do this she advised me to return to St. George's on the Private Nursing Staff, then I could have my name placed on the roster kept for this purpose. It seemed strange, going back to St. George's and being a sort of 'Ulster.' The private nurses wore the sisters' veil of authority, and when a ward sister was ill or away for any length of time it was one of these private nurses who took over temporarily. Shopping one day in Crawford Market I met a nurse who used to be a student with me, and remembering my friendship with Pamela, she gave me her address in Bombay, with the telephone number. I gave her a ring, and the following evening Pamela and her husband came for me in the little car they owned. I was taken to their flat and told to visit them whenever I was free.

Though they made me welcome, I was not happy with them as I could see that relations were strained between husband and wife—and because they had three children, I thought this very sad. Pamela was running a Paying Guest establishment which did not meet with her husband's approval. She was attractive and did not lack admirers. The good looking frivolous married women in India never did! One day she told me that right from the start her marriage was not happy. Pamela had been very spoilt by her father and aunt. The tastes that developed: model gowns, expensive entertainment and the races had to be curtailed once she married the handsome Italian. This was the start of the trouble and the admiring P.G.s with which she always surrounded herself did not help. She surprised me by the great interest she took in my 'Peshawar adventure.' The army and English society now had a special appeal for her, and she seemed to envy me my contact with them. She appeared to be ashamed of her Italian name, and once confessed to wishing she had been strong enough to have gone through with her training.

"Then you and I might have gone up to Peshawar together and had fun."

"Yes," I thought, "WHAT kind of fun!" And I thought of the lucky subaltern who had unwittingly escaped!

I now heard that a new nurse from Calcutta had joined the Private Nursing Staff, and one night we met at dinner only to discover that we already knew each other. She was one of the crowd that had joined Merrill and myself at the Flying Club whilst I was on a visit to Calcutta, She kept eyeing me in a speculative kind of way, and after dinner invited me to walk in the garden with her. After asking me what I was doing here—she informed me that Merrill had married again.

"She came out and they were married here in Bombay."

"So he's added to his *harem!*" I remarked.

"What do you mean?" she asked.

"Only that he has two ex-wives about—that *sultan* didn't waste much time, did he?"

I had one interesting case while waiting my turn for a 'homeward-bound' patient, an appendicectomy. Neville Wadia, the good-looking son of a well-known influential philanthropic Parsee business man—Sir Ness Wadia. I remember this case for two reasons; the first being that 'specialling' him at nights I was free in the afternoons. One afternoon, having tea with Pamela in the Taj, we were joined by a crowd of young people she knew; I was introduced as 'Neville's Nurse.' Then I had several girls bombarding with questions and later when I left I had messages to take back to my patient. They made me feel very important. However, I had to give up the case as a 'homeward-bound' patient had turned up for me. The second reason was the handsome cheque I was sent by Sir Ness, with a letter of thanks for nursing his son for a fortnight.

Now I was ordered to 'Mental.' 'Mental!' The one place I had hoped during my training never to see again. Here I found my case a strapping seventeen-year-old Irish girl. She was lying quite still, worn out after a violent storm which had passed. Her history case showed that something had upset her on the voyage out, and the Spanish Civil War was blamed. She was going to Australia in company with some nuns: one evening when the nuns were about to enter the cabin they were met with abuse and missiles. Reading the case history my mind flashed back to Mrs. Brown, our Eurasian champion missile thrower, and I thought, here we go again. In the past seven years I had often thought about the patient I was going to shepherd across the sea. In my imagination I could see a nice, quiet, not-very-ill man or woman—preferably a man—whom I was forever pushing round the deck in a wheelchair and who enjoyed a glass of sherry twice a day and always bought me one. Then he was accommodating enough to want tucking up early, leaving me free to enjoy the romance of ship life that I had heard so much about.

However, taking over from the hospital staff I was given a grain of comfort. To help with this difficult patient another nurse was to accompany me. She, I was happy to find, was a girl who had been a student nurse with me. Connie Adams was now on the permanent staff of, St. George's. She had to be sent as no other 'freelance' was available, I think it was on the 7th November that we left Bombay on the *Mooltan* which had docked on arrival from Colombo, her last port of call. The patient was given an injection of some hypnotic drug, probably scopolamine—twilight sleep—before we left the hospital; and we boarded the ship as soon as she had disembarked the passengers. We were to nurse her in the two-berth Isolation Cabin on the poop

S.S Mooltan—Where Irene met Eric

deck which was put out-of-bounds to the other passengers. Though we were aware of our responsibility for this patient's safety and health, we were excited to be going to England.

It was also Connie's first trip and the night before we sailed we got together making plans: we had decided to share the watch, twelve hours on, twelve off, and tossed for the first spell of duty, which neither of us wanted as we knew that it was in the first few hours that friendships were made, dining accommodation fixed, and deckchair sites grabbed. It is hardly necessary to say I lost the toss. As I had been away from Bombay for some years I had lost touch with all things salty. Connie revived my memory by saying, "Now remember, no flirting with the ship's officers, we know that they only pick up the nurses to while away the evenings. You want to keep your eye open, my girl, for the real thing—a likely husband. You and I are not getting any younger."

So with this matronly advice coming from someone who was perhaps a little younger than myself, I followed the stretcher taking Molly to the Isolation Cabin. We had put her in a strait-jacket before leaving the hospital: now she was lifted, still unconscious, and put into bed. As there was nothing I could do for her just then I unpacked her belongings. Then spent the time leaning over the rails watching the other passengers come aboard. After a while I took Molly's temperature, pulse and respiration, and no sooner had I charted these than the surgeon visited me. He noted her condition and then left. After we cast off from Ballard Pier I sat just outside the cabin door enjoying the fresh air keeping an eye on my patient. Slowly the Gateway of India and the Taj Mahal Hotel receded; I waved madly. Although I could not see them I knew Pamela and her crowd were sitting on the balcony. One of the fellows had told me, "When the *Mooltan* pulls out we will drink a toast to you."

As Bombay got dimmer I had a moment of sadness. A few of the old die-hards going on their usual six months' leave after three years went through the ritual of consigning their *topees* to the waves, and pink gins and whiskies down their throats. About midnight Connie came to relieve me; she was looking very white and her blue eyes were strained. "Green! I have had a terrible time," she said, leaning on the spare bunk, "I have been sick almost continuously since we left Bombay: I never thought it was going to be quite like this."

"You poor dear. Anyway there's not much you can do for her," and I nodded towards the patient, "She is still unconscious, but I have

246

taken her temperature—and she has been visited by the surgeon—it's all down in the report books. Now she is all yours." Then as I stood up I felt it again, and exclaimed, "Connie! I do feel queer, I have felt like this off and on for hours, but I did not realise what it was; now I know!" And with that I hurried away. I managed to get a little sleep that night, or really what was left of the night, but I now experienced a sensation I had never known before. I was frightened of being enclosed in the small space of my cabin—it was a clear case of claustrophobia—and though the nurses had laughingly warned us to keep our cabin locked after we had been informed that we were to have a two-berth cabin to ourselves, I was never able to do this. Instead I just drew the curtain.

Waking next morning, I was very tired, and after dressing, I joined the passengers for soup and biscuits on deck at about ten o'clock. I had this standing with my back against the rail facing the crowd, and then I noticed many eyes on the ribbon pinned to my uniform. After a while I walked round the deck and was stopped by a sergeant who was escorting a number of families 'Home;' unable to restrain his curiosity, he asked bluntly.

"That ribbon—what is it, Sister?"

"The Frontier Medal, 1930-31," I replied.

"I thought it was; But—but—how did you get it—I mean——"

To end his confusion I said, "Just for having a good time when we were at 'war' with the Afridis." Now I was being perfectly truthful, but *he* thought I was being facetious.

"I don't believe you: I know a lot of our fellows would give anything to possess one of those."

Now we took a turn or two round the deck together and he pointed out his wife and children. The army families were keeping together and among them I noticed a Eurasian girl with her two small children who were much browner than their mother. "Are they going 'Home' for the first time?"

"Yes," he replied, "I expect she will find it tough—in more ways than one. I cannot stand these mixed marriages, it's the children that stick in my gullet," and the dirty look he threw at those inoffensive babies made me want to pick him up and heave him overboard. Susie, I am sure, would have done it!

After an early lunch served to me in the vast dining saloon, which I had all to myself, I went up to start my second spell of duty. Connie reported that our patient was now conscious, and as she was quiet she had removed the strait-jacket. I took one look at the open cabin door, the low deck rail and the rolling sea beyond and said, "Hmm. . . . . ." Though I knew we could not expect to keep her tied up all through the voyage. After Connie left I tried to talk to Molly, but failed to get a reply; I then tried her with a drink—she refused this by pressing her lips together. Next I set about dusting and tidying; but Molly's eyes which followed my every movement had a most disconcerting effect, so abandoning this I sat just outside the door facing her.

After a while, when the ship started rolling, I felt queer again, so went in and flopped down on the empty berth—now watching Molly at close quarters I was quick to see the change in her colour. She had gone puce! I jumped up and felt her pulse—this was poor; taking her temperature I found it was high—immediately I rang for the orderly who went for the surgeon. He ordered heart stimulants, and she had these injections regularly. We fought to prolong her life—but it was hopeless. When Connie arrived for her second spell she was amazed at the change. I told her that she would not finish her watch—and asked her to send for me when she needed my help, which she did in the early hours of the morning. After we had done our job—we handed the body over to two sailors who were waiting outside. We went quickly down to our cabin ready for the first real good sleep we knew we were going to have—being together.

It seemed as if we had only slept a few minutes when we were awakened by an officer who had come to inform us about the burial arrangements. Naturally we had to be present. And just after dawn going up to a deck that was new to us, we found several officers already there. The two sailors who had taken over from us now came running up some stairs, then a very small lift behind us stopped, one of the sailors stepped forward and opened the door and we saw the tall weighted sewn-up canvas shrouded body standing upright in a corner. The sailors now lifted this out and carefully placed it on deck where a portion of rail had been removed. The shrouded body was now placed in a convenient position on a trestle, I believe, and covered with a large Union Jack.

When all was ready, at some pre-arranged signal, the ships engines stopped, and we drifted on peacefully over the Arabian Sea. This is not done for any reason of reverence, but to avoid any possibility of the body consigned to the deep getting mixed up with the propellers. As is customary, the "Man Overboard" code flag was also hoisted whilst the service was held. I remember that at the words, "*We therefore commit her body to the deep.* . . . ." when it was slipped overboard from under the flag, I closed my eyes. Connie told me later she had to do this also.

"Green. What an experience—and our first voyage, too!" said she, voicing my thoughts. We were back in our cabin getting out of uniform, which we packed away quite happily. This release from duty was so unexpected that we sat now and talked of the future. We were naturally happy at the thought that we would be free like the other passengers to enjoy the rest of the voyage.

Alas! Even as we sat planning, wireless messages were flashing between the ship and Bombay. When St. George's Hospital was informed of the death of our patient, Nurse Adams was recalled. She was to put ashore at Aden to take the first available boat back to Bombay. We were very disappointed and went to the purser's office: we begged him to send a reply asking permission for Connie to continue the voyage. This was refused, and at Aden, the day after the burial a few hours before dinner, Connie had to go ashore, and I leaned over the rail waving 'Goodbye' to her.

It is a queer thing now looking back trying to write this story, twenty-five to thirty years later, some big events seem hazy and I have to dip into the 'Souvenir Casket' for help, yet some little things, such as the red and white gingham dress that I was wearing that night, stand out in my memory: though perhaps in the light of what followed nothing to do with that evening was 'little', and so it has remained alive all these years.

As I gazed sadly at the launch taking Connie to the brightly lit town of Aden, a voice at my elbow said, "You will feel lonely now your friend has gone; won't you come and have a sherry with me?"

I turned to find a young man—later I learnt his name was Eric Edwards and he was twenty-seven—standing at my side. He did not look a 'wolf' so I accepted his offer. From him I heard that most of the passengers knew about our patient dying, and he told me he had been one of the very few to see the burial. "It's a pity we cannot alter the seating arrangements to have dinner together, but will you have coffee with me later?" I agreed, and this became a regular evening date. He would collect the coffee and then come for me. After coffee we paced the deck, danced if there was dancing, or merely sat and talked. He was friendly and helpful—never anything more. Whilst this puzzled me it, was also a relief. The nearest he got to being familiar was when he lightly touched my finger tips one evening as my hands rested in my lap to ask, "What's that?" He was pointing to the bright red nail varnish—the prompt reply, "Pig's blood" made him laugh.

Occasionally during the day we met to play deck quoits or table tennis, but our regular rendezvous was for coffee. I told him about the trouble I was having in getting fresh water to wash my hair, which I did at least twice a week. There was always plenty of salt water on tap in the bathrooms—but the fresh water had to be fetched in pails from some remote corner by the stewards, and they only appeared for this chore in the evenings. When he learnt that I wanted this water in the afternoons after *tiffin*, so that I could 'finger set' my hair in time for dinner, he arranged to get it himself. This was one of the first kind things he did which marked him out from the other young men I had met.

This willingness to help, and to expect no return, he was more like the middle-aged, 'pepper-and-salt' understanding *wallahs*—yet he was young! He told me a little about himself after he found out that I was travelling to England for the first time. He seemed worried when I told him of my arrangements with Queen Charlotte's, I had written to the matron and told her that I was in Bombay waiting to work my passage across. She had replied to say that when I arrived in London she would see me and fix something: I hoped it would be all right. He was not so sure. "What if she cannot accept you at once—what are your plans then? London is a big place for a girl to be in alone—big and dangerous."

I told him I was being met at St. Pancras by Dick and Ann Veryard, my R.A.F. friends from Peshawar, and they had very kindly asked me to stay with them for a while before going up to London. "I shall no doubt be going over all this with them, and I am sure they will help me." He was happy to hear this. In exchange he told me a little about himself; he had been born in Bihar, where his father had been an indigo-planter, and had lived in India until he was fourteen, when his father retired and the family returned to England. His mother had been born in Durban, so the 'little travel bug' was well in his blood, and when the opportunity came for him to go abroad, he immediately took it. He was now going home on a very short leave to settle some private business. As he did not mention a wife I took it he was single.

I now met the man he was travelling with—they were both in the same firm in Delhi. I disliked David Jones the moment I saw him, and my instinct was not wrong. Next morning as I stood alone by the rails he joined me and only after a moment's conversation asked, "Are you

Welsh? You speak slightly with that accent." Now I knew this was utter nonsense as every trace of the 'chee-chee' had long since vanished. He was either being deliberately offensive or trying to show me how clever he was: the no-one-can-fool-me type. I now guessed that after leaving them the night before they had discussed me and Edwards, who had a good knowledge of India, had, as my mother would say 'put two-and-two together.' He probably told his friend in confidence what he suspected. Jones, now having shot his barb, followed it up by discussing his friend. "What do you think of him? He seems to be taking his trouble well!" And he gave a derisive laugh.

"Has he a trouble?" I asked, "I wouldn't have guessed!"

"I should think not! With him dancing and playing games and...." he hesitated, then went on, "..... his wife has recently died."

The disapproval in his voice told me plenty. I guessed he was a little envious of his friend's easy manner and natural friendliness with everybody—or perhaps he envied him his freedom?

"Well! If what you say is right, I think he is very brave. Surely its better for him and for everyone he comes in contact with that he should not be gloomy!" Then excusing myself I left him. Thinking over this bit of news I realised now why Eric Edwards was different from the other young men I had met; being a widower had made him nicer I decided. Anyway it was nothing to me whether he was single, married or a widower—I was having a very good time, playing games and dancing with anyone who asked me, and though Connie had said, "Keep your eye open for the likely husband," I was not taking her seriously, as I had heard too often that friendships made on a voyage were passing affairs—*NOT* to be taken seriously, so I grabbed all the fun I could get. Being in 'general circulation' I had all my sherries paid for by different fellows, and this way my conscience did not suffer.

About two days out of Aden, a large middle-aged man whom I had seen watching me took the opportunity an empty deckchair offered by my side to flop down and start a conversation. "Do you know I intended asking you to have a drink with me after your friend left at Aden, but that young whipper-snapper beat me to it." We sat and talked for a while until the lunch gong sounded. That evening I seemed to have finished dressing sooner than most people—and sat alone on an almost deserted deck—my middle-aged friend now joined me, and after a while tried to become familiar. He was most hurt when I snubbed him, "I thought you were a sport! Nurses....."

"Are hot stuff? Is that what you were going to say? I've heard that

251

before, but please Mr. . . Mr. . . I've forgotten your name, please try and understand that some nurses are particular."

"Well, you seem to be pretty thick with that whipper-snapper, you spend most evenings. . . . ."

"Talking," I said, again interrupting, "but I shall not ask you to believe that—it will be beyond you—Excuse me!"

I told Edwards about this scene and he was disgusted. "Some fellows think any girl travelling alone is game. I'm glad you told him off."

"Anyway if you see the wolf making for me please come to my rescue," I asked.

Before we got to Suez arrangements were being made for a trip to the Pyramids and Cairo. Eric Edwards came and asked me to join him. "I would like you to come as my guest, please. You see I don't like leaving you all day with the wolf."

"That's very kind of you, and I am grateful, but I could never accept so much as I have no way of paying you back. Thank you all the same."

He tried to get me to change my mind. "I'm joining forces with Hoppy my Scots pal, but you come along, too, we both want you to come. I wish you'd change your mind before these forms go in." Again I thanked him but refused.

"Don't worry about the wolf," I said, "I'll cope! You see I'm used to them. I met many on the Frontier."

Then telling me to be good he went away. Going through the Suez Canal was to me a day packed with interest. I kept darting from one side of the ship to the other trying to see everything that went by. The familiar khaki of the British soldiers lining the banks waving and cheering made me think of Mhow, and I was a little hit homesick. At Port Said after dinner a table companion, an elderly man, expressed surprise that I had not been asked ashore by my young fellow, I corrected his mistake, he then suggested we go ashore. "Just for a little walk—to stretch our legs." This was not very romantic, but better than nothing. However it was not a success as three Egyptians selling "feelthy postcards" upset the old man.

I added to his embarrassment by asking, "What is it they are trying to sell you? Can I see? Perhaps I'd like to buy some."

"It's some rubbish; and not for your eyes," he replied. The pedlars persisted until the old man got angry, "Oh, come on," he said, "It's no use. At least it will be quieter on the boat." It was! But I did not like it! The lights of Port Said, the music coming from the various cafes, the general air of excitement all had an effect on me, and the women returning to the ship with their bunches of red roses made me feel neglected—my escort had been too old or too mean to bother with this romantic rubbish.

Late that night Edwards appeared with a large bunch of red roses which he gaily presented to me—he never knew how close he came to being kissed! After we sailed I decorated my cabin with the roses—having this to myself was nice in a way—I could spread myself; but I was still unable to shut the door. This rather worried me as I knew I should. Each night after drawing the thick green curtains across I pegged it at the sides then would lie reading for a little before switching off the light. So that night leaving Port Said I lay reading, when a voice at my head which was near the door made me jump—looking up I saw the wolf, who looked very drunk. He stood there staring down at me, and then asked, "Who has brought you all those flowers? I bet it was the whipper-snapper." He had got the curtain pulled aside, but before he could move, I quickly put my hand up to the push button for the night steward.

"If you don't go away at once, I'll ring for the steward, or I shall scream the place down!" This last threat was too much for him, he disappeared. Quickly I jumped up and closed the door; my claustrophobia was now cured.

The days slipped by between Port Said and Marseilles, each day getting a little colder. The officers had changed from their white tropical uniform to the dark navy blue. Now instead of crowding the decks people huddled in the saloons. Some of the bridge schools that had been going since the boat left Bombay were now augmented, more patronised the library and tried to find quiet corners to read in peace. The bars were always popular, with the cheap price of beer and spirits, and the almost continuous smoke haze reflected the cheap duty-free cigarettes available. We steamed through the Straits of Messina on a bright sunny afternoon, with the twin towns of Reggio on the 'toe' of Italy and Messina on Sicily looking neat and clean from the distance at which the vessel passed.

The same day, just before dusk, I was in the ironing room pressing a frock, when Eric Edwards came looking for me. "Look at Stromboli in action!" he said, pointing through the port-hole, "The Lantern of the Mediterranean" looked interesting so I left the ironing and we rushed up on deck. This volcanic 'safety-valve' is nearly always simmering and erupting gently and intermittently. We noticed the little township on this remote island and agreed that although it looked a pretty sight with its twinkling lights we should not fancy living under those risky conditions. Now the passengers going overland from Marseilles were busy with their arrangements, the baggage room was opened daily, and there was an air of excitement. Eric Edwards surprised me one evening by saying, "Look here, why don't you come overland with me. I'll gladly stand the expense; you see I don't like leaving you with these wolves."

I stared at him and then asked, "Why are you doing this? Surely its very unusual!"

"Perhaps, but you see I admire your courage. You tell me you have saved for years to take this training and here you are about to face a strange country and an English winter—Oh! What I mean is if I can make things a little easier for you—it will perhaps be a help to you, that's my only reason."

"Yes, I realise that now, and I apologize for the question, and though I am very grateful, I cannot accept."

So we parted at Marseilles. I remember going ashore here with an Italian who took me to one of those wayside stalls, and we had the wonderful *bouillabaisse*. Eating this, I was reminded of Merrill who had said, "One day I want to take you to Marseilles and give you *bouillabaisse*." And then his description of this fish-soup made poetry.

After we left Marseilles and Gibralter I got colder and colder. Apart from the climate changing with the disappearance of the sun the passengers themselves changed—they seemed to be withdrawn, remote and cold; this I found depressing. I wished now I had gone with Eric Edwards.

I will never forget my first sight of Tilbury: the gloom of a late November day. And fog! Nothing welcoming: here I truly got cold feet, and waiting to go ashore I thought what if Dick and Anna Veryard forget to meet me, and if I cannot get into Queen Charlotte's? And suddenly I felt very much alone and lost. Then I heard a voice calling my name, and looking round I saw a page being followed by an elderly woman. The lady introduced herself and then gave me a letter to read which she said explained everything.

"Gosh! This is jolly decent of him."

"So we also thought, Miss Green—your young man must be very nice!"

"My young man? Why, I hardly know him! I only met him at Aden!"

On arriving in London Eric Edwards had written to the Y.W.C.A. and arranged for me to be met at Tilbury by one of the matrons, and if necessary, I was to be taken to the Y.W.C.A. and looked after until I left for Queen Charlotte's. All expenses were to be met by him. "So you see, here I am to meet you and now, where is your luggage?"

From that moment I was made to feel as a child. She had a commanding air, and not only managed me but managed the porter! I had arranged to travel with some young people to St. Pancras, but at the sight of my companion they evaporated. I could hear them all laughing and chatting in the next carriage—whilst I sat demurely by my escort answering questions. She was very curious about Eric Edwards, but I could only tell her the little I knew about him.

"Did he not arrange to meet you or write?"

"No," I replied, "why should he? But if you let me copy the address he has given you, I shall certainly write to him from my friends' house to thank, him."

"Well, I never knew any young man could be so thoughtful—you are a lucky girl to have met him."

At St. Pancras I was relieved to find those dear people Dick and Anne Veryard waiting for me—Dick was very amused when this old lady almost asked him to sign for me. At last we were free from her and left for Victoria and Thornton Heath in Surrey. I spent a happy week with the Veryards. The day after I got there I contacted Mary Pinto, now Mary Porter, to tell her I had a tin of curry powder for her which her mother had given me at the last minute before I left Mhow. When Anne heard about this curry powder she asked me to make a curry for her. I had only a flimsy idea how to set about this, but decided to have a try. I must have had the flame too high, as after burning my sliced onion I added the curry powder, and soon the pungent smell of burning curry enveloped the house—it was terrible. Anne was brave: after throwing open as many windows as she could she said, "Never mind, it will probably taste better than it smells!" She was sadly mistaken.

Mary Porter replied from Watford and asked me to spend Christmas with them. I was very glad to get this invitation because I was not sure whether the hospital could accommodate me in December. Before replying to Mary, Anne and I went to London, Whilst I went to Queen Charlotte's Hospital in Marylebone Road to be interviewed by Miss Edith Dare, the matron, Anne went shopping. As all my papers were in order I was told I could join the batch of trainee midwives in January. Having had a general trainings and being a paying pupil, I would finish the course in six months. If one was not prepared to pay, the course for a trained nurse was eighteen months and two years for a 'white nurse'—the untrained pupil midwife. These 'white nurses' were distinguished by the all white (including the belt) uniform they wore.

Back at Thornton Heath I answered Mary's letter and told her how happy I was to accept her invitation. Now I wrote to Eric Edwards thanking him for his kind thought in having me met at Tilbury, and I let him know that I was fixed to start at Queen Charlotte's in January. Anne was very intrigued about this young man. She agreed with the Y.W.C.A. lady's sentiments that it was very unusual, very kind and thoughtful, for a young man to go to so much trouble over a girl he hardly knew, on New Year's Day I started in Queen Charlotte's. I could hardly believe, standing in those wards, that I was there at last. This 'midder' was about to become a reality after being a dream for years! I found it hard going into training again after the soft time I had had in Peshawar and private nursing—the old ache returned to my feet. However the work was interesting.

I found myself with another trainee in a post-natal ward; here we had thirty mothers and babies to care for. Now for the first time in my career I had to turn myself into a *matherani,* and did not relish the position! I often wondered what those untouchables in the King Edward Hospital at Indore would have said if they could have seen their Matron *Sahib* flitting round with bedpans! Besides bed-baths and temperatures we had to serve meals to the patients. But all these tasks were easy compared to dealing with those hungry howling babies.

Teaching them to suckle I soon came to the conclusion that there could be no animal as stupid as the new born human. He had to be fed at three or four hourly intervals; we would pick up a baby and take him to his mother: to make it interesting glycerine was smeared round the nipple and the baby's mouth held against this. Very rarely did he get the idea at once, he would more often than not lick off the glycerine, then let go and howl, whilst searching frantically round missing the nipple every time. Now the struggle started, pressing his mouth against the breast appeared to make him angry. The fact that for the first three days there was practically nothing there did not help, hut it was a vicious circle—if he suckled well it encouraged the flow! If the baby did not get the idea or if the mother got nervous, which most of the new ones did, the flow was retarded. Very few of those women made good 'cows,' yet in India the half-starved villagers, mostly living on dry *chappaties* and a chilli, had enormous breasts and a copious supply! Civilisation had its drawbacks, I guessed.

After this struggle the baby had to be weighed and was expected to put on between three-and-a-half to four ounces: if he had not he had to be returned to his mother. Again glycerine was the bait. Again the infant, (usually a boy—they were more stupid and lazy than the girls), licked off the glycerine and then howled with rage, and the entire performance was repeated. Reading the scales whilst a wriggling baby tried to commit suicide made me cross-eyed. All this had to be done to time, one dare not be slow or the time-table, so important in all hospitals, was disorganised. Here I found being on time was even more important than in 'General'. If the babies were slow in feeding, the mothers hurried over their own meals in order to make up time and this affected the milk supply; a calm unflustered woman made more milk. So one had to work quickly, calmly, carefully and cheerfully in the midst of Bedlam.

Bathing those babies was a terrifying experience; the 'Staff' demonstrated once. The 'white nurses' in this had the advantage—they practised on dolls in the prep. schools, but we trained ones were expected to be bright! So thirty babies had to be bathed in a given time, and how one or more of those slippery eels was not drowned by me I do not know. I found the custom of addressing these patients as 'mother' strange, and had the difficulty in understanding the Londoner's Cockney accent. A puzzled patient, after looking at me as if I was not quite right in the head, asked, "As you speak English so well why can't you understand me?" I could not very well reply, "Mother, your brand of English is new to me," I was often told by the nurses, patients or shopkeepers when I first went there, and got muddled with the money, that I spoke English well. This seemed to surprise them. They expected broken or *babu* English, *à la Peter Sellers*. I could not always stop to explain that being born in India did not necessarily make one an Indian, that I was an Anglo-Indian and English was my 'mother-tongue.'

After I had been there a fortnight I heard from Eric Edwards; he told me he had business in London and suggested we had dinner together somewhere. Before he left for India we met a second time; the nurse I shared a room with felt sure a romance was developing but remembering the saying, "*Ships that pass in the night. . . . . .*" I refused to get excited.

After I had been in that ward for four to six weeks I was sent to ante-natal. Here I met another girl from India who told everyone she was an Indian, and as she was quite brown and only wore *saris* when 'off-duty' she was believed. However, in confidence, she told me she was really an Eurasian and until she came to England had never worn *saris*. Puzzled, I asked, "Why the deception?"

"You see, Green, I was warned they don't like half-castes in this country, and as I am so dark I have decided to call myself an Indian."

"Hell's Bells, Grace, now I *know* we are a bad lot; in India you probably smothered yourself in powder trying to look white, and you would never have worn a *sari* for anything, yet here you reverse the whole thing."

"Yes," she replied, meditating, "life is certainly very hard for us coloured ones."

One day home sister said to us at breakfast, "This evening I have ordered a curry especially for you two girls: you will like that?" We assured her we would, and all day I thought of that curry. Full of expectation and hunger, we rushed to the dining-room after duty. I took one look at the huge bowl of dirty brown slops set before home sister, and stifled a groan. To make matters worse she served us generously, and a little later asked how we were enjoying it. Grace could only sigh. Kicking her under the table, I murmured something polite. Going up to our room, Grace and I decided we would make a curry ourselves. There were gas fires in the rooms, and when sitting up late swotting, we would make cocoa or coffee: sometimes even cooking bacon and eggs. Grace had a tin of curry powder, so we bought onions, eggs and potatoes. I told her about the ghastly failure my curry was at Thornton Heath. She assured me she could do better. Leaving her to cook I took her 'smalls' with me and retired to the bathroom. Returning half-an-hour later I was met by the unmistakable smell of curry gone wrong. I flew into my room. "Quickly! Open the windows, Grace," I said, flinging those wide, "cover that stuff, or we'll have sister after us, you can smell it for miles!"

Trying to swallow this I found her effort was only slightly better than mine.

"It's not very nice," admitted Grace ruefully.

"Perhaps we haven't the proper ingredients," I replied. Then thinking of the one I had made in Thornton Heath and the one served to us by home sister, and now this latest effort, I said aloud, "Oh, Curry! What abortions are made in thy name."

"Green!" said Grace, shocked.

"That, my dear, is what comes of learning to be a midwife—but shall I tell you something, Grace? I now make a firm vow that the first thing I do when I get home will be to learn how to cook a curry from my mother, who makes this dish better than any I have tasted elsewhere, and that includes the finest hotels of India."

In ante-natal pregnant women reporting for the first time for this treatment had their history taken and recorded, various tests were made, then they were advised as to diet and exercise. They were now seen regularly by us until their babies were born. In this department we were taught palpation—examination by hand—and we went from cubicle to cubicle examining and learning. In one of these cubicles I caught up with a male student, and was pleased when I discovered twins, which he had missed. We had a number of these students from the different hospitals. However, later I did not shine at one of the lectures. These were given in a large theatre with rows of seats in tiers all round for the students and nurses. In the centre was a surgical table, with an obliging patient; at these lectures I always took good care never to catch the eye of the lecturer, especially when he wanted someone, anyone, to palpate the patient and give results.

This particular day I was not to escape. He looked around seeking a victim and pointed, "You!" Quickly I looked away, but I was not quick enough, then again I heard, "You!" Whilst I kept my eyes averted the nurses I sat between nudged me; now I had to look at him and he said, "Yes, I mean you." Feeling like a fly about to enter the web I walked down to the centre: with all those eyes on me I just floundered. I could not do a thing right or give a correct answer, and was only too thankful, after having made it clear to everyone just how stupid I was to creep back to my chair after I was dismissed. We were also given lectures on the care of the newborn baby by Sister Tutor. Now I am very fond of scrambled eggs, but from the day we were told that the normal stool of a baby looks like scrambled eggs I have never felt quite the same about these.

I think it was after ante-natal that I did my turn in Labour Ward; here we did eight-hourly shifts, and it was bleak getting up at 8 a.m. to start the 4 a.m. shift. We were always given a hot meal before going on duty, but as one never managed to get much sleep until late, owing to the traffic down Marylebone Road, this shift was never popular, Our hostel was on a corner and we got the roar of the traffic from two busy roads. In those days when Queen Charlotte's was on Marylebone Road our abode had a huge stork on the roof. "But why on the nurses' quarters—why not over the hospital?" most new girls asked. The answer was that this was more conspicuous as one drove up Marylebone Road. "Too bad if the stork made a mistake and dropped the babies in the nurses' quarters!" said one facetiously.

"No stork is dropping a baby for me," answered another as we walked towards the nurses' home, our red-lined blue cloaks billowing out in the breeze. "After this little lot I never want to see one of those horrors again."

It goes to prove how strong the mother instinct must be when in spite of this training, and the horror a girl experiences when she sees a baby being born for the first time, that most nurses eventually marry and become mothers.

The delivery room was next door to the labour ward in which about six beds were always occupied by women in labour, and the nurse had a hectic time rubbing backs—which was very comforting—serving meals, giving hot baths and other treatment to encourage them to get a move on, and keeping them all under supervision. Yet one had to get each one to the delivery room at the right moment; too soon and one crowded in on a case in progress. Too late meant the disgrace to the nurse of a baby born in the ward. All this left one mentally and physically exhausted after an eight hour shift.

However tired, the nurses from abroad never turned down the chance of going to the live theatre. Complimentary tickets were sent to all the hospitals for the nurses, and as we were always given good seats, in those days evening dress was the rule. So all dressed up, going by bus to Golders Green, or rushing round on the underground, then to end the evening standing round a mobile canteen drinking coffee and eating sandwiches with a crowd of happy young nurses was, for me, a girl who had spent most of her life in upcountry cantonments in India, an exciting experience.

When 'on district' we were transferred to the district nurses' home, which was adjacent to the hospital. This house had its own domestic staff, and was run by the district sister. Here we nurses lived, ate and slept, always with an ear open for the door bell. On answering this we usually found a small boy—holding a Charlotte's record card to show he was genuine, and not someone calling on a false errand. His laconic "My mum has started," was hardly necessary. I was surprised at the difference in some of the homes we visited. Some were quite luxurious, others moderate, whilst the majority were poor, some in the extreme. Rags instead of sheets and sometimes even brown paper. Often we had to turn the father and children out of the one tiny room to sit on the stairs whilst the baby was being born, but the warmth, the friendliness and gratitude expressed made up for the discomforts we experienced. Without proper washing facilities, or even a chair, a dirty damp room, narrow stairs, a tiny courtyard with a dustbin and wet clothes hanging on a line in a sooty atmosphere, was 'home' for many in those days. I was shocked, as I thought this sort of poverty existed only in India.

It was whilst I was on a case in one of these poor homes feeling cold and tired that my malaria came back with a vengeance. In the morning I asked 'father' to get me a taxi: I felt unable to face waiting for a bus whilst carrying my basket. Just as the taxi pulled up I had a sudden attack of nausea, and was sick on the pavement. Getting into the taxi I lay back feeling miserable, and before the journey ended I was sick again in my apron, which I had managed to pull off only just in time. The taxi driver had missed nothing, and as I fumbled for change he remarked, in his cheeky Cockney voice, "Its catchin' Miss!"

"What's catching?" I asked, stooping to pick up my basket.

"Mornin' sickness," he replied with a chuckle, and drove away before I could think of a rude enough reply.

I met another of these cheeky Londoners 'on district.' This time a lad of sixteen or seventeen, I was in the underground rushing from one station to another with this boy on my heels. In a fairly deserted subway he came uncomfortably close to me, and putting a hand on my basket asked with an impudent gleam in his eye, "Got a baby in there, nurse?"

I wanted to swing out with my basket, but thought better of it and replied, "I'm giving them away— do you want one?" Then I ran! In these baskets we carried all that might be needed on a 'delivery', and returning to the home after a case or a visit our first job was to sterilise everything and restock. Each nurse had her own basket for which she was responsible. If the nurses were busy they sometimes borrowed each other's baskets, but mine, with the unfortunate initials I.M. before the 'Green', was left severely alone! Eric Edwards was now writing quite often and even I began to think he was interested; this gave life a rosy hue again. After getting through one of the exams, I wrote and gave him my good news. He was kind enough in replying to enclose a postal order, which he told me to use at a florists as a reward.

My next move was to the branch at Hammersmith—to the Isolation block. Here the new Queen Charlotte's was being built. The nurses lived in a lovely house with a garden, a little away from the Isolation block, and it was pleasant to see trees, and to hear birds singing again.

After finishing my time in Isolation I was given a day or two free in which to get 'cleaned up' before returning to Queen Charlotte's I took the opportunity; and spent a pleasant day with Anne Veryard. Before the final exams, or before we left the hospital, we had to have a certain number of 'deliveries' to our credit, so I returned to face many a night fully dressed on a sofa in the hospital waiting for a nurse to summon me to the delivery room when a women was about to oblige, I remember going with the nurses to a large building somewhere in London for the Central Midwives Board exam, but cannot remember where. I was also given the Queen Charlotte's certificate on the ". . . . . . . management of the newborn infant," and the Queen Charlotte's Nursing and Midwifery certificate.

After the exam for the C.M.B. we crowded into the nearest cafe, and over cups of tea and sticky buns, discussed the paper. We were mostly nurses there and were soon arguing about these; whether the questions were as easy as they appeared, or whether there were any catches. Apparently the cafe was a regular haunt of the nurses after these exams and the establishment took a keen interest in these proceedings.

The Purser's Table

Before I returned to India on the *Majola*, about the second week in September I left Charlotte's to stay with Mary Porter. I have only one incident to write about on this somewhat dull voyage out. An Australian woman shared a cabin with me, and she was quiet and rather dowdy. She asked me if I was going to see about seating arrangements in the dining saloon, but I had no friends on board and so told her I was not interested and was prepared to sit anywhere. Getting to the dining saloon the first evening I followed the steward to a table. He pulled a chair out for me and then left. This table seated six—two on either side end one at each end. I found myself at a side with a vacant chair to my left—a place had been laid there. On my right, the end place had not been laid. Opposite me sat my cabin companion, and beside her sat a married woman with a loud 'haw-haw' accent. At the remaining end place sat an unmarried woman whom I was later told was an army nurse.

In reply to my polite "Good-evening," which I offered with a friendly smile, I was given a frosty reply. Then these two women started an animated conversation, excluding my cabin companion, Mrs. Johnson and myself. That we were being snubbed was obvious, but why? We had to wait until the next evening to find out. On the second evening of the voyage most people changed into evening clothes. Mrs. Johnson asked me if I was changing and added, "Wear something pretty." I guessed we were both thinking along the sense lines as that is just what I intended to do to show those hoity-toity know-alls that I could dress as well as anybody. When I got to the table I found the three women already seated, and though I should not say it, I knew as I sat down I had shaken the two female *koi hais*. Mrs. Johnson's smile of satisfaction and gentle kick also told me plenty.

When they had recovered they repeated the tactics of the previous night. Dismayed, I thought if they keep this up right through the voyage it is going to be fun for us! Trying to start a conversation with Mrs. Johnson was hard work, for those women spoke so loudly that gentle Mrs. Johnson refused to compete. I could not help wishing that someone had been seated to my left, but though the place was again set the chair remained vacant. After we two had eaten our soup in almost complete silence the spell was broken. The steward appeared followed by a ship's officer, the purser. After apologising for being late this gentlemen took the chair beside me.

Now I was beginning to see light, and he had hardly sat down when those two women pounced. I am not going to try and describe the pantomime that now started, sufficient to say that I was spellbound by their performance. They did not let a second pass without, addressing the poor young man; when one stopped for want of breath the other took over, and this yapping went on to the end of the meal. It was made clear to me that they had read all the books that were to be read, had travelled in all the countries of the world and had eaten all the most expensive, luxurious dishes these countries had to offer. Poor Mrs. Johnson and I sat silent through this babel. When he could the officer included us in this conversation, but he was not given much chance. However, towards the end of the meal, when the two women were arguing between themselves about something, and had carelessly dropped their guard, he grabbed his chance, and in a low voice asked me to have coffee with him.

I was surprised and pleased, surprised that though they had worked so hard and thought they had him hooked, they had failed entirely. I was pleased that I had the chance now of giving them a smack-in-the-eye, and I thoroughly enjoyed the rest of the meal. After dessert, in a lull when both women were breathless for a moment, the officer turned to me and said, "Are you ready? Shall we go?" At my nod and smile he stood up, and with his hand on the back of my chair said, "Will you excuse us? Miss Green and I will have our coffee in the lounge." He now drew my chair away, and though this was a 'proud moment' I dared not look at those women before walking out.

Later in the cabin Mrs. Johnson told me, "I did. I deliberately turned and faced them as much as to say, 'Now you have been snubbed.' Their mouths fell open and they could not have looked more foolish!" We hugged each other and laughed until we were exhausted.

"This frock has certainly paid for itself. I skimped and scraped, and even put the money a friend sent me for flowers towards it; but I have no regrets now. So you know, Mrs. Johnson, I always have luck when I wear white," I told her, thinking of Eric Wilkinson's party in Peshawar.

"It was not your frock, my dear. Those two seasoned 'tabbies' overplayed their hand. He must have met many like them on these voyages."

All the same I preferred to think it was my lucky white frock! After we had left the table, Mr. Purser—I called him this for convenience—and I had coffee in the lounge, then he suggested a walk on deck. When we got outside he stood in a sheltered place after asking my permission to light a pipe, and we then paced along slowly in silence. After a while I began to feel a frightful dummy; those women seemed to have sapped me of all intelligence and I could not think of anything to speak about, they had said it all.

"I'm afraid you will think I'm very dull—I don't seem to have any conversation," I said, apologising.

"Thank God," he replied, with such relief that I laughed out loudly. So we paced, hardly speaking, now and again pausing just to lean over the rail. Then after-half-an-hour of this he excused himself, pleading work and left; no doubt feeling he had done his duty for one evening—entertaining a passenger—whilst I, feeling completely satisfied with my evening's work, went to look for Mrs. Johnson in our cabin. The next night after coffee we walked again before sitting on deck with our chairs close together, feet on the rails, watching the ship's lights reflected on the waves. The two furies now passed behind us, I saw them as I was sitting forward, but my companion, who was lying back did not. "They'll think we are flirting," I said teasing.

"Who will?" he asked, sitting up and looking around.

"Our table companions."

"Well, Miss Green, if you care about what they think, chase them and tell them that I am happily married, and do not flirt with the passengers."

"Thanks for the warning, Mr. Purser, now I shall not waste my time falling in love with you. Actually I am breaking a rule—going against advice given me '. . . . .never have anything to do with ship's officers.'"

"Then why did you agree last night to have coffee with me."

"Because I would have broken any rule to get even with those women," said I, unthinkingly.

"Thank you," replied Mr. Purser, indignantly. "And now as we seem to understand each other shall we make this a permanent date?"

"Oh, yes please, I am not going to lose you to either of them now."

"You make me feel like a dog's bone," he grumbled.

Henry and Doreen met me at Bombay, and we travelled back to Mhow together—it was lovely seeing Mama again. "Did you really see the king's house, Irene?" she asked.

"Yes, Mama. They call it Buckingham Palace." Then I asked, "When are the Pintos coming over? I have heaps of messages for them and Susie from Mary. When does Susie get a holiday again, I am longing to see her."

"Sit down, Irene," said" Mama, "I have something sad to tell you."

Then I was told that about four months ago—about the time I was taking the exams,—Susie had, without consulting her family, thrown up nursing to become a nun; she was now in some mission place in the jungle training for this.

"But why? Why?" I asked, "bewildered.

"It had something to do with a sergeant she met at the S.&.T." answered Mama. "That and the colour business."

"Yes, Susie certainly had a complex about that."

"She was much too clever," added Doreen. "If she had been like the rest of us, she would have allowed *Kismet* to work things out."

"It's not Susie I am worried about, its Mrs. Pinto, she feels this terribly," said Mama, sitting down heavily with a sigh, "You see, girls, she feels that one way or other this colour bar has deprived her of all her children. Mary was only too happy to go to England with her sergeant who was ashamed of his coloured father-in-law. Sammy has never been near them since the day many years ago doctor showed him the door because he married an Indian Christian nurse. . . . . . 'bringing more black blood into the family instead of trying to improve the strain,' he raged. Mrs. Pinto told me all this in confidence."

"And now Susie does this, poor Mrs. Pinto," I said, taking Mama's hand as I could see she was very sad.

"Yes, she is poor," said Mama. "In spite of their wealth from the restaurant: *I* can feel sorry for her."

The heavy emphasis on the "I" made Doreen enquire, "What do you mean, Mama?"

"That I am rich in the love I get from my daughters, and that God in His kindness allows us to stay together." Mama was thinking of Doreen as she spoke now—she could have been living in a posh house in the railway colony with Henry, but to be near Mama she was sharing the nursery wing of Champak bungalow with her father-in-law.

Soon after my return I contacted Colonel Nick and asked him to help me get a permanent job somewhere in Central India. In the meantime I had a case or two: the Parsee community learning they had a S.C.M. in their midst soon had me busy, and I began driving round Mhow with my basket. Then I heard from Pamela, who had found out from a new P.G. of hers that I had come out on the *Majola*. She wrote and asked me to visit her.

"There is something I wish to see you about—a suggestion I want to make to you; come and spend a month with us."

Full of curiosity, I decided I could spend a fortnight with her. Then I heard from Eric Edwards, who had been transferred to Calcutta; he wrote asking if we could meet again. He had sent me a "welcome-home" telegram when we docked in Bombay, and this had given me much pleasure, so now I replied proposing we should meet in Bombay. I had told my family about this kind young man and though Mama had not said much she had a certain gleam in her eye. "He sounds too good to be true, nab him, my girl, nab him," advised my outspoken little sister.

On arriving at Pamela's flat I felt something was wrong, and after a while asked where her husband was. "He's on tour," she answered, tight-lipped, but I felt this was untrue; then I noticed the large photograph of the good-looking Italian was missing from the honoured place on the piano. I then asked her why she wanted to see me. "To get all your news," she replied, smiling.

"Don't tell me you have dragged me all those miles just to hear my news, I could have told you the lot in one letter," I said, exasperated.

"No Mouse,"—(this name after all this time startled me)—"I have something to suggest, but it will keep until after lunch, the men will be in soon." At lunch round her table were the P.G.s who had their offices close at hand, and were able to get away for this meal. At dinner I was told they all appeared.

After lunch when we were once again alone she told me she and her husband had parted, and she wanted me to make my home in future with her. The two older children were at school in Simla, and Baba, who was five, could sleep in a cot in her room, whilst I had his little back room.

"But, Pam, I have to earn my living!"

"Yes, silly, and you can do that from here, I bet there are not many with the C.M.B. diploma in Bombay and you will get many cases. Don't say 'no', think it over the next few days you are here."

Then I told her of my ambition to get a post as matron, with a nice house thrown in so that I could offer Mama a home. She asked if I knew of such a job going spare, and seemed relieved to hear I did not. Then she asked about my stay in England, and the voyages. "Don't leave anything out, tell me all about the fellows you met—your flirtations—I want to hear it all!"

"Flirtations! Do you realise, my dear, that I have been working hard and studying, you cannot get those certificates by playing, you know!"

"But what about the boats? Come now, don't be a dark horse, tell me about the poor ship's officers you have been leading astray."

So I told her about Eric Edwards, about his many kindnesses, ending with, "The morning I left Mhow to come here I heard from him, he is coming to Bombay to spend his annual leave, and you will meet him in a couple of days." To my surprise she did not seem pleased with this news.

"Where will he stay?" she demanded.

"He is going to live with a family, people his firm knows."

"Mmph. . . . he could have come here."

"Pamela, I could not suggest that without knowing how you were situated—your rooms might have all been taken."

"Yes, but we landladies have an arrangement between ourselves about the overflows. Anyway, what is he like? I mean what does he *look* like,—tall, dark and handsome?"

"No, on the contrary he is only a little taller than I am, and fair, and he wears glasses."

"Glasses!" she exclaimed, disgusted, "Mouse, couldn't you have chosen someone more romantic looking?"

"I didn't choose him, he chose me! At least I mean he came up and spoke to me first, and has showered me with kindnesses ever since." I was confused and angry at the scorn in her voice; however, calming down I said quietly, "You know, Pamela, there is more to be considered than mere good looks."

But she was not impressed, and when Eric Edwards arrived, and showed from the beginning that he had no time for her, she was further annoyed. She was so accustomed to being the centre of attraction that it never occurred to her that a fellow could fall for someone else with her around. To sit about in her flat consuming cocktails was not his idea of a holiday, so Eric Edwards confided to me, and we spent almost every day sea and sun bathing at Breach Candy. we had our lunch and tea under the shade of the huge striped umbrellas, keeping our heads and the food under cover. It was very annoying to have a tasty morsel, *en route* to one's mouth, snatched away by a *chil* or hawk. These birds glided, about the skies just for this purpose, and swooped when occasion demanded. The unsuspecting visitor went in danger of losing not only his sandwich but also part of his finger.

Returning to town in the evenings Eric would leave me to go to his own digs to change. Most evenings we had Pamela in our company either in a foursome or a large party. One evening I had finished dressing, and stood with my back to the door by an open window manicuring my nails. Pamela entered quietly, but her angry shout "Mouse." made me jump. Looking round and seeing we wore identical dresses I exclaimed, "Hell's Bells!" and laughed.

"I don't think there is anything to laugh at—WHERE did you get THAT dress?" she demanded.

"Off-the-peg quite cheaply at a sales in a large department store in London; where did you get yours?"

"Mine was not bought cheaply, and certainly not from any department store. 'Yvonne' assured me it was a model. . . . . ."

"Well," I said, breaking in. "I know there is at least one more like these as I bought it for Doreen; you see, when I was trying this on I said to the girl, 'I would like this for myself, but I know it would suit my young sister even better.' She then told me she had another upstairs, and went up for it. I say, Pam, won't it be fun If the three of us were to be seen wearing identical dresses at the Taj. or somewhere, the Bombay public would think they had all gone cross-eyed!"

"That is unlikely to happen, after tonight my *ayah* will be given this to cut down for her daughter."

I could see now that I had only added to her anger in my attempt to make light of the situation. "I'm sorry you feel like that about it, I shall have to wear, mine until it falls apart, and Doreen likes hers so much she has already decided to have it copied at the first sign of wear."

Pam stood fuming. "I can't wait to get to 'Yvonne's' to give her a piece of my mind: I'd like to go and change only there is not time— there goes the bell. . . . . ."

It was Eric Edwards, who walked into a tense situation. "Hello!

269

Twins. You do look nice," said he looking at me, then he corrected himself. "Both of you."

That evening we went to the Taj, and leaving the Ladies' Room I was walking up the corridor when I met a fresh-looking young man, whose face was so familiar that passing him I halted and turned round. He was doing the same thing, and we both laughed. "The *Majola*, he said, smiling. "Of course! How stupid of me."

I answered, "Well, how do you like India?" And we stood talking for a few minutes. Then we moved along up the wide stairs together, pausing to chat now and again. There Pamela, who had come looking for me, found us. I introduced David Rees to her, and regretted it almost immediately. Her opening words were, "Where do you live, Mr. Rees?" And when he told her she exclaimed, "That dump! Surely you are not happy there? Oh, I am sure you are not—you must be used to something better, I imagine."

"Well!" he said, looking embarrassed, "I suppose it could be better. . . . ."

"Of course it could, you come round and see my place, that is where Irene and I live. Come to lunch tomorrow."

I looked hard at that young man, trying to warn him, but he either did not know me well enough to decipher my stare, or he was already lost and chose to be blind. After we left him Pam said, "Mouse, where did you find him? What a peach!" And she beamed at me with approval, but I was not happy.

"I don't think he will be able to afford your establishment, Pam—all that drinking. He's younger than the crowd you have there. . . . ."

"Oh, we'll manage. I want him, he's English." And as I was about to ask what she meant, she silenced me as we walked up to our party. Eric Edwards and I were asked to return to lunch next day; beaming on Eric she said, "You will be company for Mr. Rees."

At lunch, one of the P.G.'s accidentally knocked the serving spoon and fork out of a dish being offered. These were seen flying about whilst the young man tried desperately to save them from falling to the floor: he stopped, then straightening triumphantly pulled a fork out of his jacket sleeve. "*Gali—Gali!*" I said, clapping my hands. The men all roared with laughter, whilst Pam turned and looked at me, eyebrows raised and unsmiling.

That night as I was getting undressed she wandered into my room and I knew she had something on her mind the way she fidgeted. At last she spoke, "Mouse, I am thinking of getting a divorce. I must

270

change my name, and I must go to England if only for a short while, as you have done. This foreign name lets me down; the English people expect to find a large garlic-sodden Italian landlady, and I don't get them here. . . . ."

"I don't think it's that, Pam," I broke in, trying to comfort her, "I think it's because they cannot afford to pay as well as the Americans and others you have here."

But she was not to be comforted, she went on as if I had not spoken, ". . . . . .then again did you notice at lunch when they all laughed at your joke; I felt such a fool as I did not understand it."

"Why? that was just a silly thing."

"Explain it, anyway," she said, sitting on my bed.

"You know when the Egyptian conjurer at Port Said produces a chicken from under his hat, or from out of your ear, he says, "*Gali-Gali*' as one would say '*abracadabra*' if doing tricks; that's all there is to it!"

"Umph, that's not all. You speak differently, you act differently since you have been up on the Frontier and mixed with those army people."

"It's just that you find me a little more sure of myself—perhaps a little less 'mousey' than before—remember I am older!—The rest you imagine."

When Eric's holiday was nearly at an end Pamela again asked me to stay with her in Bombay. My hesitation seemed to annoy her, and she tried to enlist the help of her P.G.s bringing the subject up at table on two or three occasions. "I am trying to get this girl to stay here and nurse in Bombay, don't you think it's a good idea?" Her faithful followers were quick to agree, but I noticed that David Rees—who had now moved in to share a room with a fellow who had agreed to this when told his rent would be reduced—remained silent. Eric Edwards just gave me a long, long look without speaking.

Sunbathing at Breach Candy he brought up this subject. "I don't think you are very keen about living with your friend—I am glad—this is no place for you: but what are your plans? On the *Mooltan* you mentioned something about a matron's job—have you managed to get that?"

"Nothing is definite, however Colonel Nick has promised to help me."

After a long silence he asked me about my family, and somehow I felt it unnecessary to tell him the 'old story.' He knew already that

I had been born in India, I merely said now, "My parents were also born out here—my father worked on the railway, and we were always very poor."

From that, with his knowledge of the country, I knew he guessed all I had not told him, but I also knew he was no snob. As he was leaving Bombay that night, Eric had decided we were to have a gala lunch. "I am going to order oysters—how many can you eat?"

We drank beer, and in that heat this made us very sleepy. Soon we had slipped out of our deckchairs and were lying on the cool green lawn. I felt sure Eric had fallen asleep: he had been quiet for so long and just as I was about to follow his example, he rolled over on to his elbows, and picking a blade of grass tickled me on my bare back. "Wake up, lazy one, I have a suggestion to make. If you fail to get that matron's job come to Calcutta, I will be able to help you in small ways. To start with you can have my car, and the driver can take you round calling on the doctors. . . ."

"Where will I live?" I asked.

"I have thought of that; there is the Lady Lytton Club for nurses at Yule House, in Theatre Road."

"Have you been kind to many of the nurses from there?" I asked quickly.

Eric smiled. "No, Miss Green. I know about the nurses because the women in our company get them when a baby is expected, or for any illness—I don't go round picking up nurses."

"Sorry, Eric, you are really very sweet. I'll have to think about your suggestion; thank you for offering to help."

"Now, what do you want for a Christmas present?" he asked, changing the subject.

"How nice, I didn't know I was going to get one. . . . . let me think. . . . what about false eyelashes?"

"False eyelashes!"

"Yes! They cost the earth, you must have noticed Pam's hasn't she been sweeping your cheek with them as you danced?"

"Mph!" he exclaimed, looking disgusted, "surely you don't mean that?"

"Why not? It would be nice to look glamorous and seductive for a week."

"Don't they wash off?"

"No! Because one does not wash—cold cream is used instead of water."

"How revolting!!"

I smiled. After he had studied me for a few minutes he said, "No. . . . they won't suit you, you are not the type."

"You mean I am too 'mousey'? How depressing!"

"All I mean is that you must remain 'you', don't try and copy your friend. She is different—we'll leave it at that."

After I saw Eric off on the Calcutta Mail from Victoria Terminus, I returned to act as hostess for Pamela, who was dining out. Sitting on the balcony I watched the traffic going round the 'Oval', with the tall palm trees making a pretty picture silhouetted by the street lights. After a while I was joined by David Rees. "Missing your friend?" he asked.

"Yes, but it won't be for long, I am returning to Mhow and work tomorrow."

"I am glad to hear that—this is no place for you."

I stared at him—"How strange for you to be saying that—it's exactly what Eric said this afternoon at Breach Candy."

Just then the dinner gong sounded. "It's been nice meeting you again," he said, "and I hope you will be very happy, I think you will be, Edwards is a nice chap."

"I don't know what you are talking about. . . . ."

"I think you do: I caught Edwards looking at you in that 'certain kind of way' very often, and he did not come all the way from Calcutta merely to sunbathe at Breach Candy, Miss Green."

Then taking him by the arm, I said, "Come along, let's get some dinner before its all finished, and stop talking nonsense."

When I got back home I found Doreen was spending a night or two with us, as Henry was away on tour. "I'm longing to hear all your news, let's have an early dinner, then get into bed and have a good long *pow-wow*," she suggested.

"Nothing I would like better—I've had too many late nights."

After a bath Mama suggested I get straight to bed with a meal on a tray. She drew a *moorah* up by my bed, and sat to listen to my news.

"Come on now, Irene, tell us everything," said Doreen, snuggling under the sheets, "has he popped the question?"

"Doreen, be quiet!" said Mama, "and don't ask impertinent questions."

"But, Mama, why does she keep us in suspense?—She has told us about everything but what we want to hear most of all. Now don't pretend, darling, you are just as anxious to get your ugly duckling married off as I am."

"If you weren't a married woman, Doreen, I'd give you a good spanking," she was told.

"That's right, Mama," I said. "Anyway, Doreen, I can't tell what there isn't to tell, can I?"

"You disappoint me, Irene, I expected you to come back flashing a big diamond ring, and telling us the wedding date, but all we've heard is how nice, how kind and how understanding your Eric Edwards is."

"And that is enough to be going on with: I am not disappointed," concluded Mama.

A couple of days later I had a long letter from Eric. He gave me the name of the lady superintendent, who was an ex-army sister, in charge of the Lady Lytton Club. Nurses who wished to do private nursing, and who did not live in Calcutta, could rent rooms there. I was reading this letter from Eric, with all its details, when to add to my confusion I had a letter from the chief medical officer in Bhopal offering me the post of matron at the Prince-of-Wales Hospital. This was done on Colonel Nicholson's recommendation, and was ;just the sort of job I had been wanting for years! Administration, organising and running a hospital—but—there was also Eric Edwards!

Doreen, as usual, put it bluntly, "I think he means business, and if you go to Bhopal, you've lost him: those attractive girls in Calcutta will see to that! A young widower in a good job won't be lonely for long. Don't be a fool, Irene, grab him whilst you have the chance." Then turning to Mama for help, she said. "Don't you think I am right, Mama?"

Mama, who had been reading Lieut. Colonel S. A. Rahman's letter, now folded it to reply. "This is a very good offer, but I don't want my girl to go on working all her life—that's unnatural."

"But, Mama, this is a wonderful chancel I could get right to the top in my nursing career if I take this; I have lots of ideas how to run a hospital, new things I want to try out. . . . ."

"And whilst you are trying them out, my girl, someone else will step in and snap up your nice, kind, friendly widower, and you'll be left to turn into another sour Sister Crabbitt," said Doreen scoring a point.

Next day Mama, finding me alone on the verandah—with both letters in my hand, staring out over the garden, wondering which move would be the wiser to make—came straight to the point. "Go to Calcutta—refuse the Bhopal offer. . . . ."

"You mean, you old matchmaker, you think my Mr. Right has at last arrived?"

"Maybe—maybe, time will show," said Mama, smiling as she stood over me to stroke my head. "Anyway, give him a chance—there are other matron's jobs for you to go after later."

"And Bhopal is a dead-alive place. Mostly Indians living there as it is a State—the few Europeans, politicals and police will all be married, Not much 'fishing' to be done there! In Calcutta there will be others besides her Eric Edwards," interrupted Doreen, who had joined us on the verandah.

As I had so often done in the past, I went with my problem to Doctor Pinto. He advised me to go to Calcutta. "Before you take a matron's job, I think you should get more midwifery experience, Irene. Go round the different hospitals and take notes—it will all be useful."

So I wrote and thanked Lieut.-Colonel S. A. Rahman for his offer, which I regretted I had to refuse.

Next I wrote to the lady superintendent of the Lady Lytton Club, booking rooms, and after a quiet Christmas, I left for Calcutta early in the New Year of 1938. I caught the Calcutta Mail at Khandwa, and after a journey of roughly thirty-six hours, arrived at Howrah where, as it was a Saturday, Eric Edwards met me. Getting into the car, I found a big bunch of lotus lilies waiting for me. We drove straight to the Lady Lytton Club. Arranging to call later to take me out to lunch he left me to get a bath and change. I was startled for a moment when we went for lunch, and the car halted before the Great Eastern Hotel. Getting out I led the way familiarly into the building. Settling to a drink before *tiffin* I smiled at the old bearer serving us, and Eric remarked, "I can see you have been here before; that old chappy knew you."

"Yes, this is part of my dirty past, want to hear it? I may tell you one day." Eric reached out for my hand resting on the table, he squeezed it and said, "Your past is . . . . the past; it's your future that interests me, darling."

It was the first time he had called me that, and hearing it I was glad Mama, had advised me to come to Calcutta. We spent a happy weekend together, and all the club saw of me was when I dashed in for a bath and change. The fact that I had a young man and car at my disposal right from the start enhanced my prestige with the club servants, who liked nothing better than to escort a *sahib* on to a verandah, offer a chair and drink—which was later booked to the nurse's account—then to knock on the right bedroom door and call, "*Sahib a gaya*." Hearing that one's young man had arrived, one hurried out in time to see the bearer pocketing the *buckshesh*. On the Monday the lady superintendent gave me a list with the names and addresses of the doctors I had to contact. Eric had sent the car for me, and after breakfast I set about this business, which took about a week to get through, as I had to take my diplomas plus the references I had from Peshawar, Mhow and Indore with me for inspection. Then it was only a case of waiting for my turn.

My first case was a rich Indian householder. Unfortunately, this was just a case of simple tonsillectomy, and did not last long—the girl whose name followed mine on the roster picked up a nice long typhoid! Strangely enough, after that first Indian case, all my others were Europeans, I cannot remember them all: one was a bachelor living in a '*chummery*', I enjoyed the fuss all the men made of me—such a change from being surrounded by women. Then there was a maternity case which Colonel Gow, the well-known Calcutta gynaecologist, took whilst I did the nursing. I remember this case as it was in a posh locality. And everything in that flat was beautiful and expensive,—It was nice being able to change my patient's bedclothes daily, throwing down real Irish linen sheets for the *dhoby* to collect and take away, and she had the most marvellous ninon and georgette hand-embroidered nightgowns. When my patient heard that I had a young man she insisted on my asking him to dinner one evening, which he and I had in a large dining-room lit only by candles.

Then I had a couple of cases in the Riorden Nursing Home. A case I specially remember was in MacLean House, on Camac Street, and if I remember rightly my patient's name was Gordon. Mrs. Gordon was the wife of the *burra sahib* of one of the large Far Eastern trading companies, and the house was more like a palace then a normal residence. Large rooms, beautiful furniture, paintings and costly ornaments. There I saw, for the first time, stools that had been made from elephants' feet, and strangely enough, surrounded by all this wealth and luxury, for the first time I heard sliced French beans called 'Scotch Peas' by the little Gordon girl—any hint or suggestion of economy in those surroundings seemed incongruous.

When Mrs. Gordon asked me how long I had been 'out', I explained I had been 'out' all my life except for the short spell when I went 'Home' to get my 'midder'. Whether it was the ribbon pinned to my dress, (I soon heard I was the only nurse in Bengal who had this) or the slight 'haw-haw' that made most of my patients, their visitors and other contacts ask the same question I did not know, but always then my thoughts would fly back to Miss Snob in Peshawar. There I had vowed I would one day go to England, get my 'midder' and return to talk of 'Home.' I was going to pretend I had just come out, even invent a family left behind in some remote little-known village, perhaps also making my father a deceased parson or doctor, as most of the army sisters did! But now after four years, having achieved my ambition to get my 'midder' in Queen Charlotte's, all this seemed petty, and I scornfully rejected the pretence. I did not care anymore what anyone thought or guessed: whether I was hardened, or just independent, or merely older and wiser I did not know. So when this question was asked, my reply was "I have been out all my life except for the short time I went 'Home' to do my C.M.B. training. If she could have heard that reply I imagined Miss Snob saying, "That little Eurasian upstart! How dare she call England 'Home'!" Thinking this I smiled whilst answering Mrs. Gordon.

After a day or two in MacLean House, I asked Mrs. Gordon if she would kindly allow Eric Edwards to look round the place. She not only gave permission, but suggested he come to dinner. When Eric heard this he said, "Now you know the real reason why I wanted you in Calcutta." That this was a facetious remark I knew, as about a month after I had arrived in Calcutta one evening, after dining and dancing at Firpos, we had gone out to the lakes, that popular haunt of courting couples. There, sitting in the car quite casually, and with an 'I-couldn't-care-less' attitude, Eric "popped the question", as Doreen would have put it. I had been waiting for this moment all my life, and expected it to be much more romantic than this, so was hurt. I sat silent and angry. Then "What about it?" asked Eric.

"Hell's Bells! We hardly know each other—a fortnight on the *Mooltan*, two meetings in London, the holiday in Bombay, and now this!"

He disagreed, "I know all I want to about you—and you know all there is about me; a childless widower with fairly good prospects. Right now I can offer you a comfortably furnished flat with servants, tennis and golf, dancing and pictures."

Then I broke in. "Don't tempt me further. I know, late mornings, tea in bed, beer in the fridge, no more night duty or fractious patients. Oh, Eric, how heavenly but,—and there is a BIG but! You will have to know more about me before we can marry, and I can't bring myself to tell you so soon—perhaps I am a coward. In a few months time, if you still feel the same way, ask me again, and I'll tell you all. Yes?"

"Whatever you tell me won't make me change my mind," replied Eric, with a smile.

I sighed, "Well, we'll wait and see."

I must have pleased Colonel Gow nursing that first maternity case, because it was through him that I was given "the case of the year," as some of the nurses called it. This was Mrs. Battye, daughter of Sir Robert Reid, the acting Governor of Bengal. Mrs. Battye was expecting her first baby in the autumn, and sometime in May or June I was told to call at Government House to be interviewed by her. Some of the nurses were upset at my getting the case, as I was new to Calcutta, but as I was one of only two holding the C.M.B. diploma in the club, it seemed the obvious choice. Why I was selected in preference to the other girl I did not know. I concluded, after tossing about half the night with excitement, and thinking over the sour looks I had collected that night in the club dining room, it may have been because of my contacts in Peshawar, the club life and mixing with the army and political families which gave me the advantage, or perhaps it was just pure luck!

Anyway, it was definitely one of my 'very proud moments.' I remember hurriedly getting some new uniforms made, and giving detailed instructions to the *dhoby* about the way I liked my 'veils' starched. Then never failing to pin the ribbon on my dress since the day I came to realise that having this made people look at me twice—especially the men—I set off one morning for Government House. I was shown into a lovely large room; after a few minutes Mrs. Battye joined me. She was charming, young and very pretty. When the interview was nearly at an end Lady Reid joined us and we had tea together. When I got back to the club the nurses bombarded me with questions. Freeing myself, I flew to my room to write and tell Mama all about this very important case. I knew it would give her a great deal of pleasure, telling her friends and rubbing it into Aunt Alice.

As if this was not enough I had a second important case just then. This was Mrs. Denham-Whyte, wife of Colonel Denham-Whyte, the eminent surgeon. 'Mrs. D.W.', as she was called by all who knew her, was head of many charitable and social activities, and through overworking for these causes, had contracted tonsillitis with a slight but persistent temperature. She was ordered to stay in bed, with a day and night nurse in attendance. I was the day nurse. And it was very difficult to keep an energetic patient in bed when she felt better. She was house-proud and a good housekeeper. I well remember the daily ritual. In the mornings the Bengali butler would appear with his book for Mrs. D.W.'s orders. Then he would *salaam* and depart to be followed by the *khansamah* and *massalchi*, carrying trays of fresh provisions for inspection; only after these had been approved was the cook allowed to start his cooking, I may say that the delicious meals I enjoyed in that beautiful house in Alipore Road were made more enjoyable by the fact that I knew of this daily routine. When my patient had a relapse and her temperature returned, the colonel decided that his wife should go 'Home' for a complete rest.

CHAPTER 32

More Adventures Afloat

I was called into the colonel's office and asked if I was prepared to accompany them to look after Mrs. D.-W. on the voyage. There could be only one answer to that question, but walking out of the office I wondered if history was going to repeat itself: would Eric Edwards now think as Merrill had done, that I was some sort of grass-hopper. Or would he understand that as a nurse I had no alternative; my patient had to come first. I wondered if he would say, "You could hand the case over to another nurse," then I should have to tell him that this from a patient's point of view was never satisfactory, and we were taught as far as possible, to see the case right through. Eric lately seemed more and more to be my Mr. Right—the Englishman I had always wanted to marry, and though young, he had the experience of an older man.

He was in the right sort of job—a comfortable home was assured right away, and he was just nicely up the ladder—not too high, where socially I might have been out of place, yet he was in the 'Officer Class'? which made the little snob in me happy! He had the right background, education and good breeding, these I had been brought up to appreciate and value. So I thought what a pity if this voyage is going to break things up between us, then I reasoned if he was serious nothing would do that. And feeling helpless about the whole thing, I set about my preparations for the voyage.

It was sometime in late May or early June that I was again on the high seas. I have a menu dated 6th June, 1938, signed by eleven table companions. This was the night of the Fancy Dress Ball held as we were sailing through the Mediterranean, and though I had no fancy dress, I enjoyed the evening. Mrs. D.-W. improved immediately we left Bombay, and by the time we arrived at Aden, she was up and about, and had no further need for a nurse. I reported for duty two or three times a day, but was always told to run away and enjoy myself. I spent hours writing to all my friends, and though Pamela and I had kept up a desultory sort of correspondence, now feeling 'catty,' I had to write and let her know that I was on my second trip 'Home.' To Eric I gave the news of the strange sort of luck or coincidence I had on these 'worked passages'. He knew that on my first attempt the patient had died between Bombay and Aden. Now Mrs. D.-W. very accommodatingly had taken one look at the sea and been completely cured!

Going overland from Marseilles was a new experience for me. The D.-W's shared a two berth *coupé* on the special 'Blue Train,' but I had one all to myself! I was disappointed to know that we should be passing through Paris about two o'clock in the morning. I hoped I would be awake if only to see the lights, or identify a landmark, such as the Eiffel Tower, but I never stirred until the conductor called me next morning with a cup of tea. Still I was pleased that I could go back to India and tell them that I had journeyed across France. Travelling from Dover to Victoria in the boat train Mrs. D.-W. asked me what my plans were, and before we parted she very kindly asked me to meet her at the Ritz for tea one afternoon.

I had made no plans or arrangements for accommodation in London before leaving India, and parting from the D.-W's at Victoria, full of confidence as the old seasoned traveller I considered myself, I left for Queen Charlotte's. I was going to see if they could put me up for the week I was to be in England. My return passage had been booked for the next outward bound P. & O., the *Rawalpindi*. If Charlotte's could not accommodate me, there was always Burnetts, the little hotel-cum-sweet and tobacconist next door, where we nurses used to buy our sweets and cigarettes, and meet our boyfriends. The home sister was sorry, but as there was not a single room vacant in the Nurses' Home, she could not accommodate me, I went across to Burnetts, where I was able to get a room. I spent my time roaming round London, and saw more in that week than I had during my whole training period there.

Then to my great joy I heard from Eric, who not only wrote, but enclosed a postal order asking me to go up to Birmingham, and visit his mother and aunt, I was unable to do this for two reasons. First there was not much time, it meant a long journey for a visit of only a few hours. Secondly, I was not very keen. Mrs. Edwards had spent many years in India, and I felt sure she would very soon discover my secret, and as there was no time for her to get to know me properly, I felt sure I would make a bad impression. So I replied to Eric thanking him and giving him the excuse about there being no time for the visit. "Why didn't you suggest this visit before I left Calcutta?" I asked, turning the tables on him. Then I went out shopping, and to ease my conscience, with his money bought him a pair of silver brushes. This will do as an engagement present, I thought, I now felt sure he would again ask me to marry him on my return, then after telling him everything we could be married. Someone else would have to take the Battye case—marriage, I heard, released one from all contracts. Oh, yes, I had everything worked out, and all was set fair!

After the treatment handed out by the two table companions on the *Majola*, I was determined to see I was placed at a large table. On the *Corfu* to Marseilles, I was one of twelve, and the atmosphere at all meals had been a happy one. At the beginning of that voyage one or two appeared snobbish, but after being ignored by the remainder soon changed their attitude. So I joined the queue forming in the *Rawalpindi* dining saloon, and found myself standing behind a man in R.A.F. uniform: we were soon chatting and the girl behind me joined in, then we three decided to sit together, but eventually found ourselves with others at a table for ten. That night Pilot-Officer Bill Hughes told me he was going out to Iraq, and when I told him I was from the Far East he was very interested, and suggested we have coffee on deck. "Then you can tell me about the East—this is the first time I have come abroad, so I have lots to learn."

So started a friendship that was to last—by post—for eight years. Except for an occasional game of quoits or deck tennis with some men Bill spent all his time with me: we played games, danced or sat away from the crowd day after day, and talked of everything under the sun except personal affairs, and never once did he get familiar in any way, I had decided he must have a girl at 'Home,' and had chosen me to while away the time, thinking I looked a safe little thing. Whilst in my company he was safe from the plotting mamas escorting their unmarried daughters in the hope that the combination of sun, swimming pool, tropical moonlight and the boat deck would inveigle some unsuspecting male into committing himself.

Before Marseilles, four of us arranged to go ashore together, spending the night out going from one *café* or show to another, but somewhere in the Cannabière Bill and I lost the other couple. I had told Bill about the *Bouillabaisse à la Marseillaise*, and with the air of an expert I led him to where they made a speciality of it. At some time or other we found ourselves at a club or *café* where the floor show included a striptease act. As I had never seen one of these before I was determined to find out if it was really as daring as I had been told.

The fact that Bill, with his serious expression, was sitting opposite me did make it rather embarrassing. He sat there looking very miserable, and I felt sure that if he could have got away without causing a scene he would have done so. When only the two proverbial rose petals and fig leaf remained to be shed, it was too much for him, and putting his head down, he kept his eyes fixed on his drink until I told him it was safe. Looking up he swallowed what remained in the glass, and grabbing me by the arm, said, "Come on, let's get out of here."

Back on the ship we parted as day was dawning. As I was making my way down the corridor in which my cabin was located I heard a voice behind me call, "Mouse!" The name and the voice both startled me; turning round I rubbed my eyes, "Pamela? Is it really you or am I dreaming?"

"Now I've caught you out," said she, bearing down on me, "I asked this morning at the purser's office where you were, and was told that you had not been to bed all night, 'doing Marseilles with a crowd of passengers.' Now who have you been leading astray? Come on confess!"

"Where have you dropped from, Pam? I thought you were in Bombay, I could not contact you when I arrived there from Calcutta, as I was busy with my patient, but I wrote to you off the *Corfu*."

"Yes, I had your letter; then as I was planning to go to Switzerland to see about a divorce I took the next boat after you. . . . . ."

"And did you get your divorce?"

"Well, my lawyers are seeing to that—they think it will be all right—then I left for England all in a rush hoping to catch you there: I was going to make you put off returning to India so that we could do London together, but when I got to Queen Charlotte's they told me you had left on the *Rawalpindi*. So I came overland, and well, here I am! And as a berth is vacant in this cabin the purser told me I could have it."

"Jolly!" was all I could find to say—I was too sleepy to think clearly, but even for her all this seemed hectic and unbelievable—lawyers, divorce, voyages, overland journey, all in ten to fourteen days. Fortunately, she was just as tired as I was, and hoping the third occupant of the cabin would come in quietly, we pulled up the bedclothes and fell asleep. On waking, I wondered what Bill Hughes was going to make of Pamela, that our *tête-à-tête* meetings would now be at an end I guessed, and I was not wrong, Bill was now shared by us. If he resented this he made no sign, and I was a little disappointed; so when the ship docked at the next port where he had to disembark I nearly fell overboard with astonishment when he put his arm round my waist and held it there whilst we watched the 'tying up' process.

Pamela, hurrying round the corner, saw us like that and said, "I don't think you want me with you," and with a wink went on her way. Later when I told her that that was the first time Bill had ever done anything like that, she just would not believe me. Before leaving the ship Bill surprised me again, just as he was about to step on to the gangway he turned and asked me to write to him. "I know your address—the Nurses' Club in Calcutta—there will be a letter for you when you get there," said this strange young man. As I had decided there must be someone in England this request was startling. Oh, well, that's the last I shall see of him, I thought, as he walked down the gangway steps—but I was wrong! He did write, and we corresponded right throughout the Second World War. Then we met briefly in England, but as we both now had other interests, it was our last meeting. Left alone with Pamela I had visions of much drinking, dancing and flirting, and was not pleased at the prospect; these pastimes had now lost their attractions for me.

Then to her disgust and my relief a job presented itself. One of the women passengers, a B.O.R.'s wife, going out for the first time with two small children to join her husband in India, was taken ill, nothing serious, and I only heard of it through the woman who shared her cabin. They had from the beginning of the voyage staked a claim to a corner of the deck, where with the help of spare deckchairs, they fenced in their children, I had admired the way they had managed those young healthy, boisterous young animals, and when I saw that one woman was missing I asked after her, and learning of the situation I volunteered to help, and from then on was 'nanny.' I fed, dressed, bathed and bedded down those two children for about ten days.

It was the first time I had any contact with healthy youngsters, and the feel of their warm, steamy bodies, smelling like clean puppies, with their tiny arms clinging tightly about me as I carried them one on each arm from the bathroom down the corridor, to deposit them with a sigh of relief on the berth, did something to me. There is more in life, I thought, than drinking, dancing and flirting, more than ambition, however praiseworthy; here was something more important, something for a woman that beat all else. And after watching them envelope their mother in kisses, I shut the cabin door silently each night on this scene with a prayer in my heart.

One evening towards the end of the voyage, I was looking out over the rails, wondering what the future held for me as the ship raced towards India, when I was joined by Pamela. We talked for a while, then she pointed to the little waves which were lit up by the lights swung overhead.

"They look pretty."

"Yes. . . . . diamonds dancing in the sea."

"Where did you read that?"

"I haven't read it anywhere."

"Do you mean you have only just made it up?"

"Yes, but isn't it silly?"

"No. . . . .and I want to know why it is that I cannot think of anything like that; what is the difference between us; Mouse, are you a poet?"

"Poet or dreamer—which? Tell me, Pam, do you smell romance in the well-scrubbed bodies of children?"

"No—my *ayah* does that job for me, thank goodness," she replied with a shudder.

"Well, there you are—that's the difference between us."

When we docked at Bombay, I gently refused Pam's invitation to spend a few days with her, and took the first train for Mhow. I spent a week with Mama, and was glad Doreen was 'on line' with her husband just then, as she would certainly have asked some very awkward questions, Mama was more tactful; if she was disappointed that I had nothing to report, she gave no sign. Then I left for Calcutta. On the crowded platform of Howrah I felt very lonely; so many people were being met by friends or relatives. Then I saw Ashad Ali, Eric's Bengali driver, coming towards me. *Salaaming*, he handed me a note, it was just a few lines, a warm 'welcome-back' greeting, but that, and a bunch of flowers I saw in the car, caused my loneliness to vanish, and feeling cheerful I sat back to enjoy the drive to the Lady Lytton Club.

When I reported my return at the lady superintendent's office, I was handed an air mail letter from Bill Hughes; that strange young man had kept his promise, and had thawed enough to be able to sign off "with love." Eric called the following night to take me out to dinner. Now I heard that he had been promoted, and was out in the

285

Hooghly district. We dined and went to the pictures, after which Eric suggested a drive to the lakes. I readily agreed, thinking now this when he is going to propose again, and on the drive there I got my story ready. I was going to hold nothing back, and was full of confidence and happiness just then, but alas! There was no proposal. Perhaps he will speak another night, I comforted myself, but another and another night went by—yet he was silent.

Then one day he asked me to go out to see his new flat, he was now at a factory on the banks of the Hooghly. Here he lived in the European compound, in a large block of flats. When we arrived, one of the *memsahibs* was waiting on his doorstep; he had asked her to act as hostess. Later he told me he had done this to show that there was nothing to hide in our acquaintance, and wanted me to be accepted by his colleagues. However, after tea, she very kindly left us, and Eric was able to show me round, the flat was beautifully furnished, even down to the fridge in the store room. I looked round wistfully; wondering if I would ever be mistress here, and thought of the little touches and improvements I would make. If Eric read my thoughts he gave no sign.

After the inspection was over, he took me out to the garden to meet the others: these were the men he worked with, their wives and children. That was the first but not the last visit. I went out there two or three times before leaving for Darjeeling, where Mrs. Battye was to have her baby in Government House, and each time I went as guest to one or other of the *memsahibs*. I felt now I was being accepted. They looked, upon me as being a possible wife for Eric: this whilst being encouraging in the face of his persistent silence, left me bewildered. One night I was asked to a dinner party, which turned out to be a hectic birthday celebration. The evening had been a steamy hot one, with thunder hanging about—a storm was brewing. Just as we were about to leave for Calcutta, taking with us a fellow who was being lent to the Calcutta office, the clouds opened and down came the rain in sheets—it poured! We were advised to wait awhile.

When the rain slackened off a bit we decided to leave. The road to Calcutta, the Grand Trunk Road, followed the winding course of the Hooghly from Bandel to Howrah in those days before there were any by-passes. For those who are interested it was a road through history, where in this thirty-odd miles the European nations had founded settlements when they first ventured to this part of India for trade. The British at Hooghly, Dutch at Chinsurah, French at Chandernagore and the Danes at Serampore all established 'factories' or colonies. These were all gradually acquired by the British by consent, exchange or sale except for Chandernagore which, in fact, remained for a time an isolated French island in a sea of Nationalist India after the British rule ended. This was also the heart of the jute spinning and weaving area, and the number of mills, with their predominantly Scottish supervisory staff, brought Dundee and Aberdeen to the banks of the Hooghly in force. The road was mostly narrow and thickly populated where it wound its way through the various jute mill areas with the smelly bazaars and crowded unhygienic '*coolie* lines' inhabited by the mill labour force.

The rain had increased again to a real monsoon downpour. Eric was driving slowly, sitting well forward, peering through the curtain of water with which the windscreen wipers could hardly cope. Eric's friend was sitting by his side, I was sitting at the back and looking between the men at the rain-soaked road. We were just approaching the level crossing by the Angus Will Golf Club where there were several irrigation tanks on either side of the road. Suddenly I thought I must be seeing things. There was a huge fish, at least a foot long, wriggling its way across the road on its belly and fins in the layer of flood water, I kept very quiet, Jock, a keen fisherman, then spoke, his voice shrill with excitement. "Crikey! A blooming big fish crossing the road! Eric, did you see it?"

"No, old chap, and I should add more soda with it next time, if I were you."

"But I saw it, too. Jack, you are right, it was at least a foot or more long,"

"Thank God you saw it, Irene, or I should, have thought I was getting D.T.s, or the Deolali Tap." And the relief in his voice was comical.

The Ghoom Road Shelter

In the autumn, one night about 8 p.m., Mrs. Battye, a woman friend of hers who was to act as companion, and I left Sealdah for Siliguri on the first step of our journey to Darjeeling. Though this departure was a private affair, a certain amount of red carpet treatment had been laid on. The station staff were very attentive, and much bowing took place. The liveried servants of Government House attended to our luggage, and my battered old suitcase had never been so carefully or respectfully handled. The following morning, about seven o'clock, we arrived at Siliguri, and after breakfast started on the car journey of about fifty-one miles. This was by way of the Cart Road, which as its name implies, was once used solely by this form of transport hauled by the patient bullock or buffalo, before the car was invented or the railway built.

Ghoom was the highest point on this road at about eight thousand feet, the road descending from here into Darjeeling itself, about six miles further on and about five hundred feet lower. It was a beautiful drive, but a very winding one, and I missed a good deal of the scenery as I was feeling car-sick. I lay back most of the way with my eyes shut wishing I was not there. Of the three I fared the worst, and when Mrs. Battye said, "For the return journey you had better take the train, Sister," I readily agreed. At long last we got to our journey's end.

We were to live in a beautiful bungalow in the gardens of Government House near the main entrance. Government House had lately been more or less rebuilt, after being badly damaged in the Bihar earthquake of 1934, I can now even vaguely remember the bright blue dome roof. This looked particularly attractive against the background of the mighty 'Snows' which stretched across the skyline looking so near but were over fifty miles away. I was at liberty to wander round the grounds, and many times stood admiring that beautiful range of mountains.

My patient usually had breakfast in bed, which I took to her. Lunch and dinner she had in the dining room with her companion. When they had finished, I had mine in solitary state. The Indian butler never failed to offer me all the wines served to them, and I never failed to accept at least one. When the baby was almost due Colonel Gow came up from Calcutta, and I helped him bring a lovely little girl into the world. At some time or other Sir Robert and Lady Reid came up also, and Government House was occupied. I have in my 'Souvenir Casket' a charming snapshot of Lady Reid holding the baby.

Then I heard from Eric—to my surprise and delight he was coming up to Darjeeling for a couple of days. As my patient was doing well, she very kindly let me have the evenings free. When he arrived Eric was shown into the sitting room—where I joined him. The first thing he did was to inspect my shoes, and then advised me to change into comfortable walking ones. "We have a lot of walking to do—and those flimsy things won't do—I want exercise and a breath of fresh air after Calcutta." Darjeeling was the pedestrian's paradise if he did not mind walking up and down hills.

Cars—except those belonging to Government House—were banned on any of the roads above the level of the Cart Road, by the station. It was a question of safety—not of privilege. The main form of transport above the car level was the rickshaw or *dandy*, the latter being a modified form of sedan chair. These were all hauled or toted by the inveterate gambling Bhuttias, who were past masters at producing realistic moans, groans and puffs to prove to the hirer how hard they were toiling to carry his lazy body from the Chaurasta to Jalapahar. At the Mount Everest Hotel we sat a long while over our dinner. Then Eric said he had something really beautiful to show me, and led me to a seat in a shelter or observation post on the Ghoom Road, somewhere below the Mount Everest Hotel. Still further below were the twinkling lights of Darjeeling Bazaar, and behind this, dominating the view, was the ethereal beauty of majestic Kinchinjunga and its attendant eternal snow-covered Himalayan peaks bathed in the light of a full moon.

This scene and the gorgeous shades of a monsoon sunset on the same peaks are perhaps two of the most colourful views—one can ever expect to see. I looked for a long time in silence then murmured, "Lovely, Eric, lovely!" then I remembered words I had read somewhere, "..... *If you are lucky you will see, and when you see you will remember.*"

I was lucky, I had seen, and I was to remember, for Eric—the silent—as he had been in my thoughts since my return from my second trip 'Home' had decided that here was the spot that we were to become engaged. I sighed after drinking in this beauty—this grandeur had a strange effect on me, making me feel sad, lonely and very small. Eric, hearing the sigh, turned to me and asked, "Why the sigh?" I could find no answer except to smile. He then delved into his pocket and brought out a tiny square box, unmistakably a ring box, and opening it he said, "Here, darling, just slip this on—left hand, third finger," and as I was about to speak he stopped me by moving the hand he had placed round my waist over my lips—"No, don't say a word, no 'buts,' 'ifs' or 'whys'—put it on first—" and as I sat motionless staring at him, he picked up my left hand and said, "Here, I'll do it," and the ring was on! "Now we are engaged and you can talk as much as you like: it will make no difference, I warn you, whatever you say."

But my throat had gone dry, and I could still do nothing but stare at him. "Don't look so scared, darling, look at your ring and tell me if you like it—if you don't I can take it back. It was bought on that agreement from Bosecks, then when you get down to Calcutta we can go round together, and you can choose any other you fancy." I knew he was talking to give me time and loved him for his thoughtfulness. As he spoke he had taken a small torch from his pocket which he had shone on the ring, but it did not need that to tell me it was lovely: in the bright moonlight the gems sparkled, a 'pigeon's blood' ruby, with a large diamond on either side. I looked, and then took a deep breath. "Do you like it, Irene?" asked Eric, softly, then snapping off the torch he replaced it in his pocket, and covered my left hand with his.

"Eric! It's *beautiful*—a far lovelier ring than I ever hoped to possess."

"Whew! .....that's a relief. Now let's finish this thing off properly. ...."

"No!! Wait—Eric," and I drew away. "You must first hear what I have to say," and though I had rehearsed my speech a thousand times until I had it word perfect, now it came out all jumbled, garbled and twisted. In the end Eric took over.

"Listen, darling, what you are trying to tell me I guessed long ago; on the *Mooltan*, as a matter of fact: you are coloured, yes?" I nodded. "Three parts European, one part Asian, yes?" After the second nod, he continued, "All right, now we have the whole thing straight—what about it? I still want to marry you."

"But, Eric, have you thought about children—Aren't you scared?"

"Not seriously—it's possible but not probable that they may be coloured, the odds against that happening are too heavy. I'll risk it—now no more talk, we haven't sealed the bargain yet—that won't do," and when I opened my mouth to speak, I was stopped—stopped in the nicest possible way.

When I got back to our bungalow I went straight to Mrs. Battye to show her my ring; I wanted to show it to the whole world, but only my patient was available. Very often during that night I felt my ring as I turned over, I wanted to be sure it was really there, and not just a beautiful dream I was having. Getting into uniform next morning I reluctantly parted from my ring—in those years jewellery of any sort, even a wedding ring, was taboo. The hours dragged that day. After giving my patient her tea I was free. Eric and I had arranged to have this meal together. At the *café* he kept teasing me as I poured out, perhaps I did use my left hand a little more than usual, and when the woman seated at the next table glanced at my ring as my hand lay prominently on the cloth—I was satisfied. After tea Eric suggested a walk—"Where shall we go today?"

"To 'our beautiful place,'" I replied.

"You sentimental little thing," he chuckled, "But first let's go down to the bazaar, it's quite a fascinating place with crowds of Bhuttias and Tibetans: the shops, too, are worth visiting." So we strolled down, and looked into a couple of shops. Then Eric saw something he fancied. This was a wall plaque, made in Bhutan or Tibet of brass, with a central figure of the multi-armed Goddess Kali. Round this figure was brass filigree work studded with semi-precious blue and red stones. The overall effect was that of a Russian icon with a distinctly Oriental character. "We'll buy this to celebrate our engagement," he said. I have been glad ever since that he did that, as visitors to our home have always stopped to admire this unusual piece of handiwork. The Goddess in her abode of the Tibetan icon is the medium that takes me back to 'our beautiful place,' and the 'eternal snows.'

After making this purchase, we made once again for the observation shelter in Ghoom Road, then, after duly admiring the scene, Eric produced a list from his pocket—names of relatives to be informed of our engagement by telegram. I was pleased to note that my mother's name headed the list—it was this little touch of thoughtfulness and kindness that had endeared him to me from the very beginning; I who had always felt the need for kindness and understanding was now to have it for always. The next list was of newspapers—in England and India—that were to be sent our engagement announcement for insertion. The only one that interested me was the *C.& M.*, or *Civil and Military Gazette*, published in Lahore, I wanted my friends—and the others, especially Miss Snob in Peshawar—to read this. Soon it was time for me to return to my patient, and as Eric was leaving early next morning, it was "Goodbye" for the time being. My patient and her baby progressed normally, and in due course, according to the agreement made in Calcutta, I was able to leave them. A rickshaw from Government House took me down to the station.

The Darjeeling Himalayan Railway, a narrow gauge track, winds its way precariously but confidently from Darjeeling to Siliguri, playfully shunting backwards and forwards to negotiate a particularly heavy gradient, or making spectacular tight circular turns to appear over the stretch of line which it has travelled only a minute or two before. There are several of these 'loops,' and the double one, reminiscent of a corkscrew, is a particularly clever piece of engineering. The tale is told that the man who planned this line died of brain fever, but this may only be a local story to impress the traveller. It used to be no uncommon occurrence for the puffing, gallant little engines to have to contend with elephants almost as big as themselves on the line, especially at night. Normally the bright searchlight and a few piercing shrieks on the whistle were enough to move off the trespasser, but if the latter was a 'must,' or rogue elephant, there were occasions when it is said a pushing competition took place to decide who should have right of way.

I enjoyed the journey down, whether because the train was taking me to Eric or because the more gentle slopes and turns were kinder to my sensitive tummy. At Siliguri I caught the Calcutta Mail. Eric had written to say that unfortunately he was to be very busy the week I returned, and was taking this opportunity of getting the car overhauled. However, we were to meet at the weekend. So arriving at Sealdah I asked the *coolie* carrying my suitcase to get me a taxi, Whilst I stood waiting for this on the station steps, I had time to think of the difference just wearing a ring had made. I did not feel lonely or neglected at not being met this time, and then realised with pleasure that I now possessed a new confidence.

In the Lytton Club going into dinner that night I walked into a mixed atmosphere. The nurses had all read of my engagement in the *Statesman*; most of them were pleased, and I was greeted with the *Wedding March* being whistled or hummed. One or two shouted, "Come on, Green, we want to see your ring." There were various comments whilst this was being inspected. "Whew. . . . . !" "Marrying a *rajah?*" "Lucky you!" A few merely raised their eyebrows, and it was easy to read their thoughts, "Well! How did she manage to pull that off?"

One of the girls thought she had the answer; this was "little James," a girl who was much darker than I was, with brown eyes and dark hair. Before going up to Darjeeling I had heard that she had become engaged to a young Englishman, a junior *box-wallah*, but as we had been on opposite shifts, I had not seen her until now. After exchanging good wishes, we decided to dine at a small table for two.

"Then we can swop engagement news," James suggested.

Sitting down I remarked, glancing at her left hand, "This seems infectious!"

"You know why it is, don't you, Green?"

"No! Except that for me—it's a miracle."

"Well, I'll tell you—it's our long hair."

"Our long hair?" I stared at her then laughed, thinking it was meant to be a joke, as she and I had long hair which for quickness sake we plaited and wore halo fashion round our heads.

"You needn't laugh! My *fiancé* said to me the other night, 'Look around you, Maggie, how many of the women have long hair—not one; you are different, whilst they look like peas from a pod.' Green! I'm sure that's the answer, our long hair."

"And I prefer to think *Kismet* is the answer, my dear James."

I spent the next day or two 'putting my house in order'. First the bankbook was inspected; this was disappointing as I had not worked long enough after graduating in midwifery to have accumulated much money. In Darjeeling, after settling my patient for the night, I had spent many a pleasant hour by the fire allowing my imagination to run riot on a glamorous trousseau: now I had to set to work and alter drastically the ambitious list I had made. Then I turned out my 'Souvenir Casket.' This was large, rather dilapidated cardboard box, in which I kept old love letters—there were quite a few from Paul and Merrill—photographs, dance and band programmes, menus, invitations, visiting cards and other odds and ends of that kind. One day I must get rid of that rubbish, was something I was always telling myself, but had never been able to take this wise action—the sentimental side of my nature had objected. Now, however, it was a different matter. So with a light heart I got down to it, and without a second glance tore through the love letters and consigned them to the waste paper basket. Then I came across a photograph of Llew, the young fellow who had come up from Lahore on two occasions to see me in Peshawar, each time bringing a leather bound volume of Kipling as a present.

As I still felt friendly towards him, his photograph did not follow the others into the waste basket. I decided to try and contact him with a view to returning it. So after throwing the rest of the junk back into the 'Casket' I called the *hamal* to clear the basket, then wrote to the old address which I had not used for seven years—this was to the head office in Calcutta, I hoped they would forward the letter to wherever he was. After 'phoning Eric and telling him how much I was looking forward to our next meeting I went to bed happier than I had been for a long time. Destroying those photographs and letters from Paul and Harvey had completely taken away such bitterness as I had been unable to shed with the passing years.

Whilst changing that Saturday evening my heart sang, "I'll be meeting *my fiancé* soon," and I made an effort to look nice. We were to meet early as Eric had said in a letter, "There is plenty we have to discuss and settle." So after dinner we went to the lakes; there Eric unfolded his plans. "Get your name off the roster to start with, you do not want any more cases." This was like music in my ears—so nice to have a masterful man to look after me, I thought. "I'll see the *padre* chap and we can be married quietly by special licence, just as soon as it can be arranged."

"But, Eric, I haven't a thing to wear," I protested, "no trousseau ready or anything. . . . . ."

"Oh, you don't want to bother with all that stuff," said Eric non-chalantly, "after we are married you can go on a shopping spree with one of the girls and get all you want."

I was shocked. "Do you mean you want me to go with you just in any old dress and get married—just like that?"

"Yes, why not?"

"Why NOT? Do you realise that you are talking about my WED-DING DAY—the day I have been looking forward to all my life, and you dismiss it——just like that—" said I, nearly in tears.

"Well! darling, if you feel so strongly about it, perhaps we can wait 'till you get a dress—that should not take long; you can get one from any of the big shops, but nothing too elaborate or showy, please."

"Oh, no, NO, Eric, you have got this all wrong! Listen darling, I am going to ask you to do something; very big for me. I can see you don't want a big wedding or show of any kind—am I right?"

"Quite right. You see, Irene, I have gone through all that once, I cannot face it again."

"Yes, I understand, and I agree, but you must also understand my view point. This will be my BIG day, and I could not be happy if my family, especially my mother, was not with me. Then. . . . ." I hesitated before going further—but Eric encouraged me.

"Go on, Irene, what do you want?"

Then drawing; a deep breath I said, "*Please*, Eric, I want to be married in the Garrison Church in Mhow—as a child I went there to Sunday School, then during the First World War my father often took us to the Parsee services. A half-sister of mine was married there—so was my sister Doreen, and more than anything in the world I, too, want to be married there."

"All right, my dear, if you want it so badly—let's arrange it that way."

"Oh, Eric, you darling, you are sweet!" and I thanked him in the best way I could. Then I continued, "But it's not going to be easy for you—meeting a lot of strangers, people of a community you have never met socially, and for whom you have no particular respect. . . ."

"Oh, I don't know. . . . ." broke in Eric.

"But I do, darling, I know what I am talking about—*all too well*. But I promise you one thing, you will be made welcome, and they will do everything, especially my mother, to make things easy for you. . . ."

"Don't worry, Irene, don't get so worked up," again Eric interrupted, and put his arm round my waist to show his sympathy, but I was impatient. I felt he was not taking this as seriously as he should: did he understand all it meant? I wanted to get him by the shoulders and shake him to make him understand! ". . . . .let me finish, Eric, and then when you have heard all, and this situation is thoroughly understood, we need, never discuss it again. My mother has always said, 'Never think that I will stand in your way, it's your happiness I want, plan your future without me. You girls must let your husbands know this, and stress the point that they will be marrying *you*, not the family.' From that, Eric, you will get some idea what she is like. Whilst I agree that we must live our own lives unhampered by maternal ties, there is also family love and loyalty. I shall naturally want to see my mother from time to time, although after the wedding *you* need never see any of my people again—that is for you to decide—but, and I don't think it's necessary for me to ask you this, at the wedding you will have to use all your tact not to hurt or embarrass any of them. You are kind enough to be able to handle this very delicate situation—Oh! It's all so difficult to tell you—you see they will be feeling awkward and shy to meet you. . . ."

"It's all right, darling, I *understand*. Don't go on distressing yourself. You forget that I was born in India, of English parents. My first four years of schooling at St. Paul's, Darjeeling, was with English, Indian, Eurasian, Burmese and even Siamese children, so I am not quite the character you are painting me without any contact with the conditions you are describing in their worst possible detail. You will probably find that your mother and I will be jolly good friends. She sounds a very sensible woman, and I admire her courageous spirit. All will be well, I promise you," and, with that promise I, who was on the point of hysteria, relaxed. Taking Eric's advice next day, I went to the office and had my name removed from the roster, and gave the date I would be vacating my rooms.

The next ten days were hectic—spent in an orgy of shopping. For my wedding I bought an expensive navy and white lace dress; with this went a little white hat made entirely of flowers. It was all very pretty, but I was disappointed, and in fact, that I was not going to be a white bride. However, I was determined to keep my promise to Eric. Then I had an answer from Llew. My letter had been forwarded, "I'll ring you when I get back to Calcutta, and we'll arrange to meet. You can return the old photograph, and I'll give you my big news." I told Eric when I next saw him about this; it did not appear to upset him, and if I was hoping for any sign of jealousy, I was disappointed. The evening Llew came to see me I wore one of my trousseau evening dresses. As white suited me so well, I knew I was looking nice. Going down the wide stone staircase I carefully held up my full skirt. Then I saw Llew at the bottom. He was looking up with a smile and as I reached the last step he spoke, "Gosh, Irene, you look as young and as pretty as you did years ago."

"And you, Llew, are still the same dear old flatterer of seven years ago. . . . Oh, my dear, how are you?" And I laughed as I reached for his outstretched hands.

"How do you do it—Ever-Green-Eve?" He was now using a name I had collected in Peshawar, and disliked.

"Oh, just by being good—and being very happy," I answered lightly, then led the way to the car standing by the porch. I had brought the
photograph down with me—Llew now took this and threw it in the
back of the car. We dined at Firpos, and then waltzed to the tune of
'Night and Day.' This haunting melody made me feel rather mixed up,
happy and a little sad, seeing Llew had brought back so much of the
past—Juhu, the sea with moonlight on the waves, warm sand, palm
trees and happy young nurses; then my thoughts wandered to Peshawar where I had first heard this lovely tune, and I was glad when Llew
interrupted my thoughts.

"Let's go somewhere where we can talk quietly, I want to find out
what you have been doing with yourself these last few years."

We went to the Botanical Gardens and found an empty seat under
the famous banyan, and talked. There Llew told me of his engagement
to an Australian girl. "Didn't you see the announcement in the *Statesman*, Irene?"

"No!—if I had I should have written and sent you my good wishes
right away; I have been travelling a good deal this year and must have
missed it."

Then Llew reminded me of his second visit to Peshawar when he
had found me rather 'pi.' "I thought you were all set on becoming a
missionary, and imagined you wearing a horrible white cotton *sari*
with *chaplis*, and carrying a Bible around."

And thinking of those good, serious minded but so often plain-
looking European women, worn out through working so heroically
against heavy odds—I laughed. "That phase soon passed—as one of
the sisters said at the time I was too fond of boyfriends and dancing
to make a missionary."

"Yes, you certainly look very unlike a missionary just now, and do
you know you have a very provocative mouth, Irene? So come on,
let's go back—this won't do; you and I are both engaged, we must be
sensible."

So on that sensible note our last meeting ended. But a couple of
days later he sent me a lovely glass cocktail set—my first wedding
present. The second present I had came from some of the Lytton Club
nurses who banded together to give me a travelling glass and leather
fitted 'make-up' case.,

Just before my last weekend in Calcutta, Eric came in to see me in
the middle of the week; after dining somewhere we went straight out
to the lakes—there was still much to talk over and arrange. We were

to be married by special license, and Eric was to get the necessary documents and papers together to send to me. He then told me all I had to do when I got to Mhow. "You'll have to move fast—rush them along—if we are to be married on the 3rd of November." Actually I was beginning to regret having agreed to this early date: I had not had the time to enjoy our engagement, since coming down from Darjeeling Eric had simply swept me off my feet rushing me along at the pace he had set. "And now there's one last thing I want to ask you to do for me, Irene—will you do it?"

"Of course!"

"You may not like it—when you know what it is: will you get your hair cut short?"

"Well!" I said, sitting up straight in surprise. "Don't you like it this way?"

"Not really, you see, dear, when I first met you on the *Mooltan* you had short curly hair, which I liked—this rather prim style does not suit you—your silly little nose does not lend itself to the dignity of that switch thing—besides which, I cannot do this—Ugh!" Eric had tried to push his fingers through my hair and had met a hairpin.

"You see what I mean?" and he licked his finger.

"This is going to make 'Little James' very sad," I said.

"And who is he, and what has your hairstyle to do with him?" demanded Eric.

"You silly darling, 'Little James' is one of the Lytton Club nurses. That's her surname, the 'little' got tacked on because she is so short." Then I told him the story of the plaits and James' theory that we had only got engaged because of them.

Eric had a good laugh.

"I know why you have got engaged, darling, and it's got nothing to do with your plaits."

So the very next day, before my good resolution to please Eric vanished, I rushed to the hairdresser and had my hair cut. Eric never realised what a sacrifice that had been, but when I thought of all he was doing for me—it seemed a small thing in comparison.

For my last weekend I had been asked by one of the *memsahibs* to spend Sunday in the compound. We spent a happy afternoon playing golf and tennis, and that night we were given a lovely carved Chinese chest as a wedding present from the whole compound. After dinner we took the long drive back. "You'll get to know the G. T. Road very well in time," remarked Eric, and added, "returning from Calcutta I always look out for the lighted Virgin Mary, and when I see Her I know I am nearly home." He was speaking of the statue on the church at Bandel. This is one of the famous Roman Catholic Churches in India, and is said to have been erected in the sixteenth century by a group of Portuguese traders, who were shipwrecked in the Hooghly near this point, but were all miraculously saved. There a statue of the Virgin Mary in a niche high up in the tower over the front entrance of the church was always illuminated at night, and when the car rounded a particular bend on this portion of winding road, was clearly visible with its friendly light

I often remarked to Eric as we passed this church, "It is very pretty." I did not know it then, but that statue was to play an important part in the scheme of things in the future. Two years after we married, and our first baby was expected, Eric would not tell me for a long time whether he wanted a boy or a girl. "I want a boy—definitely, surely you have a preference?" But he would not reply, he did not want to add to my disappointment. Then one day, in a weak moment, he confessed to wanting a son. So from that day every time we passed that church, I always said a prayer, "Please, Virgin Mary, let it be a son." Some people said I was lucky when in due course my son arrived, but I preferred to think my prayer had been answered.

Then two years after John's birth another baby was expected. Again passing the church I would look up at the statue and silently pray "Let it be a girl this time, Virgin Mary." Again the know-alls thought it was just luck when my daughter was born, but I knew otherwise. However, this portion of the Old Grand Trunk Road was by-passed towards the end of the Second World War to make it easier for the army convoys to reach the many camps established along this famous highway. One wonders whether any traveller, knowing the ancient original track, now deviates from the straight course to say a little prayer to the patient Bandel Virgin Mary.

In *Champak* bungalow, I took Doreen to see my trousseau the day I arrived. She admired everything; then I opened the cardboard case in which was packed very carefully, in layers of tissue paper, the wedding dress. Shaking it out I asked, "How do you like this?"

One look at her face gave me the reply, "Oh, Irene! Mama is not going to like that. . . . ."

"Yes, I know, my dear, but I promised Eric 'no show.' It would look silly to wear a white dress without the usual trimmings, veil, bouquet or wreath. So it had to be a coloured dress, and I thought the navy and white lace smart, as you know I look dreadful in pastel shades, being sallow."

After listening in silence Doreen disdainfully tossed my navy aside saying, "This is going to spoil everything."

Then we decided to consult Mama.

"Call her and see what she thinks, Irene."

Mama was, as usual in the kitchen supervising, but when I told her why I wanted her, she hastily left everything—not even waiting to lock the store-room door, which was most unlike her, and hurried along with me—I could see her smiling and felt wretched. I showed her the trousseau first, then the wedding dress. To my surprise she admired all. Then folding her hands in her lap in eager anticipation said, "Now show me the wedding dress."

"But, Mama, I've shown it to you—that's it," and I pointed to the navy and white lace. "I told you that was my wedding dress when I took it from the box."

Looking incredulously from Doreen to me she said, "But that's not a wedding dress, it's a dinner dress."

And Doreen muttered, "I thought she hadn't got it right first time."

Then though I had written and explained it all—Eric being a widower not wanting a show, and that I should not be wearing white, I now had to go through it all again. As I spoke I could see Mama was upset.

"Irene, I understand all you say, I understand his reasons—but it's your BIG day—and, my child, you will look a widow in that," and then Mama got up and left us without another word.

"I knew it, I knew she'd be upset," said Doreen.

"Oh, shut up. You've already said that more than once," and I flung the navy and white, with the other stuff, back into the suitcase. Clearing my bed I flung myself on to it.

"Now you just listen to me, my girl," said Doreen, coming to stand over me. "You have done so much to give her this happiness—I mean, coming home to be married. She has been going around telling all her old cronies, 'my Irene is coming all the way from Calcutta to be married from her old home.' Cannot you now write to Eric and make him understand. If he is as nice as you say he is, he'll agree."

"Of course, he's nice, and he'll agree—but that's not the point—I wanted to keep my share of the bargain—no, Doreen, I can't do it."

Then the next few days slipped away—there was so much to be

done. Doctor and Mrs. Pinto were giving me the cake and refreshments as a wedding gift. Mama, Vi and Doreen were seeing to the other expenses. We were very busy and should have been happy but for that wedding dress; which hung like a cloud over us, blotting out the fun and excitement that a wedding causes in all families, especially amongst the women.

One day Doreen came in just as Mama and I were about to begin our lunch: without a by-your-leave she took a plate off the dinner-wagon, and helped herself. "That's nice! I expect you've had a whacking great meal in your own house, then you come here to eat ours—no wonder you are so fat!" I remarked, winking at Mama.

"For that rude remark I won't give you the juicy bit of news I especially came in with."

"Oh, Doreen, *please* do tell!"

Smiling, she kept me waiting, then spoke, "You'll never guess who I met in Sunderlals." He was our Hindu cloth merchant in the bazaar—"Vivienne Marrowful. Her brother-in-law has been sent to Mhow from Neemuch." Then she explained to me. "Dorothy married a sergeant in the S. & T. when you were in Charlotte's—it's the highest they've managed." And thinking of those far-off day, she smiled.

"Well! What's the juicy bit?" I asked.

"Sunderlals was showing me the cheaper quality *crepe-de-chines*—he knows by now not to produce anything expensive for me; then because she was standing there, I said, 'No, this won't do, Sunderlals, it's for Irene, Miss Sahib's wedding day, I must look well: nothing cheap will do as she is marrying a *burra sahib*.'"

"Doreen! You cat, how could you!" I was shocked.

"She'll never grow up," said Mama getting up to leave the table, but I could see her smile.

"There's more, Mama, wait!"

"No, I've no time to sit and listen to your rubbish," but as she passed Doreen, Mama patted her gently on the head.

Then when she had left the room, Doreen turned to me and continued, "That was too much for Vivienne, as I knew it would be, she had to ask, 'Who is Irene marrying, and what is his job?' I then told her your Eric was an officer in 'civvy street', and told her his designation and the name of his firm."

"Oh, Doreen, really you should not have done that—anyway, what did she say?"

"Nothing. She just went 'Mph,' I felt like saying 'Mph to you, sour puss'—but do you remember what they said in Neemuch? They were not going to marry below the officers' rank. And how they used to show off to us at those garrison dances when they had so much and we so little."

Then we both sat silent, thinking of those old days. Doreen at last broke the reverie by saying, "Irene, *can't* you do something about that dress; it's making Mama very unhappy. I know what's in her thoughts, all that old-fashioned nonsense about virgins always marrying in white, and all that. . . . ."

"Meaning that if I'm not in white I'm no virgin? Well, they can think what they like."

"Oh, it's not the old cronies I'm worried about," explained Doreen, "It's Mama—she sort of feels 'let down.' Can't you write and tell Eric everything and see what he says—get him to telegraph his reply."

"No, there's no time for anything like that now—if we are going to change anything we'll have to act now and I'll have to explain later."

"You mean. . . .?"

"I mean, my dear, that I'll be a white bride or bust—come on—let's go to Sunderlals!"

"Hurrah! Mama, Mama!" and Doreen and I rushed into the kitchen. "Can't stop to explain all now," said she, grabbing hold of Mama and kissing her with excitement, "We are going to get her a wedding dress made—and there's only three days left!!"

"A WHITE wedding dress, Mama!" I shouted over my shoulder, as I rushed after Doreen. Now Mhow Bazaar was not the place where a bride-to-be would normally shop. Most of the girls, army or railway, went into Bombay for their requirements. So running along the road, we knew we would have a difficult time in finding anything.

"I doubt if we'll find any orange blossom here—you'll have to make some."

"I can't!"

"Why not? That should be easy after the arum lilies and all the other flowers you have made."

"That's not it—it's just that I am far too excited: I couldn't sit to anything like that now."

"You poor old girl," said my little sister sympathetically.

After searching round two or three of the fairly big shops, we went on to Sunderlals—we were hoping to avoid him as Doreen said, "Now that he knows about your wedding, he'll probably guess that we want the material for a wedding dress, and push up the price—so let's miss him if we can." But it was not easy; the other shop merchants showed us heavy expensive brocades and satins, or cheap shoddy stuff—nothing between. Then at Sunderlals we saw it—just a few yards left of a white ninon with a chenille flower and leaf pattern. Then the pantomime started—Doreen pretending it was not for a wedding dress, trying to get him to reduce the price, but Sunderlals, who had known us since we were children—was not bluffed. In the end it was our old tailor, Behrulal, who had made clothes for us over many years, who shamed him into reducing.

Behrulal had his tailor's shop just opposite Sunderlals, so it was very convenient—one would call out to him, and he would cross the road carrying fashion books under his *arm,* to sit on the floor of Sunderlals shop. We soon found a simple pattern, and after begging Behrulal not to hang the dress when ready in the shop for all to see from the road—which is what he and all the tailors did as advertisement—we went in search of a veil and orange blossoms. On leaving Behrulal Doreen said, "We were lucky he agreed to make your dress, he has been getting very independent lately—more and more of the army officers' wives are getting him to make their dresses—they have lately found out the '*dirzee* mades' are cheaper than the models from Bombay—he refused to work for some railway people last week—told Mrs. Brown, 'I only work for the officers' *memsahibs*.'"

"It's a pity some of the young railway girls don't take up dressmaking. . . ."

"Strange you should say that, Irene, only the other evening at the Institute we were discussing the growing independence of the bazaar traders, and someone suggested our railway girls being taught dressmaking, and perhaps baking at the convent. . . . ."

Then Doreen paused to ask one of the cloth merchants if he kept wedding veils. He shook his head, so we continued up Main Street.

"Well, what happened?" I asked.

"Nothing, as you might have guessed. You know what Anglo-Indians are—too sleepy to bother, 'care-free' we are labelled; but I know another adjective that suits equally well."

"You mean—lazy?"

Doreen nodded. I had to get behind her to let a *tonga* pass. When abreast again, I said, "I don't agree with you, what about the men on the railway, no one can call them lazy: think of the drivers and firemen on those engines in the summer. The guards and ticket collectors and other juniors coping day after day patiently with the mobs on the stations: then what about the I.M.S.—our doctors?"

"I was really thinking of the women, Irene."

"Oh, were you, then what about the nurses?" I asked indignantly, ". . . . .if it were not for the Anglo-Indian girls taking to this, where would the hospitals be?"

"Sorry, I had forgotten about them, but they are only a small crowd; on the whole the women are lazy."

"*Chulo bhai chulo,*" called a *tonga- wallah*, and again we went in single file. Catching her up, I continued. "No, Doreen, that is unfair, not lazy—only asleep; what they went is awakening, something to happen to shake them."

"Such as what?"

"I don't know. . . . ."

"*Kapra-wallah* wedding veil *hai?*" This to a shopkeeper sitting cross-legged on the carpet, so engrossed in his account book that he had not noticed the prospective customers standing before him.

"*Nai* Miss *Sahib*, but I got plenty *topees.*"

As we walked on, disappointed, Doreen finished the discussion on the Anglo-Indians by saying grimly, "Well! It will have to be something jolly big—something really serious to do that!"

The sequel, or answer, came during the Second World War when the Anglo-Indian women woke from their long *siesta* to don khaki, and to use their hands and brains most effectively. As we walked along Main Street, we were hailed on all rides by the shopkeepers clamouring for custom. "Missy *Sahib*, come here, I got very beautiful things." "*Memsahib*—here come, have I very cheap." "Come here, I have it." When asked if he had a veil, the answer was, "I have plenty good hats." Not a few of these men called out, "Doreen *baba*, Arene *baba*, come and buy from old Motilal—" or "Come to old Ramial, *baba*." These were the old merchants who had been supplying the family since 1914. They seemed unable to realise that time had passed, and we were now adults. We found this way of being addressed embarrassing when 'Tommies' were about. Those men knew *baba* meant 'child,' and, why two grownup women were being called *babas* left them puzzled.

On a later occasion in Mhow, after our return from Eric's first home leave for ten years, during Independence Day celebrations on August 15th, 1947, I had taken the children out to see some of the flag decked streets. We were walking up the Mall, and I saw a sweeper woman ahead bent over her broom; when we got abreast, she thoughtfully waited for us to pass before continuing to disturb the dust, which is what this chore amounted to, sweeping the dust from one side of the road to the other, and the leaves and other debris to the sides of the road. Then the first little gust of wind in passing blew it all back again. They were paid very little for this unhealthy job, but the women who usually took it on were somewhat compensated when they came across a patch of fresh cow dung, which they carefully scooped up and dumped into the basket carried for this purpose. This was later 'pat-a-caked' into 'cowpats,' stuck on a sunny wall to dry, and then used as fuel for cooking or warmth, instead of being used on the land starved of any fertilisers.

Usually a baby clung to his mother's hip. It would from time to time be dumped on the roadside whilst a patch was swept, then lifted, and mother and child moved along. Very often the *matherani* was seen sitting under a tree feeding her baby whilst resting and chewing either a *pan* or wad of tobacco. This very old untouchable, as I now saw she was, suddenly threw down her *jharu* and rushed across the road calling, "Arene, *baba*. Arena, *baba!*" I looked at her for a moment before recognising *Chamali-Rani*. *Chamali* means 'jasmine'—*Rani* a 'queen'. This was the name a cruel young Moslem bearer of ours, had given this pock-marked sweeperess, who had been off and on in our service since 1914. she had finally left us, when for economic reasons after my father's death, we had to dispense with her services. The last time I had seen her was when I had helped out at the British Families Hospital about three years' previously. She had then been the head *matherani* there—and I was surprised now to find her at this lowly task.

"What has happened, *Chamali*, why did you leave the hospital?"

"*Hai mai baba*, after the British *log* left there was too much of this," and she rubbed her thumb and first finger together, in the sign that in well understood in India. "I could not give, so I lost my job. Then one day as I swept this road I noticed for the first time that the *gora-log* had gone, and most of the houses on the Mall were now filled by these *kutcha buchas*—half-baked children." This was her not very polite way of describing the Hindhi merchants, who apparently knew what to expect from the Moslems on the partition of the country into India and Pakistan, and were getting out of the latter part of the country whilst they could into a part allocated to India. As we stood together talking of the old days a light trap, merely a cane seat on four wheels drawn by a sprightly little pony, came down the Mall. Behind the reins sat a Hindu lady in a beautiful *sari*—the wife of one of the Indian officers, I guessed. Behind her, balancing precariously on a tiny platform, stood a groom. As the trap came by us the driver gave the pony a smart crack with the whip to get him moving, or to draw attention to herself. I could guess the thoughts of the *syce* from the expression on his face. *Chamali* summed it up. "She should be behind her *chukki*"—this is the small wheat grinding mill found in most Indian homes,—"not behind a pony aping the *memsahib*."

As I prepared to leave she asked me wistfully, "When will the *goralog* return, *baba*?" This I felt unable to answer. But I heard that question often, not only in 1947, but in 1954 when I returned to India on a short visit. The servant class could not reconcile themselves to the changes. The old *kitmughars* and *khansamshs* felt it was infra dig to be serving their own kind.

But to get back to the search for the wedding veil. At last one was found; when the tin storage trunk was opened, the top layer was grey with dust and silver fish scuttled for shelter.

"This is not going to be very good, but we'll have to manage," muttered Doreen.

Then after another frantic search in another tin *peti* under the stairs, the merchant produced a small box of wax orange blossoms. These, too, were very old and dusty, but we gladly bought them—however we got both cheaply. Going home I told Doreen. "The only grain of comfort is that the whole rig-out won't cost much, and after what I have spent on the navy and white—it's a consideration: though I am going to look a comical sight, moth-eaten veil, orange blossoms past their prime, and a dress that can't have the traditional long sleeves because the material won't run to it. . . . . ."

"Well, for goodness sake, don't let Mama know any of this: she will probably not notice the shortcomings. Seeing you in a white dress, complete with veil and orange blossoms, will make her happy: remember it's for her sake you are doing all this."

"Yes, and that thought will have to fortify me when I meet Eric at Khandwa and tell him about the change. . . . ."

Then Doreen interrupted to add wisely. "Remember to point out that you absolutely refused to have a bridesmaid or any other trimming—just for his sake. He'll be comforted, and will forgive you."

The following day I walked into the kitchen and was just in time to hear Doreen tell Mama, " . . . . I could have told the old silly a lot more. . . ." then she stopped abruptly on seeing me.

"Yes, go on—now who have you been discussing me with? You both look guilty—and I am not going to move from this spot until I hear the worst."

"It was Mrs. Boodrie, Irene, I met her just outside Behru's shop; I went to tell him he had to have your dress here tonight latest for a fitting. She overheard this, and joined me as I walked back. 'So, Irene's at last getting married. I hear he is an Englishman. My! Isn't she frightened?' 'Frightened? Why should she be that, Mrs. Boodrie?' 'Oh, man, everyone knows the English have very bad tempers, that is why they have red faces like the monkeys.' 'Don't be silly, Mrs. Boodrie, you don't want to believe such nonsense.' And I was hoping to shake her off, but she clung: she was hoping to get a little bit of news to peddle around, 'Well, I hope that poor *bucha* will be happy, she is a very proud one, I know.' 'Do you, Mrs. Boodrie? Well, you are wrong, my sister is not proud, why do you think that?' 'Everyone knows she could have married Charlie or other railway boys years ago, but she waited for a white man—so I say she is proud.' 'You are right about her only wanting to marry a white man, but pride has nothing to do with it: if you want the real reason ask Mama when you meet her alone—she will tell you.' Then to get rid of her I dived into Franjees where I knew she would not follow as she owes them a lot of money for drink," ended Doreen on a breathless note.

All I could find to say to this was, "The old cat!"

The next morning I left for Khandwa where I was meeting Eric. On the journey to Mhow I told him about the white dress, and he took it so calmly that I could have shaken him! "If I had known you were not going to be upset, I'd have bought a proper white wedding dress at "Stella's" instead of that navy thing. Oh, Eric, you have messed up things." But he could not see it, bless him. In Champak, meeting my family Eric was perfectly sweet. He put all at ease by walking up to my mother with outstretched hand to say, "I am shy and terrified—I want to make a good impression on you, but I expect I'll blunder— you must help me, Mrs. Green."

At this they relaxed, as they had been feeling exactly the same way.

"We'll help each other, Eric, to make our girl happy. That is what you and I want, isn't it?" And as I stood between them, they each put out a hand, Eric to take me round the waist—whilst Mama took hold of my hand; so linked together I looked from one to the other and smiled thankfully.

"*Inshallah!* We will all be happy together from now on."

"Amen," said Mama, whilst Eric looked on smiling. He had been given a room in the nursery wing, sharing this with Captain Busby, whilst Doreen and Henry moved across to our side of the house. We had to sleep on the verandah the night before the wedding, as the large bedroom next to the sitting room had been turned into a sort of reception room. My family had done their best to make my wedding a BIG day, and I have been grateful all these years for the happy memories, which I cherish.

Waking early on the morning of the wedding Doreen called out, "Bride! How do you feel?"

"Terrible."

She laughed. "Yes, I know, that's how I felt—but you'll live!"

That afternoon I saw her and Henry busy with the bridal car someone had lent us—they were decorating it under the *Champak* trees at the back of the house. The two flowing ribbons were being tied to a huge horseshoe made entirely of white paper flowers. Mama saw me watching them and told me it was meant as a surprise. Doreen had been making the horseshoe for days in a friend's house. I was very touched, and thought, "Little Irene is to get some trimmings after all!"

After lunch, Mama advised us all to have a short rest, and although I lay down, I was unable to sleep, but just dozed occasionally. In the half-way stage between sleep and wakefulness I heard an agitated voice calling, "Sister Green! Sister Green!" Turning over I thought, I was in hospital, and someone wants me; but I was having such a *beautiful* dream, it was my wedding day! Then Doreen settled matters by springing out of bed, and shaking me.

"Irene. Someone wants you." walking out to the verandah, I saw an old Parsee doctor, for whom I had worked when private nursing in Mhow; with him was another man. "Sister, we want you on a case—it's urgent, please come at once. . . . ."

I stopped him. "Just a minute, Doctor Mistri—I am very sorry but I cannot accept this case as I am getting married in a couple of hours time."

"You must stop it—put it off——" said the old man, getting excited, "—your duty comes first to the sick, I shouldn't have to remind you. Sister. . . . cancel these arrangements, we cannot lose such a valuable nurse, that would be folly."

I looked at him in amazement, then Mama walked out and took a hand. "Now, Doctor, it's no use getting angry, she has given up nursing—she gets married today, and you must go somewhere else for

IRENE IN HER WEDDING DRESS AND THE BRIDAL CAR

your nurse."

"I cannot do that, Mrs. Green, at such short notice, she should have informed us doctors, then we could have arranged to get another nurse into Mhow."

Now Mama thought he was turning nasty, so with an edge to her voice she reminded him that I had not nursed in Mhow for at least a year, and as he had managed then, he could manage now. Beaten, the doctor turned to me. "You'll be sorry for this, Sister, you are throwing up a good career. . . . ."

"Yes, to take up one that's even better; now excuse us, Doctor. . . Goodbye!" said Mama, bringing the scene to an end.

They disappeared round the corner of the house, and we three turned to move inside when we heard the doctor again calling, "Sister Green!"

"Oh! Here he comes again," said Doreen.

"Sister! I'll send you a wedding present—God Bless you!"

"Well, the silly old fool! There's still some good in him," said Mama.

Helping me to get dressed a little later Doreen, who was pinning the old veil in position, was nearly in tears: pinned up in one place, it tore away in another. In despair she said, "I can't do any more; you'll have to go with it like that, and for goodness sake be careful, don't get it caught in anything or the lot will collapse. . ." Then to cheer me up she added, ". . . . .and remember to walk slowly. When you rush you have an ugly waddle, so walk up the aisle *slowly*: remember you are a bride, not a duck."

"Thanks, sister dear."

She ignored that, "I have told Henry to hold you back if you are inclined to run." Then she handed me my small bouquet which from a sentimental wish of mine had been made from the *champak* flowers, mixed with some greenery from the cantonments' gardens. She went as far as the door, then to my amazement suddenly turned back and kissed me before running down the verandah. My brother-in-law and I waited until all the family had gone, then we walked to the car standing under the porch, where all our servants with their families and friends waited to see me. As the car drew sway they *salaamed* and called "*Ram! Ram! Arene, baba!*" Getting out of the car Henry and I handled that veil as if our lives depended upon it; concentrating on this I forgot the rest of the warning given me only a few minutes earlier. At the church door we peered in nervously, and I saw Henry run a finger round his collar. That suddenly made me brave. "Come on, Henry, let's get it over." With that he grabbed my arm, and away we went—he marched—I waddled.

At the reception, when Doreen was able to get near us, she muttered, "You were dreadful, that WADDLE! Perfect duck."

I laughed. "Darling what did it matter? What did anything matter as long as I married my Eric."

"You are quite mad," was the reply, as she moved away.

The reception proceeded as all such affairs do. Henry proposed a toast to which Eric replied, and when he spoke of me as his wife I was very proud. Then in the pause that followed Mrs. Boodrie, uncomfortably encased in corsets, produced a loud and long 'burp' of relief, which so startled Mama that she spilled some wine as she was lowering her glass. A ghostly silence followed, Mrs. Bowman, who was hard of hearing said, in what she thought was a whisper, "If only Boodrie ma would not chew *pan* and *hing* (asafoetida) all day, she would not be so naughtee." This did not help to break the uncomfortable silence. Then Eric, my Eric, acted. Quite casually he left his seat and strolled over to where Mrs. Boodrie sat on a sofa. Lowering himself slowly he reached out for a sandwich.

"Ah, Mrs. Boodrie, these must be good, I see you have been enjoying them—do you know that I show my appreciation exactly the way you do when I have enjoyed something really tasty."

At this the others, taking the cue, broke into smiles, and the chatter was restarted. I looked gratefully across to Eric, and remembered that line from Kipling's *If*. ". . . . *If you can walk with kings, nor lose the common touch.*" I do not know about 'walking with kings' but Eric had the 'common touch' all right; he could, and can, very soon put people at their ease.

Very soon Eric had Mrs. Boodrie happy, and they were smiling and chatting gaily when I walked over. As Eric stood up I took his hand and asked, "Well! Mrs. Boodrie, what do you think of my Englishman—not frightened of him, are you? He's really quite harmless, I assure you, in spite of his red face." I smiled sweetly at the confused lady, who now had the grace to look ashamed.

"What was that about?" asked Eric, looking puzzled, as I led him to where Doctor Pinto stood alone.

"I'll explain later, darling."

"Doctor Pinto, this is my Eric. I have been longing for you two to meet. Darling, this is my very good friend and adviser."

As Doctor Pinto had also been to school in St. Paul's, Darjeeling, they had something in common, and were soon exchanging recollections. Then the best man came up and claimed Eric's attention, and I was left alone with the doctor, who now handed me a note. "It's from Susie for you: I don't know how she has managed it, because they don't allow a novice to write to anyone, apart from her parents,—and that's only occasionally."

"Oh, I am *so* happy! I have thought of her very often today, as years ago we arranged that when either of us married, the other one would be her bridesmaid. That was before we took up nursing. Then we decided to go into partnership after graduating; we were going to open a nursing home or something—then— then—well, you know what happened. . . . ."

"Yes, I know, dear child—Susie could not face facts—she ran away—but aren't you going to read your letter?"

"Not now, I dare not: I can't, ever bear to look at that dear handwriting with its silly long-tailed 'n's' and 'm's, I shall want to cry, and I can't do that—the mascara will run; I shall read it when I am alone tonight."

"But you won't be alone tonight, my dear, you have forgotten you got married an hour ago." And I saw the twinkle in his eye. Then he added in a sad voice, "And you won't be needing your old doctor friend's advice anymore." Then brightening his tone he said, "But seriously, Irene, promise me you won't cry—my dear, she is happy— happy in her own way." But as he moved away I saw he looked sad.

Then Doreen came up to me and whispered, "Mama says to break it up. None of them will leave early: the army people and the European families from the railway might, but Mama's old cronies will stay 'till every drop of wine and every crumb has been finished, and old Mrs. Boodrie will get more drunk every minute."

Then I saw Eric and the best man move out towards the Nursery Wing—so I slipped away to my old bedroom—where Vi came in to help me. When I was ready, Mama came in to say "Goodbye". This was the moment I had dreaded, and though she tried very hard not to cry she did, and in spite of the mascara, so did I, and the stuff ran down my face. Then I had to go and wash and make up all over again. Doreen, coming in to see what the delay was about, grumbled at us both and pushed Mama out of the room, saying, "I can't understand you, Mama, first you say you want your girls to marry, then when they do—you cry! You should be happy, she has at last managed to catch

312

her man!"

That was the last I saw of Mama alone until the following year—on the verandah I could just see the top of her head as they crowded round Eric and me, pelting us with rice and rose petals. Eric grabbed my hand and we rushed down the steps towards the car, we got in and he drove away. I looked back once and waved to the crowd, then looked ahead, down our long drive, towards the gates of Champak bungalow where the servants' children had gathered to shout *"Ram! Ram!"* We drove on down the Mall towards the setting sun, and happiness—the happiness I have known for twenty-two years.

Epilogue
(Yorkshire 1961)

My mother died in 1946 whilst I was in England with Eric and the children. I do not have to write that I was upset, but my sorrow was lessened a little when I returned to India in 1947 and saw the chaos after partition. I was grateful then to God for taking her before she was told that her "dear British soldier boys" were leaving India forever. The final service they rendered her in return for the hospitality the boys of many regiments had received over the years was to act as pall-bearers for her funeral. My sister was standing on the verandah, wondering about all the arrangements for the internment, when a soldier, who was a complete stranger, walked up the drive and told her how sorry he was to hear the news, and asked if there was any way in which he and his friends could help. This offer was gratefully accepted. It was a blessing that my mother did not know that many of our community were being left to the mercies of the new governments. Those left considered themselves "The abandoned ones" or "*Nobody's children.*"

Partition had its crumb of comfort for some. Many considered it was a blessing in disguise as it would mean the end of this community and its disintegration which would not be a bad thing. Others maintained that in Europe or England the community would gradually be absorbed. Marrying only whites in time there would be no Eurasians left. So they thought, and it seemed a reasonable theory. The other day I had cause for reflection. I was window shopping when a young English girl with a pram joined me: we started chatting then, as I am fond of babies, I bent to look into the pram. The little very brown baby with its 'fuzzy-wuzzy' hair startled me. Then her husband came out of the shop and they moved away: he was a great big African. Looking after them I thought—here we go again! A new coloured community in the making in England itself. What are the dying race of old *koi hais* and *burra mems* going to say to this new turn of events?

Middle age has mellowed the outlook on the problems as I viewed them when younger with all the attendant fears and complexes. After drafting the story I wondered how my family would react—would they find it embarrassing? The first one to ask was my husband: I found him at his favourite pastime, reading, and managed with great difficulty to detach him from his book, to hear me through. In the end he said calmly, "well, it's your story! And if you feel better for writing it—splendid! No, it won't bother me, darling, if you want to publish it—good luck to you!"

The next one I encountered was my nineteen-year-old son at his favourite sport—food-hunting in the kitchen. After hearing excerpts of what I had written he said, "Splendid, now the chaps in school will know—if your book gets published—that I was not telling a tall one when I said I was one eighth Indian and one eighth Portuguese. They think I am more interesting that way!"

This surprised me because though I had told them when we first settled in England in 1950 that I was partly coloured I had felt they had not appreciated the point of my explanation—they were too young. And as we had never discussed this again I thought they had forgotten what I had told them, but John, with his mathematical mind, had worked out the percentage of the mixture and proudly, it appeared, had spread the word around.

Now I went in search of my daughter, who was not very successfully trying to acquire a tan in the unhelpful English climate. She was lying on the grass, sunbathing. "Ah, mummy, you can rub this tanning lotion over my back now you are here, please," she said, then settled to listen to my story. "Well, I think all the fuss they make about the colour business is silly! White, black, brown or yellow, they can all be very nice and all very nasty if they wish, so what?"

After hearing those remarks I decided to go ahead, and if this story has helped to give a better understanding of the life and unusual anxieties in a community where mixed marriages have taken place then I feel it has served its purpose.

LEONAUR

ALSO FROM LEONAUR
AVAILABLE IN SOFTCOVER OR HARDCOVER WITH DUST JACKET

PLAINS WOMEN *by Lydia Spencer Lane & Lodisa Frizzell*—Two accounts of American Women on the Western Frontier. I Married a Soldier or Old Days in the Old Army by Lydia Spencer Lane, Across the Plains to California in 1852 Journal of Mrs. Lodisa Frizzell by Lodisa Frizzell

THE WHITE SLAVE MARKET*by Mrs. Archibald Mackirdy (Olive Christian Malvery) and William Nicholas Willis*—An Overview of the Traffic in Young Women at the Turn of the Nineteenth and Early Twentieth Centuries

"TELL IT ALL" *by Fanny Stenhouse*—The Ordeals of a Woman Against Polygamy Within the Mormon Church During the 19th Century

TENTING ON THE PLAINS *by Elizabeth B. Custer*—The Experiences of General Custer's Wife in Kansas and Texas.

CAPTIVES! *by Cynthia Ann Parker, Mrs Jannette E. De Camp Sweet, Mary Schwandt, Mrs. Caroline Harris, Misses Frances and Almira Hall & Nancy McClure*—The Narratives of Seven Women Taken Prisoner by the Plains Indians of the American West

FRIENDS AND FOES IN THE TRANSKEI *by Helen M. Prichard*—A Victorian lady's experience of Southern Africa during the 1870's

NURSE EDITH CAVELL *by William Thomson Hill & Jacqueline Van Til*—Two accounts of a Notable British Nurse of the First World War. The Martyrdom of Nurse Cavell by William Thompson Hill, With Edith Cavell by Jacqueline Van Til

PERSONAL RECOLLECTIONS OF JOAN OF ARC *by Mark Twain*

FIELD HOSPITAL AND FLYING COLUMN *by Violetta Thurstan*—With the Red Cross on the Western & Eastern Fronts During the First World War.

THE CELLAR-HOUSE OF PERVYSE *by G. E. Mitton*—The Incredible Account of Two Nurses on the Western Front During the Great War.

A WOMAN'S EXPERIENCES IN THE GREAT WAR *by Louise Mack*—An Australian Author's Clandestine Journey Through War-Torn Belgium.

THE LOVE LETTERS OF HENRY VIII TO ANNE BOLEYN & OTHER CORRESPONDENCE & DOCUMENTS CONCERNING HENRY AND HIS WIVES *by Henry VIII and Henry Ellis*

A LADY'S CAPTIVITY AMONG CHINESE PIRATES *by Fanny Loviot*—The Adventures of a Lady Traveller During the 1850s

LEONAUR

ALSO FROM LEONAUR
AVAILABLE IN SOFTCOVER OR HARDCOVER WITH DUST JACKET

A DIARY FROM DIXIE by Mary Boykin Chesnut—A Lady's Account of the Confederacy During the American Civil War

FOLLOWING THE DRUM by Teresa Griffin Vielé—A U. S. Infantry Officer's Wife on the Texas frontier in the Early 1850's

FOLLOWING THE GUIDON by Elizabeth B. Custer—The Experiences of General Custer's Wife with the U. S. 7th Cavalry.

LADIES OF LUCKNOW by G. Harris & Adelaide Case—The Experiences of Two British Women During the Indian Mutiny 1857. A Lady's Diary of the Siege of Lucknow by G. Harris, Day by Day at Lucknow by Adelaide Case

MARIE-LOUISE AND THE INVASION OF 1814 by Imbert de Saint-Amand—The Empress and the Fall of the First Empire

SAPPER DOROTHY by Dorothy Lawrence—The only English Woman Soldier in the Royal Engineers 51st Division, 79th Tunnelling Co. during the First World War

ARMY LETTERS FROM AN OFFICER'S WIFE 1871-1888 by Frances M. A. Roe—Experiences On the Western Frontier With the United States Army

NAPOLEON'S LETTERS TO JOSEPHINE by Henry Foljambe Hall—Correspondence of War, Politics, Family and Love 1796-1814

MEMOIRS OF SARAH DUCHESS OF MARLBOROUGH, AND OF THE COURT OF QUEEN ANNE VOLUME 1 by A. T. Thomson

MEMOIRS OF SARAH DUCHESS OF MARLBOROUGH, AND OF THE COURT OF QUEEN ANNE VOLUME 2 by A. T. Thomson

MARY PORTER GAMEWELL AND THE SIEGE OF PEKING by A. H. Tuttle—An American Lady's Experiences of the Boxer Uprising, China 1900

VANISHING ARIZONA by Martha Summerhayes—A young wife of an officer of the U.S. 8th Infantry in Apacheria during the 1870's

THE RIFLEMAN'S WIFE by Mrs. Fitz Maurice—*The Experiences of an Officer's Wife and Chronicles of the Old 95th During the Napoleonic Wars*

THE OATMAN GIRLS by Royal B. Stratton—The Capture & Captivity of Two Young American Women in the 1850's by the Apache Indians

LEONAUR

ALSO FROM LEONAUR

AVAILABLE IN SOFTCOVER OR HARDCOVER WITH DUST JACKET

A DIARY FROM DIXIE *by Mary Boykin Chesnut*—A Lady's Account of the Confederacy During the American Civil War

FOLLOWING THE DRUM *by Teresa Griffin Vielé*—A U. S. Infantry Officer's Wife on the Texas frontier in the Early 1850's

FOLLOWING THE GUIDON *by Elizabeth B. Custer*—The Experiences of General Custer's Wife with the U. S. 7th Cavalry.

LADIES OF LUCKNOW *by G. Harris & Adelaide Case*—The Experiences of Two British Women During the Indian Mutiny 1857. A Lady's Diary of the Siege of Lucknow by G. Harris, Day by Day at Lucknow by Adelaide Case

MARIE-LOUISE AND THE INVASION OF 1814 *by Imbert de Saint-Amand*—The Empress and the Fall of the First Empire

SAPPER DOROTHY *by Dorothy Lawrence*—The only English Woman Soldier in the Royal Engineers 51st Division, 79th Tunnelling Co. during the First World War

ARMY LETTERS FROM AN OFFICER'S WIFE 1871-1888 *by Frances M. A. Roe*—Experiences On the Western Frontier With the United States Army

NAPOLEON'S LETTERS TO JOSEPHINE *by Henry Foljambe Hall*—Correspondence of War, Politics, Family and Love 1796-1814

MEMOIRS OF SARAH DUCHESS OF MARLBOROUGH, AND OF THE COURT OF QUEEN ANNE VOLUME 1 by A. T. Thomson

MEMOIRS OF SARAH DUCHESS OF MARLBOROUGH, AND OF THE COURT OF QUEEN ANNE VOLUME 2 by A. T. Thomson

MARY PORTER GAMEWELL AND THE SIEGE OF PEKING *by A. H. Tuttle*—An American Lady's Experiences of the Boxer Uprising, China 1900

VANISHING ARIZONA *by Martha Summerhayes*—A young wife of an officer of the U.S. 8th Infantry in Apacheria during the 1870's

THE RIFLEMAN'S WIFE *by Mrs. Fitz Maurice*—*The Experiences of an Officer's Wife and Chronicles of the Old 95th During the Napoleonic Wars*

THE OATMAN GIRLS *by Royal B. Stratton*—The Capture & Captivity of Two Young American Women in the 1850's by the Apache Indians

Lightning Source UK Ltd.
Milton Keynes UK
UKOW040611101212

203290UK00002B/2/P